Exploring J.R.R. Tolkien's *The Hobbit*

Corey Olsen

Exploring J.R.R. Tolkien's
The HOBBIT

Houghton Mifflin Harcourt • *Boston* • *New York* • *2012*

For information about permission to reproduce selections from this book,
write to Permissions, Houghton Mifflin Harcourt Publishing Company,
215 Park Avenue South, New York, New York 10003.

www.hmhbooks.com

Library of Congress Cataloging-in-Publication Data
Olsen, Corey.
Exploring J.R.R. Tolkien's The Hobbit / Corey Olsen.
p. cm.
ISBN 978-0-547-73946-5 (hardback)
1. Tolkien, J. R. R. (John Ronald Reuel), 1892–1973. Hobbit.
2. Middle Earth (Imaginary place) I. Title.
PR6039.032H635 2012
823'.912 — dc23
2012017316

Book design by Melissa Lotfy

Printed in the United States of America
DOC 10 9 8 7 6 5 4 3 2 1

To my mother and father
Jeremiah 33:3

Contents

Exploring J.R.R. Tolkien's *The Hobbit*

Introduction

I HAVE LOVED J.R.R. Tolkien's books for as long as I can re-member, though I must admit I don't recall exactly how old I was when I first read *The Hobbit;* somewhere around eight, I believe. My very first reading of *The Lord of the Rings* and *The Hobbit* doesn't stand out in my memory, probably because it was followed immediately by my second reading and then my third. I have read the books at least once a year for the rest of my life to date. I was not, in some ways, a stereotypical "Tolkien nerd" as a teenager—I didn't learn Quenya, I never taught myself to write Tengwar, and I have never worn a pair of rubber ears. My relationship with Tolkien has always been about reading and re-reading the books, immersing myself in the stories, in Tolkien's world. No matter how many times I read them, I find there are always new discoveries to make.

Tolkien's works served for me, as they have for many, as a gateway to the Middle Ages, inspiring an enduring fascina-tion with medieval literature. (Tolkien's books should proba-bly come with some kind of warning attached: Caution! May Turn Readers into Medievalists!) I ended up getting my PhD in medieval English literature, and when I was hired as a pro-fessor at Washington College in Maryland, I was soon able to realize one of my life's dreams: in addition to my courses on Chaucer and Arthurian literature, I also began to offer a course on Tolkien.

Teaching Tolkien's works at the college level was just as much fun as I had expected it to be. In one way, that class was very different from any other class I had ever taught: most of the people who took my Tolkien class were people who had already read Tolkien, and many of them already considered themselves fans. As a medievalist, I had never had that experience before. I never had people sign up for my Chaucer class because Chaucer was their favorite author. No one had ever come up to me after class to show me the ragged and dearly loved copy of Chrétien de Troyes's Arthurian romances that her parents had first read to her when she was seven. I never had a student who was a regular contributor to a *Piers Plowman* fan site and who customarily attended Langland conventions dressed up as Conscience or one of the theological virtues. Generally, the first order of business in teaching medieval literature is lowering students' defenses against it and convincing them that although it is strange and foreign to us, it is still fun and worthwhile. My Tolkien students, by and large, needed far less convincing.

I found among my Tolkien students an obvious hunger to learn more and study the books more thoroughly. I also found numerous obstacles that students wanted help to overcome. Casual fans found many things about Tolkien's writing difficult to understand, and some of his books difficult to get into at all (especially *The Silmarillion*). Many students, even those who had read Tolkien's major works many times, confessed that they skipped over the poetry as they read, and that the songs and poems just didn't seem all that important or relevant. All in all, I found that what students both liked best and profited from most was the opportunity to read carefully and slowly through the texts, working out the meanings of tough passages and seeing how the ideas in the story came together.

I taught my Tolkien course several times, but as I advanced in my academic career, I became increasingly dissatisfied with the other half of my professorial duties: the world of scholarly publication. Professors, of course, must "publish or perish," as everyone knows, but I found the world of scholarly publication frustratingly limited. I would be greatly surprised if many people reading this introduction have ever read the articles on Sir Thomas Malory or even on Tolkien that I had accepted early on in my career. Typical academic books and journals circulate not to thousands, but to hundreds, or even to dozens, of people. They tend to be priced so high that only research libraries can afford to purchase them, and therefore the general public has little or no access to the work that most scholars do. Increasingly, scholarly publication has become in practice a closed conversation among scholars and some of their students. I knew that there were tens of thousands of people in the world who had the same desire to learn more about Tolkien that my college students shared, and I wanted to engage them in a conversation to which everyone could be invited.

In 2009, therefore, I started my podcast and website called The Tolkien Professor (www.tolkienprofessor.com). I started by posting lectures, and I was astounded by the response. Within a month of launching the podcast on iTunes, I had over a thousand subscribers, and in a year the podcast had had over a million downloads. People were even more excited than I expected about the opportunity to take part in a serious academic conversation about Tolkien. I began having recorded discussions, holding live call-in sessions, and hosting online seminars. I have been having a tremendous amount of fun talking to both dedicated Tolkien fans and new Tolkien readers alike over the past several years and helping to facilitate a deeper appreciation for Tolkien's works.

This book brings together the lessons I've learned in the classroom, the experiences I've had through my podcast, and the love I've always had for Tolkien's work. There is nothing I enjoy more than walking slowly through a great book with a group of people, taking the time to notice important details and keep track of themes that often slip by when you read on your own. I hope that you too will enjoy the journey.

Exploring *The Hobbit*

Many people, I have discovered, get nervous at the prospect of a literary critic discussing a work they love. Too many people have had unpleasant experiences in high school English classes in which they were made to disassemble works of literature, and they don't want to see that grisly fate befall a work they actually value. This book, however, is not called *Dissecting The Hobbit*. I will not be acting as an amateur psychiatrist (or psychic), claiming to tell you what was in Tolkien's mind and why as he wrote the book.* I will not be enthron-

---

* When I use quotations from *The Hobbit* in this book, I generally attribute them to the narrator of the story, rather than to Tolkien himself. I do this in part to draw attention to the character of the narrator, who is an important figure in this story, and in part because I want to make a distinction between the many occasions on which I am pointing to what the text says and the far fewer occasions on which I am explaining a theory of my own about Tolkien's ideas. As a rule, I do the latter quite seldom. I make no claims to be able to read Tolkien's mind posthumously, and in most of this book I will simply be discussing the patterns that we can see in the published text. I do

ing myself on the judgment seat as the arbiter of taste, telling you which bits of *The Hobbit* are good and which are bad. In the end, this book just sets out to do a little more of what I suppose you already do yourself: reading and enjoying *The Hobbit.*

In *Exploring J.R.R. Tolkien's The Hobbit,* we will take a journey through the story, looking carefully about us as we go. It is easy to rip through a book that you like at top speed; the main thing I hope to do is to slow things down enough to be able to see more clearly what is unfolding in the story as we go. We will take notice of the recurring themes and images in the book, thinking about the ideas that the story keeps coming back to and developing along the way. We will listen closely to all the songs and poems Tolkien has built into the story, for they reveal a great deal about the book and especially about the characters who sing or recite them. If we walk slowly and pay attention, we may find that our perspective is enriched by the journey as much as Bilbo's was, and that our eyes have been opened to marvels that we never expected to see.

Along the way, we will see the cultures and characters of several new peoples: the Dwarves, the Trolls, the Goblins, the Eagles, the Elves (of both Rivendell and Mirkwood), and the Men of Lake-town. We will meet a few remarkable characters with whom we will be invited to linger, so that we can get to know them better—such as Gollum, Beorn, and Bard

---

not claim to know whether Tolkien himself thought about those themes and patterns consciously or not. I have tried, therefore, not to attribute ideas to Tolkien himself unless I believe there is good evidence that Tolkien consciously intended those ideas.

the Bowman. Most of all, however, we will see several central ideas that come up repeatedly throughout the book:

1. *Bilbo's Nature:* In Chapter One, we learn that Bilbo is the child of two very different families, the Tooks and the Bagginses, and that his Baggins side and his Took side push him in very different directions. The interaction between these different impulses in Bilbo is one of the central realities of Bilbo's character, and Tolkien's handling of the balance between Bilbo's Tookish and Bagginsish* desires as the story proceeds is subtle and complex, not following the simple patterns that we might expect.

2. *Bilbo's Choices:* There are several moments in Bilbo's journey when he comes to a crucial decision point, when he must take a huge step forward on his own. Waking up alone in the goblin tunnels, coming to his senses to find a giant spider tying up his legs, setting out down a dark tunnel to confront a dragon in his lair—these are the particular moments that define Bilbo's character as the story progresses, and the narrator lays great stress on them.

3. *Burglar Bilbo:* Bilbo's adventure begins when he is identified by Gandalf and hired by the dwarves as a professional burglar, and throughout the story we are reminded of Bilbo's relationship with his official position. At first, Bilbo's hiring seems like a rather absurd human resources failure, but his

---

* Tolkien uses the adjective *Tookish* numerous times, but he never uses the much sillier corresponding word *Bagginsish.* That term is my own invention, and I must admit that I enjoy how clunky and comical the word looks—there is something about it that seems to me to capture the discomfort and awkwardness so often associated with Bilbo's Baggins side during his adventure. However, since this word is not in fact used in the book, I've tried not to get carried away with it.

burglarious career ends up going in some quite surprising directions.

4. *The Desolation of the Dragon:* When Bilbo and the dwarves finally approach the Lonely Mountain, they find that it is surrounded by a wasteland that the dragon has made by his very presence, choking off the life that once filled those fertile lands. In the second half of the book, however, we begin to see that the physical desolation that the dragon has created also serves as an image for the destructiveness of dragonish desires: the "dragon-sickness," as the narrator calls it. Each character confronts these desires, and in some ways the dangers they face only increase after the dragon himself is killed.

5. *Luck:* Bilbo and his friends are the beneficiaries of a peculiar run of both good and bad luck in their journey, and the narrator draws our attention to it quite forcefully on several occasions. In addition, we learn in Chapter Three that the quest of the dwarves is bound up with the fulfillment of old prophecies, which come more and more plainly to the center of the story as Bilbo's journey continues. Through the interactions between the choices of the characters and the frequent interventions of luck, Bilbo's story challenges us to think about the relationship between fate and human choice.

6. *The Writing of* The Hobbit: At several points, we will pause to look at the construction of the story and the secondary world that Tolkien has made through that story. *The Hobbit* is a story that is very self-conscious of being a story, as we are reminded when we see Bilbo actually writing the book in its last pages. Tolkien enjoyed thinking and writing about stories and their growth, and as we read, we will take a look at how Tolkien frames the story, and how the tone of the story grows and changes.

I have laid out my discussion of *The Hobbit* chapter by chapter, so that it is easy to read it alongside the original. I have also included subheadings in each chapter, however, so that those who would like to skip ahead to trace a particular theme forward in the book may conveniently do so.

Which *Hobbit*?

Readers familiar with *The Lord of the Rings* may have many questions when they read this book. Why do I avoid using the proper names for people and places? The Lonely Mountain is named Erebor, and the Elvenking is named Thranduil, for instance, but I never use either of those names in this book. There are also far more substantive problems. In *The Fellowship of the Ring*, Gandalf makes a big deal about the fact that Bilbo was "meant" to find the Ring; why don't I talk more about the significance of the finding of the Ring of Power? For that matter, why do I spend so much time talking about the dragon-sickness but no time at all talking about the corruptive influence of the Ring on Bilbo? When Gandalf leaves Bilbo and the dwarves and heads south, he is going to join the White Council in kicking Sauron out of Mirkwood; that's a really big moment in the history of the Third Age of Middle-earth. So why do I barely even mention it? It might sound almost as if I am pretending ignorance of Tolkien's full story.

The answers to these questions are all connected, and they have to do with which version of *The Hobbit* I am discussing in this book. In order to explain what I mean by that, let me give a brief overview of the history of Tolkien's writing of *The*

Hobbit. I think of the story of *The Hobbit* as developing in three different stages, which I call the Solo Stage, the Revision Stage, and the Assimilation Stage.

The Solo Stage

The Hobbit was published in England on September 21, 1937, by George Allen and Unwin Ltd. Tolkien had published a few poems previously, but *The Hobbit* was his first big publication. For many years, this book was the only piece of literature that anyone associated with Tolkien, and it was so popular that Tolkien's publishers pressed him to write a sequel. He began working on a second book, which was supposed to follow in *The Hobbit*'s footsteps, and he and his friends called it "The New Hobbit" for a while. The writing of the second book did not at all go according to the plan of either Tolkien or Allen and Unwin, however. What started as another short hobbit adventure story for children grew, eventually, into *The Lord of the Rings.*

I call this stage the Solo Stage because for years after its publication, what was printed in *The Hobbit* was all that readers knew about Middle-earth. I do not mean to suggest that it was the only story Tolkien was thinking about. The mythological stories of the ancient history of Middle-earth—the stories later developed, collected, and published as *The Silmarillion*—already existed in more than one draft, and it is fairly clear that Tolkien was connecting Bilbo's story to that world when he was writing *The Hobbit.* But there were only a small handful of people who knew this; it would be decades before any more of the story of Middle-earth would be revealed. For the most part, what we can read between the covers of *The Hobbit* was all there was.

The Revision Stage

The Lord of the Rings may have begun as a sequel to *The Hobbit*, but before long it took Tolkien in quite a different direction. The new story did begin with a few story seeds harvested from *The Hobbit*, but they grew in surprising ways. For one thing, Tolkien found that the new book he was writing was no longer a children's book; he was rather afraid that that alone would make it unsuitable as a sequel. More importantly, however, both the new story and the world it inhabited grew and expanded far beyond the scope of the story Tolkien had told in *The Hobbit*. Nowhere was this more evident than in the primary connection between *The Hobbit* and its sequel: Bilbo's magic ring.

When Tolkien published *The Hobbit*, the ring was nothing but a magical ring of invisibility that Bilbo found on his journey. It was Gollum's ring, but although it was Gollum's greatest treasure, he was not originally enchanted or corrupted by it in any way. When Gollum proposes the riddle-game to Bilbo in *The Hobbit*, he tells Bilbo that he will give him a present—meaning the ring—if Bilbo wins. When Bilbo does win, Gollum finds himself stuck, for he only then realizes that he has lost his ring somewhere and now has no present that he can give to Bilbo. Gollum is extremely sorry, and he apologizes to Bilbo over and over again. Bilbo tells him that it is quite all right, and that Gollum can just show him the way out instead of giving him his prize. Bilbo is not entirely honest with Gollum here, for he has already guessed that the ring he found in the dark in the tunnel and which he has just lately rediscovered in his pocket is the very present that Gollum meant to give him, and thus he knows full well that he is getting a double reward. Bilbo is rather in a pinch, however, so it is hard to blame him too much. Gollum shows Bilbo to the exit, where Bilbo waves a cheerful goodbye to him, and the two go their separate ways. Throughout the rest of his adventure, Bilbo makes use of the magical ring, and it turns out to be just as useful as Gollum had told him it would be.

If that story sounds nothing like *The Hobbit* that you know, there's a reason for that. The summary I just gave is of the story as it appeared in the first edition of *The Hobbit* in 1937; it is the original story of Bilbo, Gollum, and the ring. As Tolkien was writing *The Lord of the Rings*, however, he put Bilbo's ring at the center of the story, deciding that it should turn out to be the Ring of Power, which the Dark Lord had lost. This choice, however, created a major inconsistency with Tolkien's treatment of the ring in the first edition of *The Hobbit*, which was still in circulation. Bilbo's use of the ring during the rest of the book could be made to fit the new conception of the Ring perfectly well, but the original version of the Gollum story and his cheerful willingness to give away the Ring was now utterly incompatible with the later story. In 1951, Allen and Unwin published a revised second edition of *The Hobbit*, into which Tolkien slipped a significantly altered version of the Gollum chapter. This later version is now the one that everyone reads, and the original version of the story has been mostly forgotten.

Keep in mind, however, that during what I am calling the Revision Stage *The Lord of the Rings* was still not published. When the revised edition of *The Hobbit* with its new "Baggins! We hates it forever!" version of Gollum was published in 1951, it was still the only story of Middle-earth available to the public. The revisions might have given some very attentive readers a hint about the direction in which Tolkien's new, larger story was headed (if they had known he was still working on one, ten years after *The Hobbit*'s publication), but they would still not have known much. The story people could read between the covers of *The Hobbit* had changed a little, but it was still all they had. The idea that Bilbo's ring has evil powers which work to corrupt him is an idea that is outside the story of *The Hobbit,* even after it was revised.

The Assimilation Stage

The first volume of *The Lord of the Rings, The Fellowship of the Ring,* was finally published in 1954, nearly seventeen years after *The Hobbit* had first been received so gratefully by reading audiences around the world. Now, at last, readers were able to immerse themselves in the much longer story that had succeeded the short children's book, and in the far more detailed world that Tolkien had developed during the long process of writing *The Lord of the Rings.* I call this stage the Assimilation Stage because in it Tolkien brings the story of *The Hobbit,* retroactively, to fit within the newer story that he had been writing and devising.

Tolkien had already revised *The Hobbit* to change the one element in it that could not be reconciled at all to the later story, and he now, through his new story, expanded on and developed many of the points from the original *Hobbit.* Gandalf had been in the dungeons of the Necromancer (when he met Thrain and got the key and map) because he was confirming that the Necromancer was really Sauron, taking shape in the world again after his defeat at the end of the Second Age. That also explained, of course, the move that the White Council made against Sauron to drive him from Mirkwood. The Wood-elves of Mirkwood received a more detailed history and even a few names, and the history of the Lonely Mountain—its settlement and its fall and re-establishment—was given its place in the larger story of Durin's folk and the history of the mines of Moria, called by the dwarves Khazad-dûm.

All of this wider story, not to mention the great story of the Ring of Power itself, was revealed in *The Lord of the Rings* and its long appendices. A long section of Appendix A, cut from the original publication, was later published in *Unfinished Tales* under the title "The Quest of Erebor." That story had the fictional frame of a conversation between Gandalf and the remaining companions in Minas Tirith after the War of the Ring, and it gave Gandalf's side of the whole *Hobbit* story, starting before his initial meeting with Thorin and describing what led up to the Unexpected Party at Bag-End.

So thorough was Tolkien's assimilation of his earlier work that even the revision of *The Hobbit* itself was incorporated into the story. In *The Fellowship of the Ring,* Gandalf and Frodo talk about the fact that Bilbo's book (published as *The Hobbit*) contained a false account of the story of his finding of the Ring. Gandalf explains that the Ring had already begun to take hold of Bilbo, and when he told the story in his book, he made up the part about being given the Ring by Gollum in order to bolster his personal claim to it. The "true" story, the revised version, was only discovered later, but copies of the original could still be found in circulation.

The Focus of This Book

In *Exploring J.R.R. Tolkien's The Hobbit,* I am discussing *The Hobbit* only as it existed in the Solo Stage and the Revision Stage described above. The reason for this is quite simple: I want us to read *The Hobbit* on its own ground. The story of *The Hobbit* as it developed and was expanded in the Assimilation Stage is not the same story; it is now merely a chapter in the story of the Third Age of Middle-earth as we come to see it in *The Lord of the Rings.* If, when we look at Bilbo and his magic ring in *The Hobbit,* we are constantly thinking about Frodo and Mount Doom, we will not really be paying attention to the ideas that *this* story is interested in.

Moreover, if we aren't very careful, we can easily cross lines and confuse details. The Gandalf who shows up at Bag-End in Chapter One of *The Hobbit* is not exactly the same character who helps to host Bilbo's farewell party in Chapter One of *The Fellowship of the Ring.* A lot happens to the guy in the seventeen years of real-world time that came between those two parties. If, for instance, when discussing what Gandalf says about Bilbo's being a burglar in Chapter One of *The Hobbit,* I were to bring in the things Gandalf says about hobbits and burglary in "The Quest of Erebor" from *Unfinished Tales,* I'd simply be muddying the waters.

I have tried hard, therefore, to be consistent in dealing only with the pre–Assimilation Stage *Hobbit* in this book. Almost all of the few references I have made to *The Lord of the Rings* are made in the footnotes. When I talk about the ring, I do not capitalize the word, for I am discussing Bilbo's invisibility ring, not the Ring of Power. I never refer to the Necromancer as Sauron, nor even to the Lonely Mountain as Erebor; I only use the names that are given and refer to the stories that are told between the covers of *The Hobbit* itself. This is also why I never refer to the Shire, for this as well is a later name, and it never appears in the text of *The Hobbit*. In another book, I may have a chance to discuss *The Lord of the Rings*. For this book, *The Hobbit* alone gives us more than enough to talk about.

Further Reading

Many scholars have been producing excellent material in the field of Tolkien scholarship for many years. If you are interested to learn more about *The Hobbit*, there are two books that you should certainly acquire. These are Douglas A. Anderson's *The Annotated Hobbit** and John D. Rateliff's *The History of The Hobbit*.† These two works are indispensable resources; I cannot recommend them highly enough. I am greatly indebted to both scholars for their indefatigable labor; their work has immeasurably enriched the study of J.R.R. Tolkien, as well as my own understanding of *The Hobbit*.

---

* Douglas A. Anderson, *The Annotated Hobbit*, revised edition (Houghton Mifflin, 2002).

† John Rateliff, *The History of The Hobbit* (Houghton Mifflin Harcourt, 2007).

I

A Most Excellent and Audacious Hobbit

Bilbo's Nature:
The Meeting of Two Worlds

The first sentence of *The Hobbit*, "In a hole in the ground there lived a hobbit," is the beginning of the story in more ways than one. It is not only the starting point of the book, but the actual origin of the story. Tolkien often told the tale of the famous moment in which this little book (and in many ways Tolkien's entire literary career) was born. He was grading student exams at his desk at home, and he was (unsurprisingly) terribly bored. Then, at the end of one essay book, he came upon an unexpected and glorious sight: a completely empty page. He said he was so relieved that he almost gave the student extra credit for it. Faced with the blank sheet, he spontaneously scribbled down this famous first line. "I can't think why," he said later. Once he had written the line, he realized he had to figure out what on earth hobbits were.

If the word *hobbit* was a new one to the reading public, the world Tolkien describes at the beginning of his story, the place that hobbits call home, seems quite comfortable and familiar. Hobbits themselves have a few peculiarities, of course, such as their small size, their furry, shoeless feet, and their tradition of living in holes in the ground. But although Bag-End might be small and have a round door, its "panelled walls, and floors tiled and carpeted" would make any twentieth-century reader feel at home (3).* Hobbits might look odd, but the narrator assures us that there is "little or no magic about them" (4). They are plain folk who love to laugh and eat and drink. The world of hobbits is a quiet and simple world, a world of ease and comfort, containing nothing very strange or alarming—an inviting world for the reader to enter.

The Baggins family serves as a representative of all that is sedate and hobbit-like. They are "considered highly respectable" by all their neighbors, who chiefly approve of their complete predictability. There is nothing at all adventurous about the Bagginses. They never "did anything unexpected: you could tell what a Baggins would say on any question without the bother of asking him" (3). The world of the Bagginses is a sleepy world, a domestic world, one that values peace and ease. In the middle of this quiet world sits Bilbo Baggins, lounging outside the door of his luxurious hobbit-hole, smoking his long pipe leisurely, and saying, "There's no hurry, we have all the day before us!" (6). This is Bilbo as we first meet him, the very image of hobbit respectability, the picture of tranquillity and comfortable living.

Into this peaceful scene, back in "the quiet of the world, when there was less noise and more green," steps Gandalf the wizard (5). Gandalf is the polar opposite of Bilbo; he is a mys-

---

* Page numbers in the text refer to J.R.R. Tolkien, *The Hobbit* (Mariner Books, 2012).

terious and eerie figure whose origin and business are not fully known. He not only goes on adventures himself, but he apparently travels around "arranging" them; Bilbo has heard the rumors that he is "responsible for so many quiet lads and lasses going off into the Blue for mad adventures" (7). Gandalf is a storyteller, as Bilbo also recalls, telling "wonderful tales" at parties about very strange and outlandish things, such as "dragons and goblins and giants and the rescue of princesses and the unexpected luck of widows' sons" (7). Indeed, Gandalf is not just a storyteller; he is a story-maker, for "tales and adventures sprouted up all over the place wherever he went" (5). We shouldn't be surprised, therefore, to find that the book we are reading turns out to be one more story that begins when Gandalf walks into it.

The meeting of Bilbo and Gandalf in this opening scene brings a confrontation between two worlds: the comfortable and predictable life of Mr. Bilbo Baggins of Bag-End, Under-Hill, and the marvelous, dangerous, and unsettling world of the adventures that tend to break out whenever Gandalf is around. The invasion of this adventurous world into Bilbo's quiet and well-ordered home is the primary action of the first chapter of *The Hobbit*.

The occasion is an extremely tame and civilized one: a tea party. This is for Bilbo in several senses an "Unexpected Party," as the chapter title suggests. For one thing, he didn't really know he was hosting a tea party. He has completely forgotten about his hasty and not completely sincere invitation to Gandalf the day before, and he knows nothing at all about these dwarves. "He liked visitors," the narrator informs us, adding with gentle understatement that "he liked to know them before they arrived, and he preferred to ask them himself" (9). For another thing, the party quickly ceases to be a civilized tea party and becomes something quite different and deeply disturbing to Bilbo's sensibilities. Bilbo goes from badly flustered to "positively flummoxed" and is finally forced to confront the inescapable, undesirable fact that "a most wretched adventure" has come right into his house (12).

The results of the invasion are rather curious. What we see is not simply the shattering of Bilbo's predictable and tranquil world as a crowd of uninvited dwarves tumble across his threshold, eat all his cakes, and undo the peace of his comfortable home in companionable chaos. Bilbo's world is not just turned upside down; it is transformed. The bright stillness of his dining room becomes the site of the dark and solemn councils of the dwarves and the wizard.

One small but significant interlude during the party illustrates this alteration very clearly: Gandalf and Thorin's display of smoke-rings. Remember that Bilbo was smoking on the lawn and blowing smoke-rings idly when Gandalf first arrived. Tolkien invites us in that first scene to associate smoke-rings with relaxation, comfort, and conviviality—Bilbo does, at first, invite Gandalf to sit down and share his tobacco with him. Thorin's and Gandalf's smoke-rings, however, are clearly magical, and even vaguely threatening. Unlike Bilbo's smoke-rings, which just float away lazily over the Hill, Gandalf's smoke-rings are predatory, hunting down Thorin's rings and popping them. Smoke-rings, once associated with quiet and respectable pleasure, can now be seen hovering ominously around Gandalf's head, making him "look strange and sorcerous" (14). When adventures and magic break in on Bilbo's life, even the quietest and most mundane parts of it are touched by magic and made strange and wonderful. Once again Gandalf is the story-maker.

The most important thing that is altered by the adventure

that Bilbo has unknowingly invited into his house is Bilbo himself. The complex set of changes that Bilbo's character undergoes will be one of the central and most intricate stories of the entire book.

Bilbo begins, as I suggested earlier, as the very embodiment of the sedate and predictable world of the Bagginses. In his initial conversation with Gandalf, Bilbo is the spokesperson for the mundane hobbit world. He and his neighbors, he explains, are "plain quiet folk and have no use for adventures" (6). The terms of his rejection are as revealing as they are humorous; he dismisses them as "nasty disturbing uncomfortable things" that "make you late for dinner." Bilbo's initial perspective is so narrow, so domesticated, that being made late for dinner apparently counts as a very serious hazard. When Gandalf suggests sending *him* on an adventure, Bilbo runs into his house in panic.

When Gandalf's world pursues him into his house the next day, his initial response is once again pure Baggins. As he hears Balin, Dwalin, Fili, and Kili discussing goblins and dragons, Bilbo doesn't understand their remarks, and he "did not want to, for they sounded much too adventurous" (10). Even when his house has been thoroughly taken over by thirteen dwarves and one wizard, Bilbo tries to gather the scattered remains of his peaceful world around him. He can be found sitting on a stool at the fireside, "trying to look as if this was all perfectly ordinary and not in the least an adventure" (12). As a good Baggins, Bilbo attempts to remain firmly entrenched in his little world, even after it has been invaded by adventure.

We must remember, however, that there is more to Bilbo, and to hobbit culture in general, than the staid Baggins element. There is a portion of hobbit society that does not stick to the hobbit norm of predictability and sedate living. This is the Took clan, whose members have been known at times to "go and have adventures" (4). The family may try to hush up such shocking incidents, but "the fact remained that the Tooks were not as respectable as the Bagginses." They are not complete outcasts from society, however, primarily because they are also extremely wealthy, "undoubtedly richer" even than the comfortable Bagginses. The narrator even lends an otherworldly splendor to the Tooks by repeating the rumor that "one of the Took ancestors must have taken a fairy wife," that is to say, married an elf.* Although we are immediately told that this rumor is absurd, we are still presented with the idea that something magical and strange somehow entered into the Took family line at some point.

The contrast between the two hobbit families to which we are introduced, the respectable Bagginses and the remarkable Tooks, is a very important one, because Bilbo himself is the product of a combination of these two elements. A Took of long ago may or may not have married an elf, but it is quite certain that Bungo Baggins married "the famous Belladonna Took" (4).† Bilbo looks and behaves, we are told, "exactly like a second edition of his solid and comfortable father"; we have seen him first defending and then clinging to the quiet Baggins way of life. But the narrator of the story believes it probable that Bilbo "got something a bit queer in his make-up

---

* In his early writings, Tolkien often used the words *fairy* and *elf* interchangeably. Although he later went on to use *elf* almost exclusively, the two words are synonyms in *The Hobbit*.

† In some editions of *The Hobbit*, Belladonna Took is called "fabulous" instead of "famous."

from the Took side, something that only waited for a chance to come out" (5).

We can see glimpses of Bilbo's Took side peeking around the corner even before the dwarves show up at Bag-End. When he learns who Gandalf is, his first response is not stern disapproval but remembered wonder. He recalls the "magic diamond studs" that Gandalf gave to Bilbo's grandfather, the Old Took (7). He remembers Gandalf's stories, which he calls "wonderful tales," even though they are stories about adventures. He seems to particularly treasure the memory of the fireworks that Gandalf used to make, that "used to go up like great lilies and snapdragons and laburnums of fire and hang in the twilight all evening!" (7). Bilbo, it turns out, is "not so prosy as he liked to believe." Bilbo's settled, Baggins life is like prose, plain and businesslike, and the magical world of Gandalf and the dwarves is more like poetry, full of wonder and marvels, but also strange and sorcerous like Gandalf's smoke-rings. Bilbo may adhere to the Baggins point of view, but his Tookish heritage does give him a tendency toward that other, adventurous life, a tendency that is lurking beneath the surface when Bilbo meets Gandalf. This is why Bilbo starts to say that life used to be quite interesting when Gandalf was stirring up tales and adventures among the hobbits, before he realizes what he's saying and cuts himself off. Bilbo may seem to be completely committed to a life of Bagginsish predictability, but his character is more complex than he will admit.

Bilbo's Took side first comes out in response to poetry, when the dwarves sing their song about their treasure and their quest. The dwarves' music brings him outside his own experience for the first time, opening before him a world beyond the simple, comforting place that he has been trying to cling to. While the dwarves are playing their instruments, even before their song begins, Bilbo "forgot everything else, and was swept away into dark lands under strange moons, far over The Water and very far from his hobbit-hole under The Hill" (14). He is transported into the land of the dwarves, and their song even brings him to share for a moment their own perspective and experience. As they sing, he "felt the love of beautiful things made by hands and by cunning and by magic moving through him, a fierce and jealous love, the desire of the hearts of dwarves" (16). For a little while, Bilbo is moved by the music and the poetry of the dwarves, and he steps imaginatively out of his little world and into their story. At this moment, "something Tookish woke up inside him," and Bilbo finds that there is a part of him that desires adventure after all.

We have to be careful not to oversimplify things, though. Bilbo is not just a bold adventurer lurking beneath a mild-mannered exterior; he is not some kind of hobbit Clark Kent in search of a very small phone booth. Look at what actually happens when the Tookishness is awakened in him as the dwarves sing. When he is briefly transported by the desire for adventure, he "wished to go and see the great mountains, and hear the pine-trees and the waterfalls, and explore the caves, and wear a sword instead of a walking-stick" (16). This sounds very intrepid, but notice how tame this little adventure fantasy actually is. The reference to the walking-stick is revealing. The narrator mentions that Bilbo loves taking walks, and that he has hanging in his hallway a large map "of the Country Round with all his favourite walks marked on it in red ink" (20). His first adventurous moment essentially boils down to a desire to take a very long and spectacular walk, without any of the dangers and inconveniences likely to attend a *real* adventure. He wants to explore caves, but he gives no thought to the vicious goblins who might live in those caves. He wants to hear pine trees, but he is apparently forgetting the fire-breathing dragon whose wings make the pine trees roar in the dwarves' song. He imagines wearing a sword, but he does not think about actually having to use it. Bilbo's first step into the world of adventure is a quite tentative and childlike one.

Even if we don't immediately notice the timidity of Bilbo's first desire for adventure, his reaction to it emphasizes the point quite forcibly. Even the thought of imagined danger sends the Took side of him into full retreat. When his imaginings are interrupted by the sight of a perfectly mundane fire in the distance outside his window, he thinks of "plundering dragons," shudders, and jerks away from the adventurous thoughts he had been flirting with. "Very quickly," the narrator tells us, "he was plain Mr. Baggins of Bag-End, Under-Hill, again" (16). When the idea of mortal danger is later thrust upon him even more forcibly by Thorin's reference to the fact that they "may never return" from their quest, Bilbo completely loses control, shrieking helplessly and falling flat on the floor (17). The "firework glare" of Gandalf's staff suddenly lighting the room has Bilbo blindly calling out "struck by lightning!" again and again. The work of Gandalf, the magical story-maker, has shattered Bilbo's secure and comfortable world as if with a lightning flash, and it seems that Bilbo's latent Tookishness stirred up by the music and poetry of the dwarves is simply not equal to it.

The real turning point comes when Bilbo embraces his Took side with his will, and not just his rather timid imagination. When he overhears Gloin's insulting assessment of him, his Tookishness rises up in force. He now wants to be thought fierce, to be able to face danger. This was the last obstacle that had to be overcome in order for him actually to embark on an adventurous career. Now when he declares himself ready to take part in the adventure, it may still involve a long walk, but it is no longer *just* a walk. He says he is willing to "walk from here to the East of East and fight wild Were-worms in the Last Desert" (19). We might suspect him of "poetical exaggeration" here, but at least he is now imagining using that sword that he proposes to exchange for his walking-stick. The fact that he still thinks of going without bed and breakfast as a major sacrifice shows that he has no real understanding of what the adventure will be like, but he is willing nevertheless. This is the moment in which the narrator declares, "The Took side had won" (18).

Even after this important turning point, it is clear that Bilbo has not undergone a sudden and complete transformation to Tookishness. The narrator tells us that "many a time afterwards the Baggins part regretted" this decision (18). Even while he is feeling "Tookishly determined to go on with things," there is still a lot of Baggins about him (22). Before he will enter into any discussions of plans or strategies, he puts on "his business manner (usually reserved for people who tried to borrow money off him)" and insists on having the whole story of the gold and the dragon made quite clear. Thorin, in some exasperation, asks, "Didn't you hear our song?" Their poetry, it seems to Thorin, is a more than sufficient explanation of what is going on. As I will show soon, the song does indeed tell the whole story and explain everything one really needs to know about the quest, and about who the dwarves are. We know that Bilbo did take in much of that, for we saw that he was stirred and even briefly enchanted by their song, but this is not enough for Mr. Baggins. He may not be completely prosy, but he still wants everything laid out in prose, plain and clear, to supplement the poetry.

As we read through *The Hobbit,* we will be keeping a close eye on the interaction between the Took and Baggins elements within Bilbo's character. The interplay between these two very different aspects of Bilbo's nature is very complex, and Tolkien will steadily resist bringing it to a simplified resolution.

Burglar Bilbo: The Chosen and Selected Burglar

Bilbo's decision to embrace his Took side, turn the handle of the door, and volunteer for this adventure is triggered by his overhearing Gloin's unflattering appraisal of him. Gloin thinks there must have been some mistake; Bilbo cannot possibly be the "fellow conspirator" that the dwarves are looking for. "As soon as I clapped eyes on the little fellow bobbing and puffing on the mat," he remarks with a snort, "I had my doubts. He looks more like a grocer than a burglar!" (18). Gloin's remark is perhaps unkindly expressed,* but it is not far wrong. Furthermore, the circumstances make his exasperation quite understandable. Remember, Bilbo is not being invited along out of pity or kindness; he is being referred to the dwarves as an expert, and they are looking to hire him as a kind of independent contractor. They want a professional burglar.

---

* Part of what offends Bilbo in Gloin's remark are the class implications of being compared with a grocer, when Bilbo is obviously not in the working class. The narrator never mentions anything related to this social insult explicitly, but it doubtless adds to the sting.

Perhaps even more surprising than the fact that the dwarves' recruiting brought them to Bag-End is the fact that Bilbo genuinely seems to care about their assessment of him as adventurer material. One might expect that a respectable Baggins would actually be *insulted* if an outlandish party of strange dwarves took him for a professional thief. Instead, Bilbo immediately wants to prove himself fierce, and to live up to the label of Burglar. What is at stake here is not merely Bilbo's own desire for adventure, but his identity. What is he, and what is his role?

It is Gandalf, the story-maker, who initiates this process. A day or two before, Bilbo might have believed that he knew exactly who and what he was. Now Gandalf has come along and scratched a notice on his door identifying him as an "Expert Treasure-hunter" (19). At first it might seem that Gandalf is playing some elaborate practical joke. He knows full well that the magical mark he drew on Bilbo's door is comically inappropriate. Coming out of the conversation he has just had with Bilbo and describing him as a burglar who "wants a good job, plenty of Excitement and reasonable Reward" is simply absurd. The notion of Bilbo's seeking excitement is so ridiculous that it amuses Gandalf himself tremendously; he laughs "long but quietly" before writing it (8). The recommendations he offers to the dwarves after Bilbo collapses in terror are no less absurd. Perhaps his claim that Bilbo is "fierce as a dragon in a pinch" can be excused as mere "poetical exaggeration," but on what possible basis can Gandalf claim that Bilbo is "one of the best" (18)? It rather sounds as if Gandalf is just putting them on.

However, though it may seem like the setup for a practical joke, when it comes to the identification of Bilbo as a Burglar, Gandalf really does seem to mean it. Rather than backing down from a joke that would seem to be in poor taste, Gandalf heatedly insists on what he has said: "If I say he is a Burglar, a Burglar he is, or will be when the time comes" (19). This is hard for either the dwarves or Bilbo himself to believe, but Gandalf firmly maintains it, overriding all objections. Gandalf declares that Bilbo is the "chosen and selected burglar" (21), a resonant and rather ominous phrase that seems to speak of more than just Gandalf's choice. Unlikely though it may seem to absolutely everyone, Bilbo is in some sense the burglar of destiny.

The Desire of the Hearts of Dwarves

We have been focusing quite a bit on Bilbo and his relationship to the adventure that comes through his door, but we have not yet said much about the dwarves who bring that adventure with them. The best introduction that we get to the dwarves, as I mentioned before, is the song they sing that briefly sweeps Bilbo away. Under the influence of the dwarves' music, Bilbo comes to perceive "the desire of the hearts of dwarves" (15). It stands to reason, therefore, that if we would like to get to know Thorin and Company better, we should take a careful look at what they sing. Let's start with the first half of the song:

Far over the misty mountains cold
To dungeons deep and caverns old
We must away ere break of day
To seek the pale enchanted gold.

The dwarves of yore made mighty spells,
While hammers fell like ringing bells

In places deep, where dark things sleep,
In hollow halls beneath the fells.

For ancient king and elvish lord
There many a gleaming golden hoard
They shaped and wrought, and light they caught
To hide in gems on hilt of sword.

On silver necklaces they strung
The flowering stars, on crowns they hung
The dragon-fire, in twisted wire
They meshed the light of moon and sun.

Far over the misty mountains cold
To dungeons deep and caverns old
We must away, ere break of day,
To claim our long-forgotten gold
(14–15).

The song begins with a stanza that appears three times during the song, and it serves as a statement of the purpose of the dwarves' quest. They explain where they are going: to their ancient underground home ("dungeons deep and caverns old"). They illustrate how far removed that destination is from them, both in terms of distance and of the barriers that separate them from their homeland ("Far over the misty mountains cold"). They indicate the urgency of their longing to return ("We must away ere break of day"). Finally and most importantly, they describe their primary motivation: their lost and magical treasure ("To seek the pale enchanted gold"). This stanza alone gives most of the explanation of what the dwarves are actually doing.

In the next few stanzas, we get an insight into the nature of dwarves. The settings within the song are all dark and ominous, full of subterranean gloom. The dwarves recall "dungeons deep" and "places deep, where dark things sleep." They do not actually boast of their underground halls or attribute any beauty to them. What obviously matters to them are the treasures that are crafted within those "hollow halls," which echo with the music of the ringing hammers.

Although the home of the dwarves sounds dark and gloomy, the works of craft that the dwarves make are, by contrast, associated with light. The dwarves catch light and hide it "in gems on hilt of sword." They string stars on necklaces and hang dragon-fire on crowns and mesh the "light of moon and sun" in twisted wire. The dwarves apparently do not need the sun in their deep and shadowy halls; their "gleaming golden hoard" is their sun and moon, the focus of their love and their passion.

When the dwarves repeat the first stanza, they change the way in which they express the purpose of their journey, from "To seek the pale enchanted gold" to "To claim our long-forgotten gold" (though it is obvious that the dwarves haven't forgotten about it, if others have). The introduction of the possessive pronoun here is important, for at this point the focus of the song turns from the treasure alone to the dwarves' relationship with it:

Goblets they carved there for themselves
And harps of gold; where no man delves
There lay they long, and many a song
Was sung unheard by men or elves.

The pines were roaring on the height,
The winds were moaning in the night.

The fire was red, it flaming spread;
The trees like torches blazed with light.

The bells were ringing in the dale
And men looked up with faces pale;
Then dragon's ire more fierce than fire
Laid low their towers and houses frail.

The mountain smoked beneath the moon;
The dwarves, they heard the tramp of doom.
They fled their hall to dying fall
Beneath his feet, beneath the moon.

Far over the misty mountains grim
To dungeons deep and caverns dim
We must away, ere break of day,
To win our harps and gold from him!
   (15–16)

The second half of the song starts with another stanza in praise of the dwarves' handiwork, but notice how the focus has shifted. Now the song emphasizes how the dwarves carved these goblets "for themselves," and that they were kept "where no man delves." We hear of the songs of the dwarves and their golden harps, but we are told that these songs are private songs, "unheard by men or elves." Having seen the love of the dwarves for their works of craft, we now see their secrecy and possessiveness.

It is in the context of this privacy, this ownership of their treasure, that they speak of the invasion of the dragon and of his violation and destruction of their kingdom. Notice that the song never actually depicts Smaug the dragon; he himself is not a character in this poem. Instead, they merely describe the effects of his coming, always indirectly. The trees on the mountain roar in the wind of the dragon's wings and then blaze like torches as he sets the mountain ablaze. The towers and houses of the Men of Dale are laid low, not by Smaug, but by the "dragon's ire," by his anger—he is depersonalized. We don't get a direct image of Smaug crawling into the mountain halls and killing the dwarves; instead we get the dwarves who hear "the tramp of doom" and then flee the hall "to dying fall / Beneath his feet"—again, the focus is entirely on the dwarvish victims rather than on the dragon who is killing them. The story of the fall of the dwarf kingdom in the Lonely Mountain that Thorin and his friends sing is told in such a way as to keep the focus on the victims killed by the dragon, and on the destruction wrought by the dragon. Those are what they want to hold in mind; they seem almost to want to avoid paying Smaug the compliment of making him the chief character of their story.

But they have certainly not forgotten him. The final stanza, the third instance of the repeated chorus, emphasizes their central purpose: to get back what was stolen from them. The new rhyming words introduced the third time through, *grim* and *dim* and *him,* indicate the attitude and seriousness of the dwarves. If we go back and look at the changing last line of the repeated stanza, we can see the overall shape of their focus in this adventure. It starts with praise of the glory of "pale enchanted gold," passes on to their claim on *their* "long-forgotten gold," and ends with their grim desire not only to recover their treasure, but to "win" it back, to seek vengeance on the dragon who stole it.

The love of the dwarves for their treasure is fierce and jealous, and it is shrouded with gloom and darkness. It starts in those deep, dark places the first two stanzas talk about, and it ends with the "dark business" of revenge. The dwarves use this phrase, "dark business," to describe their plans right after the song has ended. After the music ceases, they all find themselves sitting in the dark, for night has fallen and the fire has gone out. When Bilbo makes to fetch a light, the dwarves tell him, "We like the dark . . . Dark for dark business!" (16). Thorin and his companions are the good guys in this story, and their people have been the victims of a terrible atrocity about which they feel very strongly for quite natural reasons. But there is undeniably something dark and unsettling about these dwarves, apart from their association with the strange and Tookish world of adventure.

Bilbo, even at his most Tookish, cannot really relate to the dwarves very well, and this moment at the end of the dwarves' song illustrates that fact nicely. Bilbo, having emerged from his brief enchantment by the dwarf song, is disturbed by the darkness, and he is divided in his mind. The narrator tells us, "He had less than half a mind to fetch the lamp, and more than half a mind to pretend to, and go and hide behind the beer-barrels in the cellar" (16). The smaller half of his mind is the Tookish part, willing to continue taking part in this strange meeting. The larger half is the Baggins part, wanting to escape these unsettling visitors entirely. Notice, however, that *neither* half sympathizes with the darkness of the dwarves' thinking. Bilbo seeks either to escape it or to illuminate it, but he cannot simply enter into it. His perspective is very different from that of the dwarves, and that separation is not simply a product of the Took-Baggins divide. As we will see throughout the book, Bilbo will never truly fit in with his companions.

The Writing of *The Hobbit:* An Introduction to Fantasy

Before we move on to Chapter Two and the real beginning of Bilbo's adventure, I'd like to take a step back to look at a wider view of what Tolkien accomplishes in this opening chapter. Tolkien was very aware of the artistic challenge he faced in writing a work of fantasy, especially since fantasy literature was far from the literary mainstream in the early twentieth century. He knew that when they encountered his story in *The Hobbit,* his readers would have to leave their mundane and comfortable world behind and invest their imaginations in a world that contains magic and unexpected marvels. In Chapter One, Tolkien gives us a model for this very process within the story itself. We begin in our safe and predictable world, and in the first chapter, we find ourselves in a world of wizards and dwarves and dragons. In this transition, we find ourselves coming alongside a protagonist who is struggling through exactly the same process, a character who himself internalizes the conflict between the mundane and the marvelous. Our first introduction to this magical, grim, and dangerous world of adventure is also his introduction, and his reluctance and difficulty in adjusting to it give us time to ease past our own discomfort and reservations. Bilbo Baggins serves as the perfect touchstone for readers, both exploring and embodying the tricky frontier between the predictable and the unexpected.

Tolkien also faces an additional challenge in *The Hobbit* in that his intended audience is primarily younger readers. As Tolkien introduces his readers to his fantasy world, we can see him showing a careful sensitivity to the children in his audience. The reader's first encounter with Gandalf the wizard is a good example. Bilbo's first recollection of Gandalf is his giving "Old Took a pair of magic diamond studs that fastened themselves and never came undone till ordered" (7). On the one hand, this is genuinely marvelous, a trick that has the splendor not only of magic but also of gemstones to fill it with wonder. This was certainly a rare and precious gift from Gandalf to his friend. However, as our very first introduction to Gandalf's wizardry, it is a somewhat odd piece of work, an impressive but rather domestic bit of magic. What it accomplishes, though, is to bring the world of magic and wizardry into contact with children's own daily routines, inviting them to imagine how wonderful it would be to have fastenings on their clothes that were not only made of diamonds, but would instantly fasten themselves at a word. Even Gandalf's most spectacular enchantments, his fireworks, recall the mundane world, for non-magical fireworks are enough to inspire awe in a child, and Tolkien invokes this experience as a launching point for his readers' imaginations. Gandalf's magical and altogether remarkable fireworks (which clearly made an enormous impression on Bilbo in his youth) give children a glimpse of how much higher the ceiling is for wonder in this amazing new world. Tolkien makes his fantasy world imaginatively approachable for his young audience while still emphasizing how magical and marvelous it is.

Tolkien is also very clever and sensitive about the way in which he introduces children to the more serious elements of his story. When Thorin is listing the splendors of the dwarf kingdom of old during his prose history of the coming of Smaug, for instance, he mentions the gold and the jewels of the dwarves, but his primary illustration of dwarvish craftsmanship is "the most marvellous and magical toys, the like of which is not to be found in the world now-a-days" (22). The capstone on his account of the kingdom's prosperity is the fact that "the toy market of Dale was the wonder of the North" (23). Amusingly, Thorin follows this statement with the ominous transition "Undoubtedly that was what brought the dragon." Tolkien seems almost to suggest that Smaug's greed was aroused mainly by their wonderful toys. In this way, Tolkien brings the greed and desire of dragons within the scope of a child's experience and imagination. He also manages to touch the treasure-lust of dragons with just a hint of frivolity, which serves to blunt the edges of its terror for his young audience.

The fact is that the story Tolkien is setting out to tell is one that is quite serious, and even at times gruesome. Thorin and his companions have been living in exile since they were driven out many years before to wander homeless and destitute in the wild. They are preparing to set out on an all but hopeless quest to take vengeance on the monstrous dragon who massacred their people and destroyed their homes. In this first chapter, however, Tolkien very persistently couples his grim story with a lightheartedness of tone. As Bilbo's house is being invaded by dwarves and his life is being turned upside down, Tolkien is careful to keep the mood light by remarking that "this was the most awkward Wednesday he ever remembered" (11). Even the massacre of the dwarves of the Lonely Mountain is made light of at one point, when Gandalf observes that Smaug would be far too fat to fit through the narrow secret passage after "devouring so many of the dwarves and men of Dale" (20). Most conspicuous of all is how Tolkien tones down the tragedy of the disappearance and death, under mysterious and horrifying circumstances, of Thorin's father by having Gandalf rather whimsically begin the story by remarking that he "went away on the twenty-first of April, a hundred years ago last Thursday" (24). Tolkien deals with solemn and frightening things, but he still strives, through comical turns of phrase, to keep *The Hobbit* from becoming terrifying.

This choice reflects Tolkien's attitude toward children and children's stories in general. On the one hand, he is sensitive to their fears, and he doesn't want to terrify his young audience. On the other hand, he has no desire to shield them completely from serious or even gruesome things. In his essay "On Fairy-stories," in which Tolkien explains many of his theories about fantasy literature, he argues that children's stories should never be simply rose-tinted, cleared of all that is dark or frightening. He insists on the educational value of good stories dealing with serious issues, with good and evil, recognizing that there *are* horrible and frightening things in the world. "Children are meant to grow up," he explains, "and not to become Peter Pans. Not to lose innocence and wonder; but to proceed on the appointed journey." He maintains that "on callow, lumpish, and selfish youth, peril, sorrow, and the shadow of death can bestow dignity, and even sometimes wisdom."*

By the end of *The Hobbit*, we will see that the tone and mood change quite a bit from the comical and lighthearted beginning. As Bilbo pursues his quest and gains wisdom and experience, the story itself will mature. In Chapter One, Tolkien gently prepares his juvenile audience for their journey, and if they remain Tookishly determined to see it through, like Bilbo, they will find that they too have gradually changed and grown during the course of the adventure.

---

* J.R.R. Tolkien, "On Fairy-stories," in *The Tolkien Reader* (Del Rey, 1986), 137.

2

In the Lone-lands

"ROAST MUTTON"

Bilbo's Nature: Neither Took nor Baggins

When the narrator is introducing Bilbo at the beginning of Chapter One, he describes the book as "a story of how a Baggins had an adventure" and adds, "He may have lost the neighbours' respect, but he gained—well, you will see whether he gained anything in the end" (4). As we go through *The Hobbit*, I want to follow the prompt that Tolkien gives us in this passage, looking out for how Bilbo changes and develops through his adventures and, as the narrator implies, what he gains from these changes in the end. In the first chapter, we looked at how Tolkien sets up Bilbo's character, establishing the conflict between his Baggins and Took natures. In Chapter Two, we will see what the soft, sheltered Bilbo's adjustment to the adventuring life is actually like.

The chapter begins with what seems like a huge anticlimax. Bilbo wakes up to find both the dwarves and the wizard simply gone, leaving only massive piles of dirty dishes behind. This hardly seems like the direction the story had been taking the night before, even if we only consider the trajectory of Bilbo's character development. On the previous day, Bilbo went through a series of internal upheavals. His imagination and emotions were stirred by the dwarves' song, but then he was reduced to fits of screaming terror by the prospect of the dangers of the journey. Finally, inspired by anger and offended dignity at being insulted by the dwarves, he made the rather unlikely resolution to accompany the dwarves on their adventure. Even though he clearly retained reservations at the end of the chapter, we are certainly led to believe that the Took side had won.

When Bilbo wakes up in Chapter Two, the Tookish determination of the night before seems to have almost completely evaporated. The narrator tells us that he hoped that the unexpected party had been just a bad dream (27). Bilbo does show a brief and residual flash of Tookish spirit, feeling "just a trifle disappointed" that the dwarves had apparently decided to go on without him. But his Baggins side swiftly takes over again. He is surprised at his slight disappointment, but he immediately rebukes himself for it, dismissing the dwarves, the dragon, and the quest as "outlandish nonsense" and chiding himself for a fool. He puts on his apron and sets himself to the "dismally real" but refreshingly unadventurous task of washing the dishes, re-establishing his former calm and predictable life. It is as if cleaning up the evidence of the party has in some sense erased it, for he even begins "to forget about the night before." He seems to be subsiding very contentedly back into his sleepy Baggins life; by the time he is sitting down to "a nice little second breakfast in the dining-room by the open window," his world seems to be restored to its former equilibrium.

Once again, adventure bursts in on him. Gandalf's sudden appearance might not be quite as unexpected as the party of the previous day, but its impact is even more disruptive. Within five minutes of Gandalf's arrival, Bilbo is dashing out the door and leaving his home behind, having made no preparations for the journey whatsoever. The most important step Bilbo will ever take, the decision actually to leave his home and his comfortable world behind and walk off into the blue, is made almost without his realizing it. The narrator says that "to the end of his days Bilbo could never remember how he found himself" outside of his house and pelting off down the lane (28). In the end, Bilbo is swept off onto his adventure without either the Took or the Baggins sides of him having much to say about it.

Since Bilbo never really resolves to leave home, he is left in a rather indeterminate state. In order for him to have made the choice, in cold blood, to cross the threshold and leave Bag-End behind, his Took side would have to have been in much firmer control than we ever saw it back in Chapter One. He may have been "Tookishly determined to go on with things" at the end of their conversation in the dark of night (22), but we saw how quickly that resolution evaporated in the morning sun the next day. The startling intervention of Gandalf shooing him out the door, however, leaves his opposing impulses still unresolved. He is physically neither packed nor prepared for the journey, and his psychological state is in similar disarray; he ends up setting off on his adventure without ever determining whether or not he wants to do so.

Bilbo doesn't even have a coat of his own to travel in, so he has to borrow a cloak and hood from Dwalin, who has a spare. The secondhand adventurer outfit is "too large for him, and he looked rather comic," we are told (29). The image of Bilbo riding along in his ill-fitting dwarf hood is the perfect representation of Bilbo's state as he starts his travels. He is traveling, both figuratively and literally, in borrowed clothes; they are outlandish, not at all respectable, and they don't fit him. The narrator drives this point home by recalling at this moment Bilbo's ultra-predictable family heritage, remarking, "What his father Bungo would have thought of him, I daren't think" (29). But what we see in Bilbo is not merely an aspiring but incompetent adventurer. Bilbo is rather glad that he sticks out in this strange group, taking comfort in the fact that "he couldn't be mistaken for a dwarf, as he had no beard." Bilbo is poised between his Took and Baggins impulses, simultaneously trying to fit in and glad that he doesn't.

Bilbo has entered a kind of no-man's land, a very awkward place in which neither side of him is satisfied. He is rapidly losing the respect of his neighbors (or would be, if they could see him), but he has not yet gained the respect of the dwarves. Thorin speaks of awaiting Bilbo's "respected person" at the Green Dragon Inn, but this seems to be openly sarcastic on his part (28). Thorin obviously doesn't respect Bilbo at all, as we can see in his snide remark the night before, offered in "mock-politeness," when he says, "supposing the burglar-expert gives us some ideas or suggestions" (21). Thorin's use of "respected" in the letter is conspicuous, given how integral respectability was to the Baggins family reputation. It is clear that the respect of the dwarves and the respect of Bilbo's hobbit neighbors are mutually exclusive, and Bilbo is currently in limbo, having neither.

The physical journey, at the outset, also parallels Bilbo's internal state. At first, they are traveling through "a wide respectable country inhabited by decent folk" (30). The frightful quest with its forebodings of deadly danger has turned out only to be a pleasant ride through beautiful country. This is just the kind of trip that Bilbo enjoys, and he begins "to feel that adventures were not so bad after all" (30). Gandalf has even brought along Bilbo's pipe and some pocket-handkerchiefs. This feeling, however, is not his Tookishness emerging with any real strength; he only thinks he likes adventures now because he hasn't had any yet. In this first stage, he is under the same delusion in which he indulged after he heard the dwarves' song, when he briefly imagined those sterile, danger-free exploits being like a good long walk.

Soon, however, they move into "lands where people spoke strangely, and sang songs Bilbo had never heard before" (30). Even this comparatively mild element of strangeness turns out to be only transitional, and they soon pass into "the Lone-lands, where there were no people left, no inns, and the roads grew steadily worse." In this chapter, Bilbo is indeed in the Lone-lands. His comfortable Baggins world is disappearing behind him, but he remains separated from his new companions as well, belonging nowhere and fitting in with nobody.

His response to the situation is to start retreating in his mind back to Bag-End, wishing he were at home in his "nice hole by the fire, with the kettle just beginning to sing!" (30). This, of course, is to be a repeated refrain throughout the book, as the narrator indicates by telling us, "It was not the last time he wished that!" The specific image of his chair by the fireside and of his tea-kettle is a perfect little distillation of his old safe, comfortable, civilized, and pleasant Baggins world, and he will frequently return to it for refuge when he is feeling overwhelmed, miserable, or afraid. The first occasion that triggers this imaginative retreat is not danger or fright, but simply wretched discomfort. They are camping in the Lone-lands, and everything goes wrong: they can't light the fire, a pony carrying food bolts into the river, and they have little food left (31). The narrator completes the picture of misery by describing the annoying "drip, drip" of rainwater on their heads under the trees. This hardship will seem quite tame in retrospect compared to some of the difficulties Bilbo will find himself in later on, but for now, it is more than enough to make him regret all this Tookish adventure and seek comfort in the coziness of his remembered Bagginsish world.

In positioning Bilbo in the "Lone-lands" stage of his transformation, Tolkien gives us the story through the perspective of a character who sits on the margins of the two worlds. By doing this, Tolkien is able to present the story from two different angles at once. We are able to share the wide-eyed wonder (and the nervousness and fright) that Bilbo feels at times as new and unimagined scenes open up before him. But at the same time, Tolkien doesn't have to ask us to invest ourselves blindly in this strange new world, either. Since it is Bilbo who is our representative in this story, we will never lose touch with his very down-to-earth perspective on this fantastic world.

Burglar Bilbo: A Beginning

In Chapter One, Tolkien calls our attention to Bilbo's identification as a burglar. As you will recall, Gandalf hotly informs the dwarves, "If I say he is a Burglar, a Burglar he is, or will be when the time comes" (19). In Chapter Two, the dwarves seem to have accepted Gandalf's word on this, at least provisionally. Yes, Thorin is probably being rather wry when he addresses Mr. Baggins as "Burglar Bilbo" in his letter (28), but their discussion in the wet and dripping woods near the trolls' campfire shows that they are at least willing to play along with the idea. They are looking for Gandalf at first, of course, but when he can't be found they turn to Bilbo, remarking, "After all we have got a burglar with us" (32). Ridiculous though it might seem, Bilbo is the only "professional" adventurer they have with them, in Gandalf's absence.

By approaching the fire that they have seen in the dark, Bilbo is accepting the title and role of Burglar for the first time in actual practice. The narrator quite subtly and amusingly recognizes that there is some doubt about whether the label fits, however. When the dwarves finally say, "Now it is the burglar's turn," the narrator adds, "meaning Bilbo," as if we might not be completely sure to whom the dwarves are referring (32). When Bilbo first steps forward as a burglar, however, we immediately learn an interesting fact. Bilbo might have looked more like a grocer than a burglar when he was standing on his doormat back in Bag-End, but it turns out that he does have the relevant skill set to be an excellent burglar. He can move so quietly that not "even a weasel would have stirred a whisker at it" (33). His first professional job does not quite end as planned, but we shouldn't overlook the fact that he does succeed in picking William's pocket. He can hardly be blamed for not realizing that the purse itself would cry out and give him away.

In *The Lord of the Rings*, Frodo will remember Bilbo's encounter with the trolls somewhat nostalgically as "Bilbo's first successful adventure."* Looking at what actually happens in

---

* J.R.R. Tolkien, *The Fellowship of the Ring* (Mariner Books, 2012), 201.

The Hobbit, this sounds like a rather generous description. His task, remember, is just to sneak up to the fire and see if everything is "perfectly safe and canny" (32). When Bilbo sees that there are three grumpy trolls sitting around the fire, he has more or less established a solid lack of either safety or canniness, and he should be skipping right back to his companions to tell them so. Instead, he takes an unnecessary risk that ends up getting them all caught and nearly eaten by the trolls. As Bombur remarks in a delightfully alliterative observation, it was a "silly time to go practising pinching and pocket-picking . . . when what we wanted was fire and food" (40). From a coldly calculating perspective, Bilbo has hardly covered himself in glory on this little venture.

The most important thing about this incident for Bilbo, however, is his conscious choice to accept and try to live up to the title that Gandalf gave him, a choice that is, from one point of view, rather unexpected. He didn't even really make the decision to leave his house and set out on the adventure, after all, and remember, this is the hobbit who collapsed onto the rug and started shrieking and quivering like jelly at the mere mention of danger. Now, he not only agrees to walk into unknown danger in a dark and ominous forest at night, but he even insists on doing a far more dangerous thing than was asked of him. Scampering back to the dwarves as soon as he sees the trolls would not only be the most prudent choice; it would also fulfill his charge. He finds, however, that he "somehow could not go straight back to Thorin and Company emptyhanded" (34). What motivates him is a desire to live up to Gandalf's recommendation, and perhaps to earn his new companions' respect. When Bilbo slips his hand into William's pocket, committing his first "burglarious" act,

Bilbo says to himself in short-lived satisfaction, "this is a beginning!" (34). It may not be an unqualified success, but it is
indeed the official beginning of Bilbo's adventuring career.

The Dwarves: Neither Giving
nor Receiving Respect

There are two moments in Chapter Two when we gain a bit
more of an insight into the character of the dwarves. The first
is the letter that Thorin leaves on the mantelpiece. The note
is extravagantly formal and businesslike, with its references
to "total profits" and "travelling expenses" and "funeral expenses to be defrayed by us or our representatives" (28). In
fact, it seems clear that Thorin is parodying formalized contract language—some of it so far over the top that it doesn't
even make sense. He states that the terms of the contract are
"cash on delivery," which sounds very proper until you think
about it for a few seconds. What is he promising cash in payment for the delivery of? What is Bilbo supposed to deliver?
The entire treasure hoard, one hobbit-load at a time? That
would be asking a lot!

In fact, I take the stilted formal language of the letter to be
a joke at Bilbo's expense. Remember that Thorin was annoyed
when Bilbo put on his "business manner" and asked for the
whole situation to be made "all plain and clear," asking for details about "out-of-pocket expenses" and "remuneration" and
such legalities. In his note, Thorin seems to be taking up that
tone of inappropriate formality and giving it back to him in a
way calculated to make it seem a little silly.

In addition, Thorin appears to be gently mocking Bilbo

for his cowardice of the previous day, when Bilbo collapsed in terror at Thorin's hint that they might never return from their journey. Thorin offers to cover Bilbo's funeral expenses "if occasion arises and the matter is not otherwise arranged for" (28). These alternative funeral dispositions, one presumes, would be Bilbo's body being lost over a cliff or washed down a river, or perhaps dragged off and ripped to pieces by wild animals, or, in the last resort, eaten by the dragon. Thorin's over-delicate and hyper-formalized allusion to the dangers of their journey sounds like a way of teasing the hobbit both for his fright and for his taking refuge when flustered in legal language.

Despite the disdain in which Thorin, at least, seems to hold their new employee and companion, the dwarves don't abandon him when he is in trouble. When he fails to return from his reconnaissance of the campfire in the woods, they come after him to see if he needs help, even before he can attempt to give the distress signal of owl-noises that Thorin assigns him. Given how low Thorin's opinion of him seems to be, one might think that he would consider the capture of such a hopeless burglar only a little loss. But Thorin and his companions instead put themselves in very real danger to rescue him. Thorin might be skeptical and haughty, but he does honor his bargains and stick by his companions.

The other interesting aspect of the dwarves' actions in this chapter is exactly how ineffectual their attempts to help Bilbo are. The dwarves prove themselves to be noble, but they also show themselves to be completely incompetent. The arrival of the dwarves at Bag-End is the intrusion of the adventurous world into Bilbo's life; they are almost identified with the wild world. Despite this, however, we should notice that the dwarves themselves are not hardened, expert adventurers at all. They might comment archly that Bilbo's lack of pocket-handkerchiefs will be the least of the deprivations he will have to endure on their journey, but when the party actually hits the road, they are grumbling for regular meals at least as loudly as the hobbit.

What is more, our metalsmith dwarves seem to have set off on their journey entirely unarmed. That might seem incomprehensible, but either they have no weapons at all or else they simply don't think to bring them along when they explore a strange fire in the dark, from which one of their companions has already failed to return—remember that Thorin is reduced to fighting the trolls with sticks that he plucks out of the trolls' own campfire. Neither alternative speaks very highly of the dwarves' resourcefulness and planning; Bilbo has not exactly signed on with the Dream Team here. Their naiveté is also quite striking. When they see the trolls' fire in the distance, they decide to investigate on the principle that "anything was better than little supper, less breakfast, and wet clothes all the night" (32). Presumably, when they are packed up in the trolls' sacks and waiting to be cooked and eaten, they start rethinking that little piece of analysis. Despite Thorin's low opinion of Bilbo, the dwarves themselves seem little more accustomed to life in the Wild than their new burglar is.

Trolls: The Cockney Terrors

If the dwarves fail to impress us as heroes, the trolls may also surprise us as villains. The three trolls are, first and foremost, comical figures, clearly designed to get laughs. They have working-class names and cockney accents, and they drink beer out of jugs. They roll around on the ground, fighting like schoolboys, whacking one another with sticks. They throw silly insults at each other, such as "lout" and "booby," and the narrator assures us (in my favorite phrase in the book) that these are "perfectly true and applicable names" (35). The trolls are genuinely funny characters.

We cannot overlook the fact that the trolls have a serious side, however. What we learn of the nature of trolls is quite chilling. They are made of "the stuff of the mountains," and they are so tied in the essence of their being to the dark that the light of the sun destroys them (40). They are living stone, animated by darkness, enormously strong, and delighting in murder. They may be funny, but they are no joke; even the elves avoid the region for fear of them.

In Chapter One, we saw how Tolkien treated solemn or frightful subjects with a comical, lighthearted touch, presenting dark things in such a way as to keep them from being too overwhelming and terrifying. Nowhere in *The Hobbit* is that strategy more brilliantly executed than in his depiction of the trolls.

We find out about the terrible aspects of their nature and the fear they have inspired in the region only at the very end of the encounter, after Gandalf arrives and the trolls are safely petrified. When Tolkien introduces us to the trolls, he sets the scene very deliberately. In describing what Bilbo sees when he looks into the clearing by the fire, the narrator doesn't just tell us that he sees three trolls. If he had, we might start off the encounter with some terrifying image of our own imagining before us. Instead, the narrator paints for us an initial scene that is quite homey, even comforting. There is "a large fire of beech-logs," mutton being toasted "on long spits of wood," "a barrel of good drink at hand," and a "fine, toothsome smell"

(33). Only after this quiet image does the narrator inform us that the "three very large persons" sitting by the fire are "obviously trolls." He doesn't prompt us to imagine the trolls until he has placed them in a comparatively non-threatening environment.

Tolkien's handling of the trolls' conversation itself is masterful. The content of their talk, taken alone, is simply horrifying. They are longing for the taste of human flesh, and one of them casually reveals that they have recently murdered and eaten enough people to fill "a village and a half" (33). He may be exaggerating, of course, but we have no reason to think he is just making it up. Tolkien softens these harrowing details by drawing attention not to what the trolls say, but to how they say it. The narrator speaks disapproving words, not of the trolls' bloodthirstiness, but of their poor grammar and impolite speech, which is "not drawing-room fashion at all, at all." Right after he makes the comment about slaughtering a village and a half, William takes a big bite of mutton "and wiped his lips on his sleeve," at which point the narrator comments, "Yes, I am afraid trolls do behave like that." The humorous part is that it is unclear which troll behavior the narrator is apologizing for—the massacre of entire towns full of people or the wiping of his mouth on his sleeve. Tolkien manages to register the trolls' savagery in his readers' minds while still diffusing it by lumping it in with their mere impoliteness and bad manners.

It is also no coincidence that when Bilbo and his friends encounter the trolls, the moments that could be the most disturbing are also the most amusing. I am thinking in particular about the many times the trolls talk about eating Bilbo and the dwarves. Bilbo getting captured and almost eaten for dinner would be terrifying—if not for the trolls' references to cookery. A troll who sizes up a captive hobbit and speculates about how much meat will be left over after the hobbit has been skinned and boned (as if he were standing at the counter of a butcher's shop) is not all that frightening. No matter how many times I read *The Hobbit*, I cannot help but laugh when Bert suggests that if they could catch a few more they might make a pie. Even Bilbo himself seems in on the joke; while he is being suspended from the troll's fist by his own hair, he stammers out witty wordplay: "I am a good cook myself, and cook better than I cook, if you see what I mean. I'll cook beautifully for you, a perfectly beautiful breakfast for you, if only you won't have me for supper" (35). Bilbo, threatened with gruesome death, nevertheless picks up on the spirit of the encounter.

The capture of the dwarves works similarly. The dwarves are popped into sacks and then forced to listen while the trolls debate over exactly how their victims should be prepared for eating. The idea of trolls pausing to have this discussion is highly comical; we might not have expected man-eating trolls to get so absorbed in a culinary debate that they forget about the one thing they must fear above all others: the sunrise.

We might perhaps find "Roast Mutton" a rather odd title for this chapter; in fact, it might be the most peculiar chapter title in the whole book. Surely the mutton itself plays the smallest possible role in the events of the chapter? Notice, though, how the title anticipates Tolkien's entire approach to the depiction of the trolls. Food is, in fact, the main focus of the episode. By referring to the mutton on the trolls' spits in the chapter title, Tolkien fixes our attention on the trolls' means of getting and preparing their supper. They are eating mutton while wishing they had human flesh, but they are "quite likely to try roasted dwarf" (33). Tolkien might have titled the chapter "Roasted Dwarf and Hobbit Pie," but that would have been horrifying. In the title, as in the chapter itself, the threat is present, but submerged.

Tolkien takes the terror out of the troll encounter, but we should notice that even through the comical touches he manages to make a serious point. The trolls are not defeated or destroyed by their enemies. Gandalf tricks them, but he does not overcome them. The trolls are the victims of their own greed and their own quarrelsomeness; Gandalf has only to stir it up and then let the trolls bring about their own destruction. In short, they are undone by their own evil. This is a general principle in Tolkien's works, and we will find examples of it everywhere. What is true of the trolls will be true of Smaug later on, and we will also find it true of Sauron and Gollum and Saruman in *The Lord of the Rings*.

3

The Ridiculous and the Sublime

"A SHORT REST"

Elves: The Valley Is Jolly

As we move from the slapstick trolls in the Lone-lands to the elves of Rivendell, we might expect to be moving from the ridiculous to the sublime. If this is our expectation, it is quickly disappointed. When we first meet the elves in *The Hobbit,* we find them bursting into a very strange song, full of lyrics like "tra-la-la-lally" and "ha! ha!" (46). For readers who know *The Lord of the Rings,* this introduction to Rivendell will seem particularly jarring, but even those new to Tolkien might be taken aback by the elves' frivolity.

The elves seem to have no dignity whatsoever. They are singing apparent nonsense from the trees (whether they are up the trees or merely among them is not clear), and their talk seems quite childish. They tease the dwarves about their long beards (47). They tease Bilbo for being pudgy. They are finally so outrageous and indiscreet that Gandalf has to shush and rebuke them like a classroom full of five-year-olds: "Hush, hush! Good people! . . . Valleys have ears, and some elves have over-merry tongues" (48). All in all, the elves seem almost as ridiculous as the trolls did.

Tolkien's choice to depict the elves in this way seems puzzling. After all, his decision to overlay the potentially frightening trolls with lightheartedness and laughter makes obvious sense; the comedy softens the horror of the man-eating monsters. But why make the elves frivolous? It seems almost to prevent us from taking them seriously at all. But we shouldn't be too hasty to dismiss them—the narrator cautions us about that. He tells us that Thorin and his friends find the elves annoying and think them foolish, but he warns us that that "is a very foolish thing to think" (47). Tolkien seems to be suggesting that there is more to the elves than we might see at first.

In order to figure out what the elves are like, we should do the same thing that we did with the dwarves back in Chapter One: pay attention to the song that they sing and see what it shows us about them. This seems especially appropriate since it is the song in particular that makes it hard for most readers to take the elves of Rivendell seriously. The narrator fully anticipates this, of course, calling the song "ridiculous" and remarking to the reader afterwards, "pretty fair nonsense I daresay you think it" (46). We need to take an unprejudiced look at it, though, if we want to understand what the elves are really like.

The elves' song sounds artless and fragmentary. Whereas the dwarves' song, especially in the second half, tells the story of the invasion and ruin of the Lonely Mountain, the elves' song consists of a disjointed series of simple questions and even simpler statements of fact, rounded out with a generous helping of nonsense syllables.

The first stanza illustrates the pattern quite well:

O! What are you doing,
And where are you going?
Your ponies need shoeing!
The river is flowing!
  O! tra-la-la-lally
    here down in the valley!
      (46)

They begin with two questions that seem like an ordinary enough conversation starter, asking the newly arrived strangers what they are doing and where they are going. True, it may be a bit unusual to *sing* that kind of question, but perhaps we could get over that little oddity. However, if we look ahead a bit, we can see that the elves already know perfectly well the answers to these questions. Their rather disrespectful remarks show that they know just who their visitors are: "Just look!" they say. "Bilbo the hobbit on a pony . . . ! Isn't it delicious!" (47). Their indiscreet reference to Bilbo's being "too fat to get through key-holes yet" demonstrates that they know all about what the dwarves are doing, down to the secret map and key (48). Bilbo marvels at the fact that the elves seem to know all about him. Why, therefore, are they asking pointless questions in their song?

If we return to the first stanza, we can see that the elves follow up their wholly unnecessary questions with two rather peculiar observations: the fact that the travelers' "ponies need shoeing" and that "the river is flowing." Why would the elves point these things out in their song? Are they mocking Bilbo and his companions for being road-worn after their long journey? Is the flowing of the river supposed to be some kind of news flash? I would guess that Bilbo spotted that for himself. These two lines seem almost as gratuitous as the opening questions.

And what sense are we to make of the last two lines? The last line, "here down in the valley," sounds like a completion of a thought, but which one? *What* is "down in the valley"? The syntax of the lines suggests, bizarrely, that "tra-la-la-lally," which sounded at first like merely rhythmic syllables without meaning, actually stands as the subject and verb of that sentence. In some sense inscrutable to mere mortals, "tra-la-la-lally" would seem to be what is happening "down in the valley."

The second and third stanzas of the song follow along the same lines. There are more crashingly obvious statements, such as the simple facts that the "faggots are reeking" (Hey, look: smoke is rising from those burning logs over there!) and the "bannocks are baking" (Wow! There are oat cakes cooking!) (46). There are also plenty more superfluous questions to which the elves already have the answers. As we have seen, they clearly know what the dwarves are seeking and where they are "making." The only apparent purpose for posing these questions would be to tease the dwarves and Bilbo about the fact that the elves already know the secret of their quest. This motivation seems most plain in the exaggerated lines "No knowing, no knowing / What brings Mister Baggins / And Balin and Dwalin / down into the valley." The fact is, the elves do know, and they seem to delight in harping on it.

The elves finish their performance with what sounds almost like discourtesy, or at least an oblivious insensitivity:

To fly would be folly,
To stay would be jolly

And listen and hark
Till the end of the dark
   to our tune
   ha! ha!
    (46)

Remember, the dwarves and Bilbo have just finished a tiring journey through dangerous country. They were nearly killed by trolls recently, and they lost most of their food supply just before that. The elves who meet them on their arrival at the "Last Homely House," instead of ushering them inside to eat and rest, suggest that the dwarves would be better off staying outside in the trees with them all night, listening to their songs until dawn. Keep in mind that they remark in this same stanza that the daylight is only just then dying, so the elves are inviting their guests to join them for about nine hours of uninterrupted "tril-lil-lil-lolly." They even compare a potential (and likely) refusal of their odd invitation to running away ("flying"), as if it were a faint-hearted or even a cowardly act.

All things considered, the elves' song doesn't seem to make any more sense when we read it carefully than it did initially. If anything, it sounds even more strange, and its singers seem even more incomprehensible. If we thought the elves silly after our first reading of the song, a second reading might make us think them barking mad.

The elves are undeniably peculiar, but even now I would point to three cues that Tolkien gives us that should lead us to be cautious about dismissing the elves as simpletons. The first is a line I have already mentioned: the narrator's parenthetical caution that thinking the elves foolish is "a very foolish thing to think" (47). The second is Bilbo's response to the elves'

seemingly ludicrous invitation to end his long and weary journey by staying up all night listening to them sing. The narrator notes that "tired as he was, Bilbo would have liked to stay
a while. Elvish singing is not a thing to miss, in June under
the stars, not if you care for such things" (47). Bilbo Baggins,
of all people, actually considers giving up rest and food, weary
and hungry as he is, in favor of listening to the elves' songs.
The lyrics of their song might be senseless, but there would
seem to be something more to that song than we might think,
judging by Bilbo's reaction. The third cue is the narrator's description of Bilbo's feelings about elves in general. We are told
that Bilbo "loved elves, though he seldom met them; but he
was a little frightened of them too" (47). Bilbo is not very familiar with the elves, but he both loves and fears them, a mixture of conflicting reactions that speaks to their strangeness,
but also hints at something higher or greater, which Bilbo
himself only imperfectly understands.

I would suggest that these passages prompt us to back up
and look at the elves and their song one more time. Notice
that the elves don't just sing the one silly song; they are almost constantly singing. They are singing when Bilbo and the
dwarves arrive. They sing as the dwarves cross the river. They
have plans to go on singing the entire night, and they are still
singing when it is time for the adventurers to leave. We might
also notice that the elves laugh almost as frequently. They
joke with the dwarves and Bilbo, teasing them and laughing at them. But they are not mere scoffers; they laugh all the
time, at almost everything. Both they and their songs are usually referred to as "merry," and their first song is described as
"a burst of song like laughter in the trees" (45). The frequent
repetition of "ha! ha!" seems to be an attempt to represent in

print the merriment of their singing. The elves are joyful, and they take delight in everything.

At a third reading, therefore, their song begins to look a little different. Their nonsense words are like laughter turned into music. Their unnecessary and teasing questions are like a sustained joke, having fun both with the dwarves' secrecy and with their own knowledge. The unconnected and obvious statements of fact are, in my mind, the most characteristic and interesting elements of the song. In those moments, the elves digress into a pure and free-floating enjoyment of the world around them. They are delighted by everything: by the flowing of the river, by the smell of the wood fire, by the baking of oat cakes, by the beards and ponies of the dwarves, and by the fading of the afternoon into evening twilight. The elves' continual singing, like their frequent laughter, is an expression of this delight, and it is the lack of restraint in the pleasure that they take in the things around them that makes them seem absurd.

If the dwarves think the elves foolish, it is very likely because they take themselves and their quest very seriously. Remember, for instance, Thorin's ponderous and even pretentious way of speaking when he is talking about their quest back in Chapter One, even pausing to point out, "It is a solemn moment" (17). These elves don't seem to be solemn about anything and would doubtless laugh if they heard Thorin say anything like that. The secrecy and solemnity of dwarves are almost as delightful as the plumpness and domesticity of hobbits—or the splashing and murmur of flowing rivers. The merriment of the elves suggests not that they hold themselves aloof from the world and its people and are laughing at or mocking them. Rather, they are connected with the world in a deeper and stranger sense, taking pleasure in all of its ways and varieties.

In the "ridiculous" song of the elves of Rivendell, therefore, I believe that Tolkien is trying to give us a glimpse of this rather mystical elvish perspective. He even brings it into a tone and mode of speech that children can understand and relate to: their laughing, teasing mode of address and whimsical words. Bilbo, who has been our representative so far in the magical world that he and we have entered together, is moved by the elves' singing, valuing it almost more than the Baggins enjoyment of food and drink and rest, even when he is weary and very hungry. The elvish exultation transcends those simple pleasures, and I believe Tolkien is trying to transmit a glimpse of that high and transcendent perspective to a juvenile audience here. It is a terrifically difficult task, and I don't think that Tolkien is completely successful, but I believe that that's what he's trying to do.

There is one other brief reference at the beginning of this scene that *Hobbit* readers often find puzzling, and I think it illustrates in brief what is going on throughout the rest of the scene. When Bilbo looks down into the valley, his rather surprising first remark is "Hmmm! It smells like elves!" (45). This comment is never explained, and we are not told in *The Hobbit* exactly what elves smell like.* It seems like an odd com-

---

* We do get a hint about the smell of elves, actually, in another of Tolkien's writings. Right around the time he was writing *The Hobbit* Tolkien was also writing a long poem called *The Lay of Leithian,* which wasn't published until after his death. That poem is the story of Beren and Lúthien, which is told in *The Silmarillion,* and which Strider sings about in the dell under Weathertop in the "A Knife in the Dark" chapter of *The Fellowship of the Ring.* In *The Lay of Leithian,* the elf-maiden Lúthien is described as being accompanied everywhere by a remarkable fragrance, the "odour of immortal flowers

ment, but it is also rather haunting; from Bilbo's "Hmmm!" it would seem that they smell extremely good, and that this fragrance moves him in some indefinable way, just as their singing does. Notice what happens right after he smells them: "He looked up at the stars. They were burning bright and blue" (45). The scent of the elves seems to stimulate him to contemplate high and lovely things, to become sensitive to beauty that he might have taken for granted otherwise. Bilbo's remark is comical, but it also points to an idea that is very difficult to grasp and an experience that is very hard to describe, just like the elves' song.

There is, of course, another side of elves; they are more than just merry singers who take delight in the natural world. They are also an ancient people with a long and tragic history, and if we do emerge from their singing by the river still thinking them silly and empty-headed, the snatches that Tolkien reveals of their history should help to counteract that. We are told that Elrond and his people are connected to "the strange stories before the beginning of History, the wars of the evil goblins and the elves and the first men in the North" (48). The narrator alludes to these stories as if we were already familiar with them, and if you have read *The Silmarillion,* you will indeed know the stories to which he is referring. But remember that when *The Hobbit* was published in 1937, and even when the revised edition was printed in 1951, those stories had not been published and were completely unknown to readers of *The Hobbit.* All we get here is the general un-

---

/ in everlasting spring" (Canto XII.3794–95). *That,* I suspect, is more or less what elves smell like, and what Bilbo was getting a whiff of on the breeze near Rivendell.

derstanding that these apparently frivolous people are directly connected to battles in which warriors of old fought against armies of terrible evil in the ancient times of heroic legends. Their story is clearly a sad one, too; the only detail we're given is the fact that there was once a great city of the elves called Gondolin, and that it was destroyed by dragons and goblins ages ago (49). The elves may be "merry folk" whose song and conversation are full of fancy, but we are also told to connect them with the mysterious and lofty "High Elves of the West," and their merriment is made remarkable by the majesty and sorrow of their history.

The central figure among the elves is Elrond, master of Rivendell, and Tolkien makes it completely impossible for us to view him as frivolous or empty-headed. His description brings together the superlatives of all the races. He is "as noble and fair in face as an elf-lord, as strong as a warrior, as wise as a wizard, as venerable as a king of dwarves, and as kind as summer" (49). Having been shown the joy the elves take in the world, we are shown in Elrond their beauty and strength and power, and even their authority. His power over evil creatures is established in the bald statement "Evil things did not come into that valley." Perhaps, by the end of the chapter, we can begin to understand better Bilbo's mixed reaction to the elves, how he both loves them and is a little frightened of them. They are homey and friendly, laughing and eager to include their guests in their merriment. But they are also high and ancient, holding an unknown power and a quiet authority. It is fitting, therefore, that we think them strange when we first meet them, for they are indeed strange to human experience, but it would be "a very foolish thing" indeed to simply think them foolish.

Bilbo's Nature: Both Took and Baggins

Bilbo's stay at Rivendell provides him more than just the "short rest" alluded to in the chapter title. In the company of the elves and the comforts of their house, Bilbo tastes, for the first time, a life that can satisfy both parts of his divided nature. It is the perfect house for food and sleep and sitting and thinking. No Baggins could want more when it comes to comfort, ease, and security. But it is also the perfect house for storytelling and singing, and the world of the old, great legends of the past still lives on there in the house of the great Elrond and his people. At Rivendell, one can actually enjoy "a pleasant mixture" of all of these things, which have never been joined in Bilbo's experience (49). At Bag-End, Bilbo's Took side was dormant. On the journey, his Baggins side protests and complains and longs to be home by his fireside. Rivendell, however, is perfect.

In Rivendell, Bilbo glimpses what an actual reconciliation between his two natures might look like: a life in which he could allow himself to be swept away into songs of adventure and tragedy and delight, and yet also remain safe and comfortable. The narrator shows us the depth of Bilbo's satisfaction by telling us the remarkable fact that while he is with Elrond and the elves, he stops longing for Bag-End. We're told that "Bilbo would gladly have stopped there for ever and ever — even supposing a wish would have taken him right back to his hobbit-hole without trouble" (48). Bilbo recognizes that even his hobbit-hole, that image of coziness and safety to which he clings when he is in distress, cannot compete with the deeper and richer and fuller satisfaction of life with the elves in Rivendell. When it is time for Bilbo and the dwarves to leave, he is not only rested; he is invigorated. His heart is "ready for more adventure" (51).

Luck: Good Fortune and Prophecy

Chapter Three brings to our attention a theme that will be increasingly important throughout the rest of the book: the remarkable good luck of Bilbo and his companions. The first pieces of extraordinary luck that we see occur at the end of Chapter Two. After the trolls are petrified, Bilbo is able to let his companions into the trolls' lair by use of a key he found on the ground after it had "very luckily" fallen out of William's pocket while the trolls were scuffling with each other (41).* In the trolls' cave, Gandalf and the dwarves find two swords and Bilbo's knife. This certainly seems like a stroke of good fortune, for the dwarves were unarmed, and the swords "look like good blades" and have "beautiful scabbards and jewelled hilts" (41).

Only in Chapter Three do we learn how extraordinary their luck has actually been. When Elrond reads the runes on the swords, he is able to tell them that they are not only "very old swords" and powerful, but they are "very famous" blades (49). They have names, Orcrist and Glamdring, and the latter of these actually belonged to the king of the ancient elven city of Gondolin. This would be rather like going on vacation to India and finding in a village marketplace a sword that belonged to Alexander the Great. The odds against it are pretty staggering; Thorin and his companions have been remarkably fortunate.

---

* In the first draft of *The Hobbit* that Tolkien wrote, the key which Bilbo found on the ground turns out to be the very key that opens the secret door into the Lonely Mountain. Only later, revising the book before its publication, did Tolkien change that key into the key to the trolls' cave and have Gandalf give Thorin the Mountain key. As we can see, therefore, in his initial concept, Tolkien was planning to make the coincidence of finding the key on the ground an even more staggeringly lucky coincidence!

But just in case we overlook the unlikeliness of that particular stroke of luck, Tolkien reasserts the extent to which fortune is favoring Bilbo and his friends through the *astonishing* coincidence of the moon-letters. When Elrond finds the runes, he explains that they would only be visible by the light of "a moon of the same shape and season as the day when they were written" (50). The letters "must have been written on a midsummer's eve in a crescent moon, a long while ago," he explains. So it isn't just that the hidden message on the map is only visible on one day in the whole year—it is only visible when the moon is in one particular phase on that one day in the year. In other words, by a truly astounding coincidence, the dwarves just happen to give the map to Elrond to read at the only time of day on the one day in *decades* that the message would have been visible. Now *that* was lucky! This isn't a stretch that Tolkien hopes we won't notice and think about, though. The narrator draws our attention to it, pointing out that there wouldn't have been another chance to read the runes "until goodness knows when" (50). We might begin to wonder at this point if there is something mysterious at work here.

Our suspicions only deepen when we consider the actual message spelled out by the miraculously revealed letters. The words are, in a sense, instructions explaining how to enter the secret side passage into the Mountain. But the only actual instruction is "Stand by the grey stone when the thrush knocks" (50). The rest is not a set of directions, but a prediction: "the setting sun with the last light of Durin's Day will shine upon the key-hole." Even that first instruction contains a prediction, of course: the knocking of the thrush. Notice that it doesn't just say *a* thrush; the message seems to foretell the knocking of a particular thrush. The sense that what we are reading is not advice but prophecy is deepened by the reference to Durin's Day. Just as only the light of this one particular moon on this one particular day could reveal the runes, so the light of the setting sun on that one special day, the day dedicated to Durin, "the father of the fathers of the eldest race of Dwarves," will reveal the key-hole (50). Thorin admits that he has no idea when Durin's Day will fall, or whether this year will be one of those special years in which that particular alignment of sun and moon and season will happen. But if it does happen that year, and Thorin and his companions manage to be standing by a particular grey stone at the right time on that particular day, and the right thrush comes by and "knocks" (though we don't know what that means), then the key-hole to the door will be revealed to him.

It would seem that there are only two sensible reactions we can have to these long strings of wildly improbable events. We can either scoff at them and find the whole story rather absurd, or we can begin to suspect that Bilbo's adventure is being orchestrated by some power beyond the wizardry of Gandalf the Grey or the wisdom of Elrond of Rivendell. They themselves, of course, have also been made the instruments of this prophecy, for it was Gandalf who delivered the map and the key to Thorin, and Elrond who happened to hold it up to the moon at the right time on the right day. Gandalf himself seems to have a shrewd suspicion that something incalculable is going on. Thorin's impulse is to dismiss the reference to Durin's Day on the map, saying, "But this will not help us much, I fear, for it passes our skill in these days to guess when such a time will come again" (51). Gandalf replies, "That remains to be seen"; he, it seems, is not so quick to dismiss the message and seems to believe that it will turn out to be relevant after all, no matter how toweringly unlikely that may seem. Gently, Tolkien is drawing our attention to the fact that there is a higher purpose at work in the events of this story, and we are being prompted to suspect that the amazing luck of Bilbo and Thorin is not accidental.

4

Over the Edge of the Wild

"OVER HILL AND UNDER HILL"

Bilbo's Nature: Into the Wild

Rivendell is called "The Last Homely House," and it stands on an important boundary. It is at the border, with all of the "respectable country," where one might possibly find good inns, to the west (30). When you get to Rivendell, as Gandalf explains to Bilbo, you have "come to the very edge of the Wild" (44). As I mentioned in Chapter Three, Rivendell doesn't just sit on this boundary; it embodies it. The house of Elrond is the place where the world of quiet comforts and the world of legends come together and coexist. The path beyond it, into the Wild, is "a hard path and a dangerous path, a crooked way and a lonely and a long" (52).

The transitional status of Rivendell, of course, has a disquieting implication for Bilbo as he prepares to journey on. It suggests that even the Lone-lands and their man-eating trolls are on the safe and comfortable western side of Rivendell. Bilbo may think he has seen a lot of danger by the time he gets there, but it turns out that his adventures have not even really begun in earnest. Bilbo shows his naiveté when he is still on the road to Rivendell. Catching in the distance his first sight of a mountain, the nearest of the Misty Mountains, he briefly imagines that he is coming to the end of his quest and that he is seeing the Lonely Mountain itself. When Balin explains that he is seeing only the beginning of the first major obstacle that stands between them and the dragon-haunted mountain they seek, Bilbo feels "more tired than he ever remembered feeling before" (43). In response, he retreats in his mind to The Hill and Bag-End, thinking "of his comfortable chair before the fire in his favourite sitting-room in his hobbit-hole, and of the kettle singing." Even while he is still west of Rivendell, the quiet world of Bilbo's home seems very far away.

On the other side of Elrond's house, Bilbo can plainly see the extent of that separation. As the travelers climb the mountain pass, the lands he has passed through stretch out below him. Bilbo knows that "his own country of safe and comfortable things, and his little hobbit-hole" are somewhere in that vista, but they are "far, far away in the West, where things were blue and faint" (52). In the title of the chapter, Tolkien points with some irony to the strangeness and unfamiliarity of the world Bilbo has entered. Tolkien characterizes Bilbo's journey through the mountains and his terrifying side trip into their depths with comical understatement as a passage "Over Hill and Under Hill." Under The Hill, of course, is Bilbo's home address, but the contrast between resting peacefully under the one Hill and being dragged by goblins under the other couldn't be more extreme.

The distance between Bilbo's new surroundings and his old home is more than geographical; he has been swept into a very alien world. It is a world in which "stone-giants" casually step out of the background and start "hurling rocks at one another for a game" (55). These monstrous creatures don't seem to be hostile; indeed they are "guffawing" and appear to be just having fun. But even the sport in the Wild is deadly and could end up with one of the party being "picked up by some giant and kicked sky-high for a football."* Even the weather in the mountains is monstrous and gigantic; up there, "the lightning splinters on the peaks, and rocks shiver, and great crashes split the air and go rolling and tumbling into every cave and hollow; and the darkness is filled with overwhelming noise and sudden light" (53). Bilbo, child of the tranquil lands in the West, "had never seen or imagined anything of the kind."

When Bilbo is ambushed by goblins, things go from very bad to much worse. Even after he is rescued from his chains by Gandalf, he and his friends are still in a terrible fix: "No ponies, and no food, and no knowing quite where we are, and hordes of angry goblins just behind" (62). Imagine that for a hobbit who used to think going without cakes at tea painful, and who considered a willingness to go without bed and breakfast an impressive degree of dedication!

Chapter Four shows us a small, frightened hobbit who is very much out of place in the Wild, but there are two points that help put Bilbo's position into context. First, we should notice that Bilbo is actually not much more overwhelmed than his dwarvish companions are. Their discomfort with the games of the stone-giants and their haste to settle into a convenient cave before they have thoroughly explored it suggest that they are feeling nearly as bewildered as Bilbo in this op-

---

* When he mentions "football," Tolkien and his original audience would almost certainly have been thinking of rugby, which Tolkien used to play when he was at school.

pressive, mountainous world. Later on, when they are running from pursuing goblins, the dwarves sound more professional and confident than the little burglar. Bilbo is complaining, "Why, O why did I ever leave my hobbit-hole!" and Bombur, who is carrying him, mocks him by imitation: "Why, O why did I ever bring a wretched little hobbit on a treasure hunt!" (63). But Bombur's condescending words are an illusion. He might talk a better game, casually suggesting that their current plight is just part of a treasure hunt, but he is not really handling the situation any better than Bilbo. The narrator tells us that Bombur is even then staggering "along with the sweat dripping down his nose in his heat and terror." Bilbo is out of his depth, but he isn't the only one.

The second thing to remember is that in the middle of all these dangers, Bilbo makes his first actual contribution as a member of the company. In the troll incident, Bilbo doesn't really accomplish anything positive, unless you count finding the key on the ground by chance. In fact, his role in the troll encounter had a negative impact, if anything; by getting himself caught, he almost gets all of the dwarves killed as well. In the goblins' cave, however, Bilbo, for the first time, takes action and saves the day. True, all he does is wake up and yell about one second before the goblins grab them, but it is still something. Bilbo might be in over his head, but already he has done enough to make the narrator say: "It turned out a good thing that night that they had brought little Bilbo with them, after all" (56). And as the narrator might say, "Not for the last time!"

The dream Bilbo is having right before he wakes up and yells is also worthy of note. This is the second reference to Bilbo's dreaming in the book so far. The first one seems quite straightforward; at the end of Chapter One, we're told that listening to Thorin reprise the dwarf song as he fell asleep gave Bilbo "very uncomfortable dreams" (26). We don't know exactly what he dreamed, but his discomfort fits in well with the internal conflict we saw in Bilbo during the Unexpected Party. Whether the song leads him to think dwarvish thoughts again, which his Baggins side would find uncomfortable, or fills his mind with fear and anxiety about the dangers of the quest, it is very understandable that he should have unquiet dreams.

Part of Bilbo's dream in Chapter Four might also relate to his internal state. Certainly his final vision of himself "beginning to fall down, down, goodness knows where to," like Alice in the rabbit hole, might evoke his sense of his life spiraling out of control as he is entering this new and frightening world (57). But in the main portion of the dream, he simply dreams of what is happening in the cave around him: "a crack in the wall at the back of the cave" getting "bigger and bigger" (56). The narrator doesn't explicitly confirm it, but it appears that those initial details of his dream are exactly what has occurred. Bilbo's dream is a true dream, revealing to him their danger and helping him wake in time to shout his warning.

We don't have enough information to understand Bilbo's dream in the cave fully, but it is a suggestive moment. It is conceivable that he is not really sleeping at first, and he is seeing what is happening in the cave in a dream-like state before slipping into a real dream about falling. But if this is a real dream, then it seems as if Bilbo has somehow received some kind of warning in his sleep, an insight into what is going on in the waking world, to which he is returned with a jolt, just in the nick of time to deliver his warning.

Goblins: Down Down to Goblin-town

The crack that Bilbo sees opening up in his dream admits into the story one of the most important sets of stock characters in all of Tolkien's stories: the goblins, or "orcs" as he will call them in *The Lord of the Rings*.* For the third time, Tolkien introduces us to a new race of creatures by giving us a song of theirs very soon after Bilbo is introduced to them. If we look closely at the harsh and cruel little song that the goblins sing as they drive Bilbo and the dwarves down into their stronghold, we will get some important insights into their nature, and into their relationship with both elves and dwarves.

The first verse of the goblins' song gives a kind of plot summary:

> *Clap! Snap! the black crack!*
> *Grip, grab! Pinch, nab!*
> *And down down to Goblin-town*
>   *You go, my lad!*
>   *(58)*

This verse retells the story of the capture of the dwarves in very simple terms: the black crack opened and shut; they grabbed the dwarves; they are taking the dwarves and Bilbo down to Goblin-town. Although the narrative of the verse doesn't tell us anything we didn't know, the style tells us a lot. This verse

---

* Tolkien uses the words *goblin* and *orc* essentially synonymously. *Orc* comes from an Old English word; *goblin* is a traditional fairy-tale label. In *The Hobbit*, when he is writing for a children's audience in the tradition of fairy tales, Tolkien tends to use *goblin*. When he moves to *The Lord of the Rings*, Tolkien favors the older word with fewer associations in traditional literature. But he uses both terms in both books to describe the same race of creatures.

is almost all action. Six of the nine words in the first two lines are verbs, and all the verbs are in the present tense. The goblins are not really telling the story of the capture in their song; they are reliving the moment, savoring the action.

The song is also simplistic and blunt. Except for the word *goblin* itself, every single word in the first stanza has only one syllable. I don't think this is designed to suggest that the goblins are stupid and unsophisticated, though. Their poetic medium fits its content perfectly. The monosyllables that they choose are mostly onomatopoetic; that is, they are just harsh sounds turned into words, such as *clap* and *snap* and even *crack,* which is one of their few nouns. "Clap! Snap! the black crack!" is so full of repeated and explosive consonants that the very sound of the line is violent. The result is a verse that would sound harsh, ugly, and cruel even if we didn't know what the words meant.

The second stanza starts off in the same mode, with four more violent, onomatopoetic monosyllables:

> *Clash, crash! Crush, smash!*
> *Hammer and tongs! Knocker and gongs!*
> *Pound, pound, far underground!*
>   *Ho, ho! my lad!*
>   (58)

This verse is not just a replay of present cruelty, as the first stanza is. Here we get a glimpse into the larger goblin culture. We can see, for instance, that all that crashing and smashing are not all purely, or at least not directly, destructive. The goblins, like the dwarves, are smiths and craftsmen. In fact, this stanza should remind us of the dwarves' own song in Chapter One:

The dwarves of yore made mighty spells,
While hammers fell like ringing bells
In places deep, where dark things sleep,
In hollow halls beneath the fells.

(14–15)

The dwarves' verse about hammering sounds a lot more attractive than "Pound, pound, far underground," but the two songs are clearly describing the same thing. The narrator's later prose description of the goblins makes the same connection. He explains that goblins "can tunnel and mine as well as any but the most skilled dwarves," and, also like the dwarves, they are good makers of weapons and tools (59). The dwarves and the goblins seem to have a lot in common, professionally.

Just as the dwarves' song reveals to Bilbo "the desire of the hearts of dwarves," so the third verse of the goblins' song reveals the true hearts of the goblins:

Swish, smack! Whip crack!
Batter and beat! Yammer and bleat!
Work, work! Nor dare to shirk,
While Goblins quaff, and Goblins laugh,
Round and round far underground
   Below, my lad!
   (58)

Once again, we get monosyllabic verbs, but this time instead of the pounding of hammers we hear the cracking of whips. The goblins do not take delight in the act of craftsmanship, as the dwarves do. Their pleasure is in sitting idly by, drinking ("quaffing"), while they force others to do their work for them. The narrator explains that goblins don't usually go to the trouble of smithing or mining for themselves; they prefer to exploit "prisoners and slaves that have to work till they die for want of air and light" (59). They are both cruel and lazy, as we can see in the lines "Work, work! Nor dare to shirk, / While Goblins quaff, and Goblins laugh," which show the goblins imagining lying around while mocking their slaves. Notice that this stanza even has an extra line; the goblins are drawing out this pleasant fantasy, lingering on it and savoring it.

The pleasure that the goblins take in their actions might also remind us, in a horrible and twisted way, of the delight that the elves of Rivendell express for the world around them. The enjoyment of the goblins, however, shows them to be almost the polar opposite of the elves. The elves, in their light and silly song in Chapter Three, found fun in everything they encountered, from the fading sunlight to the worn horseshoes of the dwarves' ponies, responding to them all with laughter. The last three verses of their song simply dissolve into delighted laughter, ending with "ha! ha!" The goblins also burst into laughter, but their "Ho, ho! my lad!" couldn't be any more different. They derive amusement not from things as they are, but from their own power over those things, their ability to destroy them or to make them suffer. The goblins' pleasure is as warped and sickening as the elves' pleasure is innocent and wholesome.

The relationship between the goblins and the dwarves is more complicated, though. They are certainly different enough, though both are known for smithcraft. The dwarves' song is full of relish in the loveliness of the works of their hands, and many of the things they describe have no obvious utility but are simply beautiful, such as stars strung on silver necklaces or dragon-fire hung on crowns (15). The cleverness of the goblins is pragmatically devoted to furthering their acts of cruelty. They "make no beautiful things"; they specialize in weapons and "instruments of torture" (59). Moreover, the narrator speculates that they invented "some of the machines that have since troubled the world, especially the ingenious devices for killing large numbers of people at once."* The goblins, unlike the dwarves, are dreadfully practical in the projects they undertake.

The dwarves share more with the goblins than just a knack for smithcraft, however. Both are associated with the darkness and find their homes in the deep places of the earth. The dwarves, you may remember, tell Bilbo at Bag-End that they "like the dark" and think it most fitting for discussing their "dark business" (16). The goblins' connection with darkness is much more complete than the dwarves', of course. The goblins surround themselves with "deep, deep dark, such as only goblins that have taken to living in the heart of the mountains can see through" (57). The goblins don't merely like the dark; they are bound to it, so that they cannot stand the sun (84). The dwarves are not so completely tied to the shadows as the goblins are, but they are nevertheless creatures of the darkness.

The darkness with which the dwarves are associated, however, is not simply literal. When they call their business "dark business," they doubtless mean it is very secret, but it also plainly seems rather sinister to Bilbo, who wants to fetch a

---

* In this sentence, Tolkien demonstrates more plainly than almost anywhere else in his fiction his own views on war and military technology. He was largely opposed to industrialization, not just because he was nostalgic for the simple life, but because he could see that factories tended to lead to bigger and more powerful bombs.

lamp. If the goblins' hearts are thoroughly shrouded in wickedness and cruelty, we must also remember the dwarves' tendencies toward vengefulness and possessiveness. Thorin and Company are not evil, but unlike the elves they are capable of meeting the goblins on their own level: underground, out of the light of the sun. The dwarves once fought a war against the goblins in retribution for the murder of their king and captain: Thror, Thorin's grandfather. The uncomfortable truth is that when the goblins are chasing Gandalf and the dwarves in furious pursuit at the end of the chapter, they are hunting them for the exact same reason: retribution for the murder of the Great Goblin.

Nevertheless, despite these similarities between them, Tolkien primarily emphasizes the differences between the goblins and Thorin's company. The closest contrast we get is once more in a song: the song that the dwarves sing in Bilbo's kitchen back in Chapter One. While whirling around the hobbit's orderly kitchen, the dwarves sing:

> *Chip the glasses and crack the plates!*
>   *Blunt the knives and bend the forks!*
> *That's what Bilbo Baggins hates—*
>   *Smash the bottles and burn the corks!*
>   *(13)*

This is only the first of three stanzas, which go on in the same direction. If we compare this little song with the goblins' song, I think we can see both the similarities and the differences between them very clearly.

The dwarves' kitchen song, like the goblins' song, is dominated by harsh, monosyllabic verbs that occur twice per line in three out of the four lines in this first stanza (line three being the repeated catch phrase of the song). The dwarves even use some of the same violent and harsh-sounding verbs that the goblins use, such as *crack, smash,* and *pound* (in stanza three: "Pound them up with a thumping pole"). The dwarves' song is playful, but it is a song about violence and destruction being done at the expense of a helpless victim.

There are two key differences between the songs, though. The first is that the violence the dwarves are threatening is quite tame and domestic compared to the goblins' terrible threats. Blunting knives and bending forks is worlds away from laughing mockingly while beaten and bloodied slaves work themselves to death amidst darkness and fear. But the second difference, of course, is even more important: the dwarves don't really mean it. They're only teasing Bilbo! Immediately after their song, the narrator assures us that "of course they did none of these dreadful things" (13). The dwarves were enjoying how flustered and "bebothered" Bilbo was, which is a bit mean-spirited, but they clearly don't intend him any actual harm.

The goblins, by contrast, mean every word of their cruel song. The first verse of the goblin song recaps what just happened, the capture in the cave. The second and third verses describe what is about to happen: the imprisonment, torture, and slavery of the dwarves and Bilbo, in which they will be beaten, whipped, and made to "pound, pound, far underground" until they die (58). Immediately after this song, the narrator confirms that the goblins plan to start making all the dreadful things in their song come true as soon as possible. They get out their whips and "with a *swish, smack!*" make the dwarves get started promptly with the yammering and bleating. The hearts of the dwarves may be tinged with shadows, but the goblins are thoroughly and determinedly wicked, as dark as the "deep, deep dark" of their holes (57).

The Writing of *The Hobbit:* Legends and Tales

In Rivendell in Chapter Three, Bilbo and the reader encounter not only adventure, but a world of ancient legends and heroes, meeting Elrond the Half-Elven and hearing of the lost elven city of Gondolin. Like the moon-letters on Thror's map, Thorin's own legendary status also becomes visible in the light of Rivendell. We always knew that Thorin was "an enormously important dwarf" (11), but back in Chapter One that seemed to mean "very haughty" and pompous as much as anything else. Thorin, we may recall, does not deign to help with the washing-up after tea because "he was too important" (12). In Chapter Three, however, we get a glimpse of how significant Thorin actually is. He is not only the exiled ruler of the lost kingdom under the Mountain, but he is the heir of Durin, "the father of the fathers of the eldest race of Dwarves" (50). The story of Thorin and his bumbling troop of followers, it appears, also stretches back, like Elrond's own, into legendary history, back to the very roots and origins of his race itself.

Thorin's importance is solidly confirmed by the Great Goblin, who recognizes Thorin's name and obviously knows stories about him. "I know too much about your folk already," the goblin lord remarks ominously (60). Of course, we the readers know a good deal less than the Great Goblin apparently does, but his comment helps us to put what we do know into perspective. Back in Chapter One, Gandalf mentions that Thorin's grandfather Thror was killed "in the mines of Moria by Azog the Goblin" (24), and Thorin alludes to the bloodshed that followed by grimly stating, "We have long ago paid the goblins of Moria" (25). Much later, in *The Lord of the Rings* and its appendices, readers would learn more about this struggle and discover that it was a widespread and terrible war, lasting for years and culminating in an enormous battle. In *The Hobbit,* though, we know nothing about the "mines of Moria." The dwarves as we have met them seem rather comical and inept, and we were not originally given much reason to think that their "paying the goblins of Moria" was more than a local skirmish. The encounter with the Great Goblin shows us differently, however. The stories, still unknown to us, about Thorin and his clan and their war with the goblins have obviously traveled far and wide in the Wild.

Our time in Rivendell and our encounter with the tales of the great war between the goblins and the elves of Gondolin also provide a new context for the references to that old conflict between Thorin's family and the goblins. We are invited to see the recent struggle between dwarf and goblin as parallel to the ancient and legendary war between elf and goblin. The Great Goblin himself seems to see it this way, as he associates "murderers" with "friends of Elves" from the beginning (59). The parallel is firmly established, and the Great Goblin's worst suspicions confirmed, when he recognizes Thorin's sword, Orcrist. The goblins, it seems, have preserved stories and legends from the old days too, and their fear and hatred of the two elven swords and anyone who bears them show how detailed and how vivid those stories are. Even the names of the swords have been remembered, for "Beater" and "Biter" are obviously not just names the goblins have given them, but simplified translations of the swords' right names, Glamdring

(Foe-Hammer, Beater) and Orcrist (Goblin-Cleaver, Biter). The Great Goblin's animosity, already aroused by Thorin's own reputation, flares into rage at this connection between the known, recent enemies of his people and their ancient foes, the Elves.

In fact, as we move through Tolkien's story, our eyes are steadily opened to the much bigger story that stretches into the distance around and behind *The Hobbit*, the story of which the tale of Bilbo's journey is only a short chapter. As readers, we remain focused on the journey of the uncomfortable and out-of-place hobbit and his often foolish dwarvish companions, assisted by the resourceful wizard Gandalf, but increasingly we become aware of the greater legends that surround it. The small peek we get at how Chapter Four looks from the goblins' perspective is very illuminating. What they see is one of the most notorious captains of their bitter rivals suddenly appearing among them, wielding the magical sword of their ancient enemies, the sword whose name has been passed down in whispers among them for centuries and which burns with a hateful light in the darkness of their caves when it senses their presence. The history to which Tolkien has been alluding from the beginning starts to come together into a great tale, full of marvels and dread. Like Bilbo, we are beginning to get acclimated to the world of adventure that is gradually unfolding before us.

5

The Turning Point

Bilbo's Choices: The First Turning Point

We may think that Bilbo is in a pretty tight place as he is being roughly carried along on the backs of the dwarves with the goblins in furious pursuit. The crucible of doubt and danger in which the hobbit's adventurous spirit is being formed and refined, however, has not yet reached its hottest and most desperate point. That point comes at the beginning of Chapter Five, when Bilbo wakes up alone in the dark.

The narrator tells us that this moment, in which Bilbo finds his ring by chance, is "a turning point in his career" (65). The finding of the ring is certainly an important moment, and if we go on to read *The Lord of the Rings,* we will look back at this moment as a turning point in the entire history of Middle-earth. But this moment in which Bilbo discovers that he is alone in the dark in the goblins' tunnels is a turning point in a much more personal way as well. This might be the worst situation in which Bilbo will ever find himself in all of his adventures. There are greater dangers which he will have to face alone later in his story, but he will be a different and more experienced hobbit by then. He has been steadily and increasingly immersed in the world of adventure through the first four chapters, but up until this point he has only been a kind of passenger, an observer. The only thing he has really done, apart from disastrously failing to pick William the troll's pocket, is shout loudly in the goblins' cave. Now, he is thrown entirely on his own resources. Mr. Baggins, who once collapsed into quivering terror at the mere mention of the possibility of danger to himself, now finds himself, a few scant weeks later, forced to find his way to the other side of the Misty Mountains through the complex tunnel network of the murderous goblins who are hunting for him, without any food or water or even a source of light. Bilbo must now become a real adventurer or die.

Bilbo felt far removed from "his own country of safe and comfortable things" when he looked back and saw it "blue and faint" on the horizon from up in the mountain passes (52). Now, buried in the utter darkness beneath the mountains, he finds himself at a practically infinite remove from his "nice bright hobbit-hole," as he poignantly remembers it after his capture by the goblins (57). Here, not even the memory of homely things can help him. His first impulse when he awakes is toward a kind of Baggins escapism. He tries to immerse himself in a fantasy of "frying bacon and eggs in his own kitchen at home" (65). These memories cannot comfort him but "only made him miserabler." He then tries to take comfort in a real rather than an imagined pleasure of home: smoking. After his failed attempt to light his pipe, however, he realizes that smoking would not have helped him, and might even have been disastrous. "Goodness knows," the narrator remarks, "what the striking of matches and the smell of tobacco would have brought on him out of dark holes in that horrible place" (66). Nothing from his old life in Bag-End can help him at all now.

What finally brings him comfort, significantly, is his sword. He draws it out and finds that it glows at the nearness of goblins, showing that it is an Elvish blade like Thorin's and Gandalf's swords. This sword is an emphatically Tookish thing to take comfort in. Remember that back in Bag-End, for Bilbo, a sword was one of the symbols of the adventurous life. When he felt a longing for adventure first tentatively stirring within him as the dwarves sang their song, it manifested itself as a desire to "wear a sword instead of a walking-stick" (16). That, of course, was only a mental image, and he immediately brushed it away. Even after he finds his little sword in the trolls' cave, he seems to forget about it most of the time. Now he suddenly discovers he has not just any sword, but a "blade made in Gondolin for the goblin-wars of which so many songs had sung" (66). At this critical moment, he is drawing his sword for the first time, stepping into the Tookish role of bold adventurer. When he does so, he finds unexpectedly that he himself has been drawn into that world of heroic legends that Elrond and apparently even Thorin inhabit. He can now see himself as a character in one of those long, ancient stories that have spanned ages of wonder and tragedy.

Instead of feeling overwhelmed, he is quite pleased. We may also remember how, in the moment in which he overheard Gloin's insult and burst back into his sitting room to volunteer for the journey, he wanted to be thought fierce. Looking at his sword, he realizes that he might now be able to make the terrifying goblins themselves think him fierce, for he "had noticed that such weapons made a great impression on goblins that came upon them suddenly" (66). The commitment he made in Bag-End to a life of adventure had been almost purely theoretical. Now, in this moment, he begins to make it a reality. He has passed the turning point in his career.

Gollum: A Miserable, Wicked Creature

The character of the goblins, which we examined in Chapter Four, provides us with a kind of baseline for the wicked creatures we will meet in the rest of *The Hobbit*. They will be the standard of comparison for all other evil creatures, and they therefore provide us with a useful benchmark for understanding Gollum's initial description. Gollum is older than the goblins, and he lives deeper in the heart of the mountains than even they do. The goblins might live in impenetrable darkness and fear the sun, but the narrator says that Gollum himself is "as dark as darkness" (68). The goblins, we are told, are cruel but not brave; they will catch anyone they can, "as long as it is done smart and secret, and the prisoners are not able to defend themselves" (59). Gollum preys on the goblins themselves in exactly the same style, taking care that he is never found out, catching and throttling goblins from behind if they come down near his lake. Even the goblins fear Gollum; to them, he is "something unpleasant . . . lurking down there" by the lake, an unknown and shadowy figure of fear (68). We are introduced to Gollum not as someone who is as evil and scary as the goblins, but as someone who outdoes the goblins in almost every dimension.

As we begin to approach Gollum, we must recognize the fact that he is the character that people are most likely to be familiar with already when they read *The Hobbit* for the first time. This is even more true of Gollum than of Bilbo, for we get to know Gollum much better as a character in *The Lord of the Rings* than we do Bilbo. Readers of *The Lord of the Rings* will find *The Hobbit*'s Gollum quite familiar and will see his encounter with Bilbo as anticipating and setting up Gollum's relationship with Frodo later on.

It is important to keep in mind, however, that this similarity was imposed on Gollum retroactively. When Tolkien sat down to write *The Lord of the Rings,* he thought of it as a sequel to *The Hobbit.** He wanted, therefore, some link that he could establish between the story of *The Hobbit* and the later story, some seed that he could take from *The Hobbit* and grow into a new story. The link he decided on was Bilbo's magic ring, but in the process of developing the story of *The Lord of the Rings,* he decided that Bilbo's ring would be much more than just a very useful invisibility ring. That change in the nature of the ring did not conflict with all of *The Hobbit,* but it did require a significant reconsideration of the "Riddles in the Dark" chapter, and of the character of Gollum in particular. When Tolkien sent his publisher some corrections to the text of *The Hobbit* in 1950, therefore, he made some very important changes to his original depiction of Gollum, making him much more like the Gollum that we read about in *The Fellowship of the Ring* and finally meet in *The Two Towers.* Thus, though the story of Bilbo and Gollum's meeting was published almost twenty years before *The Fellowship of the Ring,* I think it is fair to say that the Gollum in *The Hobbit,* as it now stands, is actually based on the Gollum of *The Lord of the Rings,* and not the other way around.

If we go back and look at the particular changes that Tol-

---

* He and the other members of the Inklings, the group of friends who met to read and discuss each other's works, called *The Lord of the Rings* "The New Hobbit" for years.

kien made when he revised Chapter Five, we can see the aspects of Gollum's character that Tolkien really wanted to emphasize. The first thing that he did was to make Gollum more thoroughly wicked than he had been in the first edition. The original Gollum was still predatory (he did hope to kill and eat Bilbo), but he was also fair and even decent. In the first edition, Gollum was rather touchingly concerned about not breaking the rules of the riddle-game. When he lost the game, he was absolutely determined to fulfill his end of the bargain no matter what, because he "learned long long ago . . . never, never to cheat" at the riddle-game.*

There is one fascinating passage that highlights the change in Gollum's character in Tolkien's revision quite sharply. Intriguingly, it is a line that Tolkien keeps unchanged in the new edition, but whose meaning he alters completely. In both editions, when Bilbo wins the game, Gollum leaves in his boat to go to his island, and Bilbo, seeing him go, thinks Gollum "was just making an excuse and did not mean to come back" (76). Bilbo's suspicion that Gollum is slinking away in bad faith is wrong in both editions, but for completely opposite reasons. In the first edition, Gollum is supposed to be fetching Bilbo a prize, a reward for winning the game. Bilbo is wrong to think Gollum is planning to break their agreement; Gollum has every intention of being true to his word, and he is returning to his island to find the ring so he can give it to Bilbo. Gollum, it turns out, is a far more honest and forthright creature than Bilbo gives him credit for.

In the revised edition that most of us are now familiar

---

* Rateliff, *The History of the Hobbit*, I.160. The full text of the first edition of Chapter Five is on pages 153–63 of Volume I of the two-volume edition.

with, Gollum leaves Bilbo, vaguely saying that he needs to "get some things" that will help him in guiding Bilbo to the exit (76). Bilbo still thinks, in exactly the same words, that Gollum is sneaking away to get out of fulfilling the bargain, and he is still wrong. Once again, Gollum has every intention of returning to Bilbo once he has retrieved his ring from the island, but in the second edition he plans to return, not to hand it over to Bilbo, but to use it to kill him. Gollum is "angry now and hungry," we are told (76). This second time, Bilbo is wrong because Gollum turns out to be far more wicked and untrustworthy than Bilbo had suspected. In rewriting Gollum's character, Tolkien removed almost all of the good impulses that he originally gave to him.

In looking at the wickedness of Gollum, we must also guard against a common misunderstanding of his character. Gollum talks to himself and debates with himself, and this might lead us to assume that Gollum's character is divided between a good side and a bad side. There are a few moments in *The Lord of the Rings* when some good impulses or nostalgic feelings can still be seen in Gollum, but in *The Hobbit*, in particular, his internal dialogue, spoken aloud, is not between a good self and an evil self.

After the riddle-game is over and Gollum has passed by the unexpectedly invisible Bilbo in the passage, Gollum stops and argues with himself about what he should do. The primary difference we can see between the two debating perspectives within Gollum here is that one is pessimistic and the other optimistic. He first says that there is no use searching for the ring, since he is sure that Bilbo has it (79). He responds more hopefully that perhaps Bilbo does not have the ring after all, and that anyway Bilbo does not know what the ring can do, and in any case, Bilbo is not going anywhere because he is lost. The first perspective cynically points out that Bilbo is "tricksy" and gloomily suggests that it is likely that Bilbo does indeed know what the ring does, and that he was probably even lying about being lost (80). The second perspective responds, with waning hopefulness, that Bilbo won't escape completely with the ring, because the goblins will certainly catch him. The first replies in panic and terror, pointing out that the goblins capturing Bilbo and getting the ring would be the very worst disaster of all and would mean certain death. To this the second perspective quickly agrees, and the debate ends with Gollum's scampering off to cut Bilbo off from the "back-door." One of these perspectives is quicker to think evil of others and to imagine terrible things happening to himself, but neither is kind, friendly, or at all well-intentioned toward Bilbo.

In his revisions to Chapter Five from the first edition, Tolkien not only makes Gollum more wicked; he also makes him more tragic and pitiable. Gollum may not have a good side, but he is not simply and repulsively evil, either. Tolkien emphasizes the sadness of his life. For instance, when Gollum suggested the riddle-game to Bilbo in the first edition, Tolkien tells us that he used to play the riddle-game at times "before the goblins came, and he was cut off from his friends far under the mountain."* There is no particular pathos here. It is, of course, too bad that Gollum hasn't been able to hang out with his subterranean friends as much since the mountains became infested with goblins, but it doesn't sound espe-

* Rateliff, 156.

cially tragic (though it does invite us to wonder who Gollum's friends might have been!).

In the later edition, Tolkien writes that Gollum used to play the riddle-game "with other funny creatures sitting in their holes in the long, long ago, before he lost all his friends and was driven away, alone, and crept down, down, into the dark under the mountains" (69). In the new version, Tolkien starts our relationship with Gollum by giving us this terribly sad glimpse into his personal history. We learn that he once had friends who sound rather like hobbits—funny creatures sitting in their holes—but that he somehow lost them and is now completely alone. We find that he is only living in the deep caves because he was driven there (perhaps by those who used to be his friends). Although he is now as dark as the darkness, he is not native to the dark. When Gandalf tells Frodo Gollum's story at the beginning of *The Fellowship of the Ring*, he calls it a sad story, and we are given a glimpse of that story here in this one sentence. Tolkien perfectly sums up his revision of Gollum's character when he has the narrator call him "a miserable wicked creature" (76), and we must keep both of these aspects of Gollum in mind as we look at Bilbo's interactions with him in this chapter, which will culminate in Bilbo's crucial moral decision as he leaves Gollum behind.

Bilbo's Nature: The Riddle-Game

The centerpiece of Chapter Five, as its title suggests, is the riddle contest between Gollum and Bilbo. Tolkien wrote the poetry for all of these riddles himself, even though many of them are based on other, similar riddles that he had read elsewhere. If we look closely at Bilbo's and Gollum's riddles, we will find that they are not a random collection of word puzzles. The riddles that each character tells show us a lot about the person who tells them. Nowhere are the darkness and misery of Gollum's existence shown more starkly and movingly than in his riddles, and those of Bilbo will teach us a lot about his perspective at this crucial moment of his life.

The riddles are not just character sketches, however—we must remember that this is also a deadly struggle, with Bilbo's very life at stake. The riddles themselves reflect this conflict, for in them we can see two warring points of view squaring off. Bilbo may only be thinking about stumping Gollum and saving his skin, but through his choice of riddles we can also see him beginning to play a part that he will play more and more explicitly through the rest of the book: the representative and spokesman of life and peace and joy.

Gollum begins the contest with his Mountain riddle:

> *What has roots as nobody sees,*
> *Is taller than trees,*
> *Up, up it goes,*
> *And yet never grows?*
> *(70)*

This riddle has an obvious personal relevance to Gollum; the mountains are his home, since he left his river valley ages before to live under the mountains. The emphasis of the riddle is on the grandeur and mystery of mountains. They are taller and greater than the mere trees of the valley. His reference to nobody seeing the roots of the mountains is touched with a slightly boastful irony that hints at a desire to aggrandize himself as well as his mountain home. He, Gollum, has indeed seen those roots; he alone lives there, beneath even the tunnels of the goblins, "down at the very roots of the mountain" (68). Gollum indirectly depicts himself as an exception to the general rule, the one person who has seen the mysteries, the knower of secrets.

The final note of the riddle, however, points in a different direction. If the first two lines emphasize the greatness both of Gollum's knowledge and of his mountain home itself, the last two lines hint at his despair. The mountains, though enormous, are not alive; they don't grow. The greatness of the mountains and Gollum's own status turns out to be a stagnant, lifeless greatness, full of darkness and loneliness.

Bilbo's response to this first riddle does not at first seem quite so revealing. Bilbo's own first riddle is the simple and relatively commonplace Teeth riddle:

Thirty white horses on a red hill,
  First they champ,
  Then they stamp,
Then they stand still.
  (70)

The narrator admits that Bilbo only tells this riddle because "the idea of eating was rather on his mind" (70). And yet this rather disturbing context for Bilbo's riddle serves to emphasize the comparative brightness and boldness of its imagery. Even when he himself is facing the possibility of being devoured, the "idea of eating" that is on his mind is a very positive one. The image of the thirty white horses on a hill, champing and stamping, is a brave, lively, and attractive one.

Tolkien accentuates the implications of Bilbo's description

of teeth through Gollum's remark that he has only six "horses" (which are probably not particularly white). Gollum's snarling, hissing, snaggle-toothed mouth is adapted to a sort of eating that is worlds away from the dignified, orderly, and refined eating of Bilbo's imaginary line of white horses, suitable for the Bag-End dining room or for breakfast on the lawn. There is little of the parade ground about Gollum's teeth.

Gollum's second riddle, like the first, is intriguingly applicable to Gollum's own grim existence. This one is his Wind riddle:

> *Voiceless it cries,*
> *Wingless flutters,*
> *Toothless bites,*
> *Mouthless mutters.*
> *(70)*

This riddle is rather creepy in what it depicts the wind as doing: crying, biting, muttering. What Gollum emphasizes about the wind is what it doesn't have: it has no voice, no wings, no teeth, no mouth. There is a kind of helplessness about this description. The heart of the riddle, of course, is an apparent paradox: the wind has none of those things and yet still performs all those actions. Yet the actions themselves are so futile, so desolate, that their accomplishment only increases the pathos. The wind doesn't roar; it cries. It doesn't soar; it only flutters. The wind is described as being nobody and having nothing, and yet it is still always biting, always crying, always muttering. This, of course, is also a perfect description of Gollum's own nightmare reality, alone at the roots of the mountain.

Bilbo's response is a riddle he makes up on the spot, and it is a fascinating rejoinder to Gollum's bleak Wind riddle. This is the Sun on the Daisies riddle:

> *An eye in a blue face*
> *Saw an eye in a green face.*
> *"That eye is like to this eye"*
> *Said the first eye,*
> *"But in low place*
> *Not in high place."*
> *(71)*

Certainly in tone and subject it is as different from the Wind riddle as can be. Where Gollum emphasizes how disembodied the wind is, Bilbo personifies both sun and flower, characterizing them as eyes in human faces and giving them human speech. Where Gollum speaks of the voiceless and inarticulate muttering of the wind, Bilbo gives us the very words the sun speaks. Where Gollum's riddle is grim and almost despairing, Bilbo's is full of light, cheerfulness, and the memory of comfortable and beautiful things.

This riddle hinges on the etymology of the word *daisy*. In Old English, which was Tolkien's main academic specialty, this flower was originally named "the day's eye," the *daeges eage,* both because the yellow center looks like the sun and because the petals fold in to conceal that center at night and unfold again with the dawn. In the Middle Ages, the sun itself was often compared to an eye, being called the "eye of the world." The riddle plays on these names, therefore, pointing to the similarity and the relationship between the sun and the daisy.

We can think about this riddle on two different levels.

On the simplest level, it is a riddle full of bright and lively things that are very dear to Bilbo, the more so because he is currently cut off from them: the sun, the blue sky, the green fields, and the flowers (of which he is especially fond, as we were told in Chapter One). When Bilbo is first dragged down into the darkness of the goblin caves, he starts pining for his hobbit-hole again, but this time, significantly, for his "nice bright" hobbit-hole, so different from the morally and literally dark goblin tunnels (57). Bilbo clearly is longing for the light and air of the outside world, and his riddle remembers them fondly.

The riddle also suggests some interesting things about Bilbo's worldview. By appealing to the likeness between the daisy and the sun, Bilbo establishes the connection between the everyday things of his world and the higher and greater order that surrounds them. Notice that the riddle is essentially a narrative given from the sun's perspective. The sun looks down on the world from the heavens and considers the daisies. We then get a direct quotation of the sun's remarks upon noticing the humble daisy. The sun emphasizes the connection between the two, recognizing that the flower is a reflection, an echo, of itself in the world. While Gollum is speaking of emptiness and solitude, Bilbo is recognizing that the things in his daily world have a place within the higher and greater order of creation as well as a likeness to those high and great things, which look down upon them in kindness. We can hardly reconstruct Bilbo's entire theology on this one riddle, but it contains some suggestive hints.

Bilbo's Daisy riddle is not, consciously, a rebuttal to Gollum's Wind riddle. When Gollum in turn responds with his third riddle, however, it is explicitly a retaliation for the sunlit riddle that he found so vexing. He finds Bilbo's riddle, that "ordinary above ground everyday sort of riddle," tiring, and it puts him out of temper. His response is "something a bit more difficult and more unpleasant" (71). His Darkness riddle:

> *It cannot be seen, cannot be felt,*
> *Cannot be heard, cannot be smelt.*
> *It lies behind stars and under hills,*
>   *And empty holes it fills.*
> *It comes first and follows after,*
>   *Ends life, kills laughter.*
>   *(71)*

The simplest way in which this riddle serves as a response to Bilbo's Daisy riddle is obvious; frustrated and irritated by Bilbo's riddle about light, Gollum tells a riddle about darkness.

This riddle, like Gollum's previous riddles, also has its autobiographical aspects. The narrator, you will remember, describes Gollum as "dark as darkness" (68), and Gollum, who is getting hungry, begins his riddle by describing the dark as a sort of idealized version of himself. Gollum hunts by stealth, invisible with his ring, undetectable until he has his fingers around the throat of his victim. Those first two lines, therefore, sound like the ultimate version of the hunting Gollum: undetectable, irresistible. The sun on the daisies may give us a glimpse of Bilbo's world that he longs for; the dark is Gollum's true world, his perfected self.

The last four lines give us perhaps a clearer insight into Gollum's larger worldview than any other part of the text. Just as Bilbo's Daisy riddle gives a small glimpse into Bilbo's metaphysical framework, so the Darkness riddle lays out Gollum's own dark theology. As he did in the Mountain riddle, Gollum emphasizes the grandeur and majesty of a thing that is associated with him personally. By pointing out that the darkness "lies behind stars and under hills," Gollum is claiming that the darkness, his darkness, is both beneath the daisies and above the sun, enclosing both the lower and the higher worlds of Bilbo's riddle. Listening to and thinking about Bilbo's riddle invites one to think of the broad, bright world above, which might make Gollum's dark, shut-in world seem small and pitiful in comparison. Gollum shifts the ground here, claiming that darkness is in fact greatest of all, and that it is actually the sunlit world that is the small, confined space, enclosed both above and below by the darkness, a mere bubble of brightness in the great expanse of night. He broadens this point even further by stating that the darkness "comes first and follows after," showing that the dark encloses the light not only in space, but in time as well. According to Gollum, all of time and space, themselves finite, are bounded by the infinite darkness.

The last line speaks not only of the vastness of the dark, but of its nature as well. The darkness "ends life" and "kills laughter." Gollum characterizes the darkness as the destroyer not only of life but of liveliness, of the kind of joy and delight that might be associated with the sun and the daisies. Notice that Gollum is not just being nihilistic here, claiming that nothing really matters and nothing really exists. That's not how Gollum talks about the darkness. This darkness Gollum speaks of is not a mere emptiness or void. Darkness is not just the absence of life and joy; it is something that obliterates them. Empty holes are not really empty; they are filled with Darkness; it is a positive thing.

This kind of talk has a disturbing precedent in Tolkien's other writings. In *The Silmarillion,* Tolkien tells the story of the downfall of the great human nation of Númenor. In their arrogance and their greedy desire for immortality, the Númenóreans eventually believe the lies told to them by Sauron, the Dark Lord who is working to hasten the destruction of Númenor. When Sauron is deceiving them into abandoning the worship of Ilúvatar and their allegiance to the powers of good, he speaks of darkness in terms similar to Gollum's. He says that beyond the world lies the "Ancient Darkness," and he claims that the Lord of Darkness is the "Lord of All" and the "Giver of Freedom."* "Darkness alone," says Sauron, "is worshipful."† If Bilbo's Daisy riddle hints at his sense of a divine order in which the mortal world reflects the glory and beauty of the heavenly world, Gollum's Darkness riddle responds with echoes of the greatest wickedness that mortals have ever engaged in: the worship of Evil and Darkness itself in the place of God.

Bilbo's next riddle seems like an almost comical letdown from the momentous and horrible implications of Gollum's Darkness riddle:

A box without hinges, key, or lid,
Yet golden treasure inside is hid.
(71)

This is the Egg riddle, and Bilbo himself doesn't think much of it; the narrator tells us he views it as a mere stalling tactic. Ironically, however, it proves the hardest riddle for Gollum

---

* J.R.R. Tolkien, *The Silmarillion* (Houghton Mifflin, 2001), 272.
† Ibid., 271.

to guess of any that Bilbo asks. In some sense, therefore, it does seem to serve as a kind of rebuttal; it gets to Gollum and leaves him flustered.

There are two things that are conspicuous about this riddle. The first is the reference to golden treasure. The whole purpose of Bilbo's journey, of course, is to seek a golden treasure that lies under a mountain, and here is Bilbo, under the mountains, making a riddle about golden treasure. But the treasure that he speaks of is not golden harps and jeweled crowns and necklaces. It is a very different kind of treasure: it is the treasure of life itself, the egg yolk that will develop into the hatchling that emerges from the egg. This is also a treasure that cannot be profitably burgled; it is a chest that cannot be opened without destroying the treasure inside.

The second conspicuous thing about the Egg riddle is how it follows upon the Darkness riddle. Gollum has just described how darkness "ends life," and Bilbo immediately tells a riddle about the beginning of life, as if reasserting the life and liveliness that Gollum would seek to suppress. We mustn't get too carried away, however, with the larger metaphysical implications of the riddle. There can be no doubt that when Bilbo is thinking of eggs, he is thinking primarily, as he was a few pages earlier, of "frying bacon and eggs in his own kitchen at home" (65). But the thought of frying eggs in his nice bright hobbit-hole is still in itself a perfectly appropriate rejoinder to the Darkness riddle. Remember that darkness, according to Gollum, kills laughter in addition to ending life. A leisurely second breakfast on the lawn is, in its own way, no less a defiance of the power of darkness than is the life of an embryo inside a living egg.

How Gollum guesses the Egg riddle again points to the differences between the two characters. The memory that finally recalls the answer to his mind is the memory of sucking eggs. Here is an activity that is alien to both positive associations with eggs. Here is neither the preservation of new life nor the peace, comfort, and prosperity of fried eggs and bacon. Gollum can only barely recall eggs, but when he does, all he can remember is greedily sucking the life out of them.

Gollum's Fish riddle steps down from the grandiosity of the Darkness riddle and seems rather to match the level of Bilbo's own Egg riddle:

> *Alive without breath,*
> *As cold as death;*
> *Never thirsty, ever drinking,*
> *All in mail never clinking.*
> *(72)*

The Egg riddle responded to the Darkness riddle by reasserting life and liveliness. The Fish riddle comes back by parodying life and confounding it with death. A fish is a perfectly natural and lively kind of creature, but Gollum's riddling description makes it sound like some kind of zombie: animate but unbreathing, and cold as the grave. The fish's relationship to the water is also horribly twisted. To Gollum's fish, the water is not nourishing and life-giving; it is an unwanted drink continually forced upon it.

This riddle also, like the Wind riddle, resonates with Gollum's own world. In Gollum's dark world at the roots of the mountains, the fish have changed over time. When Bilbo first encounters the lake, he thinks about the fish "whose fathers swam in, goodness only knows how many years ago, and never swam out again, while their eyes grew bigger and bigger from

trying to see in the blackness" (67). The fish thus form an in-
structive parallel to Gollum's own career, and their description
recalls his at many points. The fish were once wholesome and
natural, but they found that the journey into the dark heart of
the mountains was a one-way trip, becoming twisted by their
starvation for light until they are merely "nasty slimy things,
with big bulging blind eyes, wriggling in the water" (67). Gollum likewise seems to have been altered by his long time underground, becoming a "slimy creature" with "pale lamp-like
eyes" (68). Gollum's description of the fish's drinking also recalls his own wretched existence. Fish are "never thirsty, ever
drinking," living a life of continual consumption and continual dissatisfaction. Bilbo's world is a world of eggs and bacon
and deep sighs of contentment; Gollum's is a world of gnaw-
ing desire and perpetual loathing.

Bilbo's response is simple but typical, taking the subject
of Gollum's previous riddle and placing it in a strikingly Baggins-like setting:

> No-legs lay on one-leg, two-legs sat near on three-legs, four-
> legs got some.
> (73)

Here Bilbo takes Gollum's parody of warm-blooded life, the
fish, and makes it the centerpiece of a very cozy domestic
scene. A man sitting on a stool and eating his dinner off a
little table while his cat sits purring at his side is an image of
contentment utterly alien to the world of Gollum's gasping,
bulgy-eyed fish. You can practically see the warm fire blazing next to the man described in the riddle, and I imagine
he will light up his pipe afterwards. Notice also the camara-

derie of the man and cat, sharing their meal. It is in every way a warm-blooded, peaceful, friendly scene that Bilbo invokes. It is no wonder that Gollum might have had some trouble guessing it, if he had not already been thinking of fish.

Gollum's final riddle, his "hard and horrible" riddle, is indeed a riddle about finality itself:

> *This thing all things devours:*
> *Birds, beasts, trees, flowers;*
> *Gnaws iron, bites steel;*
> *Grinds hard stones to meal;*
> *Slays king, ruins town,*
> *And beats high mountain down.*
> *(73)*

Gollum describes time as the destroyer of everything. The riddle illustrates a concept commonly associated with time, especially during the Renaissance, and articulated in the Latin phrase *Tempus edax rerum*, usually translated "Time devours all things."

What is particularly interesting about Gollum's treatment of this traditional idea is how systematic it is. Look at how Gollum lists the things devoured by time. In line two, time destroys living things, the bright and comfortable world that Bilbo's riddles have so persistently recalled. In lines three and four, it destroys iron, steel, and stone: the elements associated with the harsher and darker world of the dwarves and goblins. In line five, it destroys civilization itself, laying waste to order and human society. This reference to king and town is particularly relevant in a story that will end with the return of a king and both the destruction and the re-establishment of towns. Finally, even the high mountain is beaten down by time, and thus Gollum includes his own world in the general destruction. The last line of Gollum's last riddle brings us back to his first riddle, the Mountain riddle, in which he spoke so boastingly of his own dark and stony home. The mountain may be the last to go in the Time riddle, but Gollum still acknowledges that it will go.

Gollum's riddle speaks of final hopelessness, the end even of his own life and world. Gollum is very ancient; even in the more cheerful first edition of *The Hobbit*, he has been in his lonely lake since before the arrival of the goblins in the mountains. Through his age-long and miserable experience of life, he is well aware of the passage of the years, which have gnawed, ground, and beaten him until, like the blind fish, he has been warped and stunted beyond recognition. This last riddle resounds with a stubbornness and a despair that speak powerfully of both the wickedness and the misery of Gollum's existence. The world that it reveals is horrible indeed, and to it Bilbo has no response.

Bilbo's Choices: Sympathy for Gollum

In the wake of Gollum's Time riddle, Bilbo can think of no more riddles. The final and decisive question "What have I got in my pocket?" is uttered by accident, Bilbo voicing his thought aloud by mistake as his hand finds the ring, for a second time, in the dark (74). The last exchange of the riddle-game is laced with ironies. The elusive correct answer to Bilbo's question turns out to be the one thing on which Gollum had "brooded for ages" (77). While he is trying to guess the answer, Gollum thinks over the things in his own pockets, trying to guess what other, less nasty people might keep in their pockets (75), when all along the correct answer is actually the very thing he himself has carried in his pockets for centuries. Bilbo himself does not know the answer to the question he asks; he learns what it is he has in his pocket only from Gollum, who failed to guess it in three tries.

And yet the greatest irony of the Pocket question is an irony unintended by Tolkien in 1937. Bilbo can think of no response to the Time riddle, but as it turns out, his last question would indeed serve as a kind of rebuttal to it. Once Tolkien later establishes Bilbo's ring as a Ring of Power, he will explain that these rings do in a sense counteract the devouring force of time, granting greatly prolonged life to their mortal owners. This relevance of the ring as a response to the Time riddle can't have been consciously intended by Tolkien in the first edition of *The Hobbit*, since he had no thought then that the ring had any such significance or power, but it is a remarkable coincidence.

In the meantime, the primary emphasis in the text is once again on Bilbo's luck. His unintentional asking of the winning question is the third time that a stroke of luck has come to his aid during the riddle-game. The first is when Bilbo is struggling with the Fish riddle only to have a cold, clammy fish jump right onto his toes and suggest the answer (73). The second is when Bilbo correctly answers the Time riddle entirely by accident, meaning to call out for more time and merely calling: "Time! Time!" (74). Three times he is "saved by pure luck." I drew attention to the extraordinary good fortune of Bilbo and the dwarves back in my discussion of Chapter Three, and here in Chapter Five luck seems to be taking a more forceful role in Bilbo's guidance and preservation.

The Pocket question also prompts us to think about the fate from which Bilbo's luck is saving him. Throughout the riddle contest, Bilbo and Gollum have stood forth as spokesmen for opposing perspectives, for light and darkness, for wholesomeness and corruption, for contentment and despair. We end the game, however, with a question that serves not to separate the two, but to establish a link between them. Both of them have had the same ring in their pockets, and we see Bilbo doing for the first time what Gollum has been doing for ages: fingering the ring in his pocket and talking aloud to it. The two have seemed like diametrically opposed principles, but in the end it seems that they might almost be "before" and "after" pictures of the same character. Although Bilbo doesn't yet recognize it, Gollum's fate should be a cautionary tale.

Even before this last question Tolkien has invited us at several points to see connections between the two characters. Gollum's riddles may reveal a viewpoint alien to his own, but Bilbo guesses several of them because he has "heard something rather like" them before (70). Gollum as well is enabled to guess some of Bilbo's riddles only because he still retains memories "of days when he had been less lonely and sneaky and nasty," of days when he seemed to live a fairly Baggins-like life, "with his grandmother in a hole in a bank by a river" (71). Gollum's dim memories show us that he was not always this way, and they also contain an implicit warning for Bilbo himself. Bilbo, too, is undergoing a change, a transition out of his quiet and happy life in his hole in the side of a hill. Gollum's memories are a reminder that such transitions are not always for the better, and even Bagginses might descend into corruption and wretchedness.

Bilbo does not seem to see this connection at first. When he hears Gollum's cries of misery upon discovering the loss of his precious ring, Bilbo is untouched and "could not find much pity in his heart," even though he does find Gollum's weeping "horrible to listen to" (79). In the final moments of his meeting with Gollum, however, Bilbo sees at last the full implications of Gollum's condition. At the mouth of the exit tunnel, with a wary Gollum standing between him and freedom, Bilbo faces a serious moral crisis. His panic and his desperation to escape at first prompt him to brutal and ruthless action. He feels that he must "stab the foul thing, put its eyes out, kill it" (81). His moral sense quickly reasserts itself, however. Indeed, he swings the other direction and is even a bit overgenerous in his assessment of his enemy. He says to himself that Gollum "had not actually threatened to kill him, or tried to yet," even though both of these things are not quite true (81). Gollum had tried to catch and kill him when he ran up the passage, and Gollum's open discussion of whether or not Bilbo would be "scrumptiously crunchable" certainly constitutes a threat (72).

But Bilbo's generosity here is not purely objective. It is driven by his understanding, in this moment, of Gollum's life and world, of the connection between himself and Gollum. He imagines himself in Gollum's position, lost in "endless, unmarked days without light or hope of betterment, hard stone, cold fish, sneaking and whispering" (81). He trembles at the thought, gripped by a "pity mixed with horror." The result is a new strength and resolve that literally propel him back to the light he was so desperate to regain. His moral choice becomes a leap of faith, a "leap in the dark" and out of the dark, and he successfully rises above both of the dark ends that awaited him there, either to be killed by Gollum or to become him (82).

Gollum's final action in this story, his "blood-curdling shriek, filled with hatred and despair," reasserts the differences between Gollum and Bilbo and emphasizes the significance of Bilbo's moral choice (82). Gollum is given over to hope-lessness, left with nothing but eternal hatred for the one who has just shown him mercy. Bilbo persists in running toward the hope of escape, the back-door, despite the fact that his compassion for Gollum's misery now brings his "heart to his mouth."

At the beginning of the book, the narrator invites us to judge whether Bilbo "gained anything in the end" (4). In Chapter Five, we are still far from the end, but we can already begin to see what Bilbo is gaining. Bilbo has passed the turning point in his career. He has ceased to be a passive victim of his adventure, and he has embraced his new life. He has even come to take pleasure in seeing his own life as part of the great, grand stories that he listened to (with obvious pleasure, despite their Tookishness) even when he lived in Bag-End. When Gollum asks him about his sword, he proudly calls it "a blade which came out of Gondolin!"—openly boasting about his newfound connection with the legends of old (69). When he discovers that the ring he found by accident is a magic ring like the ones he had heard about in old tales, his "head was in a whirl of hope and wonder" (80). Bilbo has come to see that, though adventures may in truth be "nasty . . . uncomfortable things" that "make you late for dinner," as he said back in Chapter One (6), it can also be rather grand to be a part of one of the great stories.

His first encounter after he adopts this positive frame of mind, however, shows a very serious side to this new world. In Gollum, Bilbo finds something not only worse than go-ing without bed and breakfast, but worse even than being tor-tured and killed by the goblins. In Gollum, he meets his moral opposite, a dark creature whose world seems entirely contrary to Bilbo's own, as their riddles repeatedly illustrate. But Tolkien shows us the connection between the two worlds, a connection that is embodied in the ring, Gollum's ring that turns out to be the answer to Bilbo's last and most personal riddle. In his final act of pity and compassion, Bilbo retains his moral stature despite the desperate circumstances. That, too, is a turning point in his life, and possibly the most momentous of all. Bilbo has squeezed through a tight place, escaping out of the darkness and into the light, and he will never turn back, even though he will have to leave his brass buttons and many other things behind him.

6

Where the Wild Things Are

Bilbo's Nature: Reintroductions

In Chapter Five, we saw Bilbo pass a major turning point in his career. Left on his own in the dark with nothing and no one to rely on, he not only survived but maintained his moral integrity, refusing to let his desperate situation justify ruthless actions. Bilbo is neither overcome in the darkness nor corrupted by the darkness, and he leaves both Gollum and the goblins behind him in the fading daylight.

As Bilbo runs down the mountain slope with his buttons rolling around on the doorstep, his worst danger seems to be over. He is still in a difficult situation; as the narrator reminds us, he "had lost hood, cloak, food, pony, his buttons and his friends" (85). But Bilbo's response to his new situation shows us quite clearly how much he has grown. Despite the trouble he is still in and all the things that he still lacks, his first thoughts are for his companions. He is concerned about Gandalf and the dwarves, and he wonders whether he should go back into the goblin caves to see if he can find them and rescue them, if necessary. He reasons that, now that he has a magic ring, he has resources which he should use to help his friends. He now seems to be thinking of himself as the professional adventurer hired by the dwarves, whose duty it is to put his expertise to work for the aid of his comrades.

The change we can see in Bilbo's attitude and outlook here is astonishing. Back in Bag-End, when he was still thinking about slinking away from the dwarves and hiding behind the beer-barrels in his cellar until they left him alone (16), it would have seemed absurd to imagine that Bilbo could elude goblins and escape from the bowels of the Misty Mountains completely unassisted. That he has not only succeeded in escaping but is planning to venture back in to attempt a single-handed rescue of the dwarves is nothing short of staggering.

It isn't that Bilbo has had a complete personality transplant, of course. He still finds the idea of going back under the mountains a "very uncomfortable thought," and he expresses his dread of the goblin caves very clearly when he thinks of them as "horrible, horrible tunnels" (85). He feels miserable about the whole prospect. But he makes the decision to go back, nevertheless. Although Bilbo's resolution turns out to be unnecessary, it shows us how much the timid little Mr. Baggins has really changed.

When Bilbo meets the dwarves again and tells them about his encounter with Gollum, he deliberately omits any reference to his new magic ring. In the beginning of *The Lord of the Rings,* of course, Tolkien is going to make a big deal of this particular moment. Gandalf will explain to Frodo in Chapter Two of Book One of *The Fellowship of the Ring* that this initial lie by Bilbo to his friends is a disquieting and ominous sign, an indication that this ring has an immediate and unwholesome effect on its possessor. As we read *The Hobbit,* however, we should remember that that aspect of this story is one that will be very cleverly imposed on it later, in retrospect. As I discussed in the Introduction, the ring in *The Hobbit,* as initially conceived by Tolkien, is neither sinister nor ominous; it is just a magical ring of invisibility—the perfect accessory to give a professional burglar a big boost in his career.

In the context of *The Hobbit,* Bilbo's untruthfulness to the dwarves is easy to understand: he wants very much to raise his "street cred" with them. The dwarves, we must recall, still don't think very highly of Bilbo. They have traveled together for a long while now, but the hobbit has so far contributed very little. As I mentioned in Chapter Four, Bilbo's shriek of alarm as the goblins are leaping out to capture them is the only positive thing he has done, and so much has happened since then that the dwarves can perhaps be forgiven for not thinking much about it. Their attitude toward Bilbo is made pretty clear by the unidentified dwarf who remarks, "He has been more trouble than use so far. . . . If we have got to go back now into those abominable tunnels to look for him, then drat him, I say" (86). This opinion is unkind, of course, and its meanness is emphasized by the fact that we have just seen Bilbo himself decide that he would do for the dwarves what they are now saying they don't want to do for him. Still, it must be admitted that from a purely practical point of view, this dwarf's opinion is understandable.

Bilbo knows it. We already saw, back at the troll encounter, that Bilbo is sensitive to the lack of respect he receives from the dwarves. The whole reason he decided to pick William's pocket in the first place was that he couldn't bear to face the dwarves without at least attempting something burglarious. Bilbo's decision to "give them all a surprise" here in Chapter Six by sneaking invisibly into the middle of their camp is motivated by the same desire: to raise himself in their esteem (86).

The story Bilbo tells of his solo adventure is plainly calculated to inflate his appearance of competence as a burglar and an adventurer. He downplays the marvel of his sudden appearance among them and his sneaking past Balin on guard, casually attributing it to his professional skill by saying that he "just crept along, you know—very carefully and quietly" (87). When the dwarves ask whether there were goblin guards at the gate, his reply is ostentatiously flippant: "O yes! lots of them; but I dodged 'em" (88). Bilbo's performance here appears calculated to counteract his rather disgraceful showing back in Bag-End, when he collapsed into hysterics on his hearthrug in front of them all. That little scene was what had led to Gloin's comment about Bilbo looking more like a grocer than a burglar, which outraged and offended Bilbo. Now that his new ring gives him such a splendid opportunity to impress his new friends, Bilbo is setting out to build up his reputation.

Bilbo's plan works, for in this moment, the dwarves look at him "with quite a new respect" (88). His sneaking in among them undetected seems to validate the quite improbable story he tells them of himself; the narrator tells us that "it is a fact that Bilbo's reputation went up a very great deal with the dwarves after this" (87). The dwarves' newfound appreciation of the hobbit is most eloquently expressed in the curiously elaborate reaction of Balin when he finds that Bilbo has crept past him. Balin takes off his hood to him and, oddly, introduces himself anew. The narrator even gives us their formal exchange in full: "'Balin at your service,' said he. 'Your servant, Mr. Baggins,' said Bilbo." Here, on the far side of the

Misty Mountains, Bilbo and the dwarves are starting their relationship afresh, meeting this time as equals.

Even Gandalf, who has been Bilbo's (rather questionable) professional reference from the beginning, seems to be impressed. At the beginning of Chapter Six, his attitude toward Bilbo is very different from that of the dwarves, but he doesn't show any more actual confidence in the hobbit than they do. Gandalf may express loyalty and affection, calling Bilbo his friend, but he doesn't say much to defend his performance thus far. He only claims that he is "not a bad little chap"—rather faint praise!—and adds that he feels "responsible for him" (86). Gandalf certainly doesn't sound as if he is talking about an esteemed colleague here; he makes Bilbo sound more like a child or a pet he is baby-sitting. Gandalf, therefore, is "more pleased than all the others" when Bilbo suddenly materializes among them, but he is also "as astonished as any of them" (87).

Bilbo's reappearance marks a new beginning, therefore, not only in Bilbo's relationship with the dwarves, but in his relationship with Gandalf. The wizard has, from the start, insisted that Bilbo is worth taking with them, but that insistence was based purely on a hunch that Bilbo would end up being important to the quest. Gandalf's statements in defense of Bilbo have tended to be in the future tense. He did state authoritatively back in Chapter One that "if I say he is a Burglar, a Burglar he is," but he felt compelled to qualify this by adding, "or will be when the time comes" (19). When he is defending Bilbo prior to the hobbit's appearance in Chapter Six, he does the same thing, predicting, "If we can only find him again, you will thank me before all is over" (86). Gandalf may believe that his assessment will turn out to be true, but not even he claims that there is much to justify it yet. Bilbo's astonishing escape from the mountains and sudden appearance among them provides the first external confirmation of Gandalf's faith. Now, for the first time, he can use the present tense with confidence, saying proudly, "What did I tell you? . . . Mr. Baggins has more about him than you guess" (88).

We are not allowed, however, to start thinking that Bilbo has been completely transformed and is now some kind of hardened master adventurer. For one thing, his perspective remains firmly grounded in immediate and mundane concerns. He is keenly aware of the physical discomforts of their situation, complaining, "My toes are all bruised and bent, and my legs ache, and my stomach is wagging like an empty sack" (92). Even in the midst of his nonchalant description of his dodging the goblin guards at the gate, he dwells with great regret on the loss of the buttons off his waistcoat. Bilbo may have turned a corner in his career, but he still does find adventures to be "nasty disturbing uncomfortable things" (6), and this one has now made him *very* late for dinner.

For another thing, he obviously does not fit in with the events happening around him, even now, just as he didn't fit into the dwarf hood that Dwalin lent him. There may be more about him than the dwarves guess, but he remains helpless most of the time. He was too small to escape the goblins in the tunnels by running away with everyone else; he had to be carried. He is the only member of the group who can't climb the trees in the wargs' glade; Dori is almost killed helping him up. He is apparently overlooked by the eagles who swoop in to rescue them from the goblins' fire, and he has to cling to Dori's legs to avoid being left behind. The dwarves may have a new and higher opinion of his abilities, but that doesn't stop Dori from feeling like a porter for having to lug

Bilbo around all the time, hauling him out of danger again and again. Bilbo has made a new beginning with the dwarves, but it is still only a beginning.

Goblins: Burn, Burn Tree and Fern

When we meet the goblins for the second time here in Chapter Six, we gain a new appreciation for their depravity. We were introduced to their wickedness and cruelty through the song that they sang when they captured Bilbo and his companions. Tolkien confirms their wickedness by the same means, through the two songs they sing around the trees in which the unfortunate travelers have taken refuge.

The narrator calls their first song in Chapter Six a "horrible song":

> *Fifteen birds in five fir-trees,*
> *their feathers were fanned in a fiery breeze!*
> *But, funny little birds, they had no wings!*
> *O what shall we do with the funny little things?*
> *Roast 'em alive, or stew them in a pot;*
> *fry them, boil them and eat them hot?*
> *(98)*

What makes this song so horrible is the frivolousness of it. We know that the goblins are furiously angry, seeking revenge on the dwarves for the killing of the Great Goblin. We are prepared for savagery and rage. But what we actually see from the goblins is revenge taken not in anger or even in grim satisfaction, but with a sickening kind of delight. Their song invokes amusing, even peaceful imagery: "funny little birds" perched in the trees, with the breeze fanning their feathers. The repetition of "funny little" establishes an almost childish tone to the first four lines, a tone that Gandalf plays on when he tries to intimidate them in response, calling them "naughty little boys" (98). The last two lines of the song, of course, give the answer to their rhetorical question: "what shall we do with the funny little things?" These lines bring about a sudden shift in tone, from light and whimsical to grim and fierce. "Roast 'em alive" is an answer that plainly reveals the cruel mockery contained in the childish tone of the song's beginning.

The list in the last two lines of the different options for cooking Bilbo and his friends may remind us of the extensive cookery debates held by the trolls in Chapter Two. (*Nobody* can seem to figure out how to cook dwarves properly!) In the context of their song, however, the goblins' cooking references are much more chilling. The trolls may have been evil, but their culinary discussions were purely practical. To them, the dwarves were a food source, and they were having an honest disagreement about how they might best be prepared for eating. The list of cookery options in the goblin song, however, is not a debate among chefs; it is an extended fantasy of torture. Tolkien sets up this particular piece of cruel humor in the very title of this chapter, invoking the imagery of frying pans and cooking fires in anticipation of the taunts that the goblins will hurl at Bilbo and his friends around the blaze. The goblins have no plans to eat the dwarves; they are just amusing themselves by imagining all of the varied and excruciating ways in which they could see the dwarves die.

The goblins' amusement is clearly demonstrated by the taunts with which they follow their little song. Maintaining the metaphor from their song, they shout to the dwarves, "Fly away little birds!" (98), taking pleasure in the knowledge that the dwarves cannot, in fact, escape. Most horribly of all, they end by commanding the dwarves to "sing," undoubtedly anticipating the screams of agony the dwarves will likely let loose as they are burned alive. That tortured shrieking is the song that the goblins are hoping to hear from these "funny little birds": goblin humor at its best.

In the second song that the goblins sing around the feet of the burning trees, they shift back to the form, rhythm, and tone of their original song back in Chapter Four:

> *Burn, burn tree and fern!*
> *Shrivel and scorch! A fizzling torch*
> *To light the night for our delight,*
>   *Ya hey!*
>   *(98)*

The first verse once again illustrates the horrid shrewdness of the goblins. In their reference to torches we can see part of the reason that the goblins considered their plan to burn the dwarves in their trees "most amusing" (97). The blazing trees will not only serve as an inescapable means of excruciating death to their hated enemies; they will also provide convenient illumination so that the goblins can properly enjoy the spectacle. Killing their enemies is good, but for the goblins the true "delight" is in being able to watch them suffer.

In fact, the enjoyment of the dwarves' suffering is the entire subject of the lovingly expanded second verse of the song:

> *Bake and toast 'em, fry and roast 'em!*
> *till beards blaze, and eyes glaze;*
> *till hair smells and skins crack,*
> *fat melts, and bones black*

in cinders lie
beneath the sky!
So dwarves shall die,
and light the night for our delight,
Ya hey!
Ya-harri-hey!
Ya hoy!
(99)

Just as in the original song in Chapter Four, this verse dwells on immediate sense experience. In that first song, they started by reliving the capture of the dwarves in the first verse, and they ended by anticipating in the third verse the imminent pain and terror of the dwarves when they were tortured and enslaved. Similarly, in this song the first verse describes in simple, ugly language the fiery spectacle that the goblins are watching at that moment, while the second verse moves on to dwell on the horrible things that are about to happen. After their first song, the goblins began cheerfully making the "Swish, smack!" and the "Yammer and bleat!" parts of its last verse start coming true right away. In Chapter Six, they time their final "Ya hoy!" celebrating the fiery deaths of their enemies with the actual lighting of the first occupied tree.

Notice also how keen and varied is the goblins' pleasure in the gruesome deaths of the dwarves. They are thinking not only about the terrible details that they will see (beards blazing and eyes glazing), but also about the finer points of what they will hear (skin cracking) and smell (hair smoldering, fat melting). All of the goblins' senses are engaged in their gleeful, morbid anticipation.

In these last two songs of the goblins, in fact, we can hear a horrible parallel to the attitude that the elves of Rivendell showed in their song. The elves sing a simple song full of laughter and childlike delight in beauty and in living things, a sensual reveling in the flowing of the river and the baking of bread. The goblins also sing songs that are full of laughter and simple delight, songs that luxuriate in sensory experience. The elves are, as the narrator will later call them, Good People; their love and joy are pure and overflowing. The goblins are very wicked people; their cruelty and malice are almost equally undiluted and exuberant. The elves celebrate life, and the goblins celebrate death, with disturbingly similar enthusiasm. I said in Chapter Four that the goblins are almost the exact opposites of the elves, and nothing illustrates this principle more powerfully than their songs. There are many strange and terrifying creatures that Bilbo will meet on his journey, but none can beat the goblins in moral depravity. Bilbo will encounter creatures more deadly, but none will take as much simple pleasure in the pain and suffering of others as the goblins do. Among all Tolkien's monsters, the goblins are the measuring stick to which the evil of all evil creatures will be compared.

The Wild: Wargs and Eagles

The narrator tells us at the beginning of Chapter Four that Bilbo and his companions have crossed into the Wild. Bilbo's adventure certainly does start to get wild pretty quickly, as he encounters great stone-giants who throw boulders around for fun and runs afoul of the goblins who take him captive into their holes. But since Bilbo is taken into the goblins' subterranean world so quickly, we don't get a chance to see what the Wild is really like, aboveground. When Bilbo emerges from the caves at the beginning of Chapter Six, we return to the Wild proper. Bilbo's alarming experiences in the pine woods on the eastern slopes of the Misty Mountains bring us into contact with two kinds of creatures who serve as interesting representatives of the Wild and its nature: the wargs and the eagles. If we look closely at these two groups, we can come to a better understanding of what Tolkien seems to mean when he calls this region the Wild.

In Chapter Six, we learn that the wargs are the allies of the goblins. The wargs are wolves, but we mustn't think that they are simply the pets of the goblins, beasts that goblins use as human hunters might use hounds. The wargs seem to have a culture totally separate from the goblins, with their own chieftain who is spoken of in parallel with the Great Goblin. They also have a spoken language which marks them out as intelligent beyond the normal scope of animals. This language, however, also most clearly betrays their low moral standing. Their speech is a "dreadful language," and to Bilbo it sounds terrible, "as if all their talk was about cruel and wicked things" (94). Bilbo can't understand their awful language, but the narrator confirms that his suspicions are quite right about the subject of their talk. The higher social functioning that separates them from other animals also betrays their wickedness. The wargs are certainly fit allies of the goblins.

The wargs, however, are more wild and less civilized than the goblins. They are much larger and more intelligent than typical wolves, but they still share many characteristics with normal animals, such as their fear of fire. Notice, however, that these bestial qualities serve to make the wargs less evil than the goblins, not more; their animal nature puts a limit on the evil they are capable of performing. When Gandalf starts harassing the wargs with wizard's fire, they can do nothing but run around in terror and confusion. The goblins, on the other hand, find the whole situation supremely funny, and they immediately contrive to take advantage of the fire themselves. The goblins, with their more "advanced" perspective, are capable of moving on to a deeper level of cruelty than the wargs alone can attain. The wargs would gladly have ripped Bilbo and the dwarves to pieces if they had caught them, but the sadistic creativity that the goblins show is quite beyond the wargs. The wargs, being more savage and wild, are less depraved than their civilized allies.

The eagles, as the enemies of the goblins and the instrument of the nearly miraculous rescue of Bilbo and his friends, seem clearly to be on the side of good and against evil. Some eagles may be "cowardly and cruel," the narrator concedes, but these eagles, the "ancient race of the northern mountains," are "the greatest of all birds; they were proud and strong and noble-hearted" (97). They show themselves to be honorable and gracious in the gratitude that they show to Gandalf for his service in healing the Lord of the Eagles on a previous occasion. The great birds certainly seem noble and heroic.

And yet we mustn't get the wrong idea about the Eagles. They are not champions of goodness, soaring about looking for wrongs to right and damsels (or hobbits) in distress to rescue. The eagles do save the dwarves, but they don't actually care much about them. The Lord of the Eagles expresses gladness that they were able to do a good turn for Gandalf, but he says that the main reason they interfered was "to cheat the goblins of their sport" (103). Saving the dwarves is more of a means than an end. The Lord of the Eagles further emphasizes their lack of investment in the dwarves or their quest when he is discussing plans for the next day. The eagles will help, but they are unwilling to put themselves in any danger in order to do so. "We will not risk ourselves for dwarves in the southward plains," he states flatly (103). Gandalf the wizard may choose to accompany the dwarves far and at great danger to himself, but the eagles are not as proactive nor as generous.

Even the eagles' enmity with the goblins is actually quite casual. The narrator simply says that they neither love nor fear the goblins. They do at times swoop down on them and drive them shrieking back into their caves, we are told, but this doesn't happen regularly or often. The eagles are not the Protectors of the Wild, the Anti-Goblin S.W.A.T. Team. The narrator tells us that they only attack the goblins "when they took any notice of them at all (which was seldom)" (97). Most of the time, the eagles don't really care all that much.

The relationship between the eagles and the "brave woodmen" that the narrator mentions earlier in the chapter is even more revealing (95). The woodmen appear to be, generally speaking, good people. Remember that they are the ones whom the goblins and wargs had been planning to attack that night. Yet the eagles are not these people's allies against the evil goblins; rather, the eagles live in open and unashamed enmity with the householders. The Lord of the Eagles notes that if the men saw them, they would shoot at them, assuming that the eagles were after their sheep. "And at other times they would be right," the eagle lord cheerfully confirms (103). The meat they bring to the dwarves that very night, in fact, includes a "small sheep" among the rabbits and hares.

The eagles are good, but they are not automatically on the side of everyone who is good, devoting their efforts to opposing evil wherever they find it. The eagles, like the wargs, are wild, sharing much in common with their lesser relatives among the beasts. Even the details the narrator gives in order to set the eagles apart as extraordinary emphasize their dual nature. The Lord of the Eagles has "eyes that could look at the sun unblinking, and could see a rabbit moving on the ground a mile below even in moonlight" (96). The eagles can and do lift their eyes to gaze at high things (remember the sun in Bilbo's Daisy riddle?), but their eyes are more often used for scanning the ground for prey. They are in conflict with human farmers as many predators naturally are. The main reason that they usually ignore goblins, the narrator tells us, is that they "did not eat such creatures" (97). They are great and noble beings, but they are, at bottom, predatory beasts.

As Bilbo is uncomfortably aware when he is up in their eyries, the eagles are not entirely safe. When he overhears one eagle referring to him and Dori as "prisoners," he wonders whether they have truly been saved at all (102). His fears are unfounded, it turns out, but they are far from unreasonable. When the eagle he is riding the next morning admits that he thinks Bilbo looks rather like a rabbit, his fears seem all the more justified. The eagles are good, but they are thoroughly wild.

As we can see, *Wild* does not simply mean "evil"—it is a good deal more complex than that. The Wild is not just the place where wicked creatures such as goblins dwell, and when Bilbo enters the Wild he is not just going behind enemy lines. Rather, Bilbo has gone far beyond his land of safe and comfortable things, entering a region where the creatures are savage and harsh. There are wicked wargs in the Wild, and there are also noble eagles, but both are fierce and predatory. The wargs show us, however, that this savagery, this connection with uncivilized beasts that both of these groups of intelligent creatures share, is not itself evil. The wildness of the wargs is the primary thing that makes them less depraved, less evil than their more civilized goblin neighbors; the wargs' savagery is, in a sense, the most positive thing about them.

We might think that the polished and secure society of Bilbo's home is presented as a superior culture, safer and far preferable to life in the Wild. The goblins, however, have plainly demonstrated that civilization is not necessarily a good thing; the cunning of culturally "advanced" people can be turned to torture, slavery, and the development of "the ingenious devices for killing large numbers of people at once" (59). The eagles also provide a caution against making several different simplistic assumptions. Good creatures in Tolkien's fiction are not always embodiments of virtue, and fierce, dangerous predators are not always wicked. Bilbo's experiences in the Wild should help us to recognize that Tolkien's world is much more complex, morally, than many people assume on a first reading.

7

The Friend of Bears and the Guest of Eagles

"QUEER LODGINGS"

The Wild: Beorn

There is no character in *The Hobbit* who embodies the moral complexity of the Wild more thoroughly than Beorn does. On the one hand, Beorn is extremely dangerous and unpredictable. Gandalf first refers to him rather ominously as an unnamed "Somebody" (107). We learn that this Somebody lives close by, that he carved the steps out of the huge rock they are standing on, and that it would be very dangerous to encounter him at night. Gandalf calls him a "very great person," which is not particularly reassuring, especially when Gandalf follows that statement by insisting that they "*must* be careful not to annoy him, or heaven knows what will happen" (108). Gandalf's initial description of Beorn makes it clear that they are taking a serious risk in approaching him.

This is all rather alarming, especially to a hobbit who is still trying to recover from the tumultuous events that Bilbo has recently been through. That night, Bilbo will dive under his blankets and hide his head after waking up to hear growl-ing and scuffling sounds outside. He fears that Beorn is going to burst in on them in bear's shape and kill them all. Bilbo is once again doing an injustice to his host, just as he did when he misinterpreted the eagles' use of the word *prisoners* back in Chapter Six. In both cases, however, the error is perfectly reasonable. Even though Bilbo was rescued from the fire by the eagle, he had nevertheless been taken to the inaccessi-ble nest of an enormous carnivore. Here in Chapter Seven, he has been taken in and feasted by Beorn, but Bilbo clearly has taken Gandalf's cautions about how dangerous Beorn is to heart. Beorn himself doesn't exactly do much to dispel his guests' fears, either, warning them, "You must not stray out-side until the sun is up, on your peril" (120). Beorn may be, in several senses, a "very great person," but his house is clearly a very dangerous place.

On the other hand, Beorn is more clearly and firmly aligned against the wicked creatures of the mountains than the eagles are. As we saw in the previous chapter, the eagles enjoy cheating the goblins of their sport, but they don't of-ten go out of their way to oppose them. Beorn, in contrast, is a determined and bitter enemy of the goblins and wargs. His acceptance of the dwarves shows clearly where his priori-ties lie. He is not "over fond of dwarves," but he is willing to welcome Gandalf's dwarf companions to his house as long as they are "enemies of goblins" (112). Apparently, anyone who fights against the goblins can't be all bad, in Beorn's book. This seems to be what is behind his particular greeting of Thorin, as well. Like the Great Goblin himself, Beorn recognizes Tho-rin's name and knows that he is the "son of Thrain, son of Thror." Beorn appears to respect Thorin for his lineage; he puts this forward as a reason why Thorin can stay. It is hard to imagine Beorn being impressed with the mere fact that Thorin comes from a royal family, however. It is much more likely that Beorn is interested in Thorin's family because they are such famous enemies of the goblins in the Misty Mountains. Beorn's fierceness against the goblins may well contribute to Bilbo's healthy personal fear of the giant skin-changer, but Gandalf is certainly right to say that Bilbo is being "silly" and that his "wits are sleepy" when he suggests that Beorn might lead the goblins and wargs down upon them (122). Scary and unpredictable he might be, but he is obviously a dedicated enemy of those evil creatures.

Although Beorn's steadfast opposition to the goblins would seem to make him a clear ally of Thorin and the dwarves, the very fierceness and bloodthirstiness of that opposition almost call his fundamental goodness into question. When Gandalf tells of killing goblins with a flash of lightning in the mountain cave, Beorn says, "Good!" (115), a growl of ferocious pleasure. His further comment, that this proves that "it is some good being a wizard, then," shows that according to Beorn, the only useful kind of magic is magic that kills goblins. It seems safe to say that he wouldn't be very impressed by magical diamond studs, and he shows impatience even at the account of Gandalf's more spectacular fireworks display in the wolf glade. "I would have given them more than fireworks!" he mutters, suggesting that Gandalf's magic is not sufficiently violent and lethal for his taste (116).

After Beorn has confirmed their story about themselves, learning that they have indeed killed many goblins, including the Great Goblin, he is delighted and goes about chuckling fiercely to himself (123). His manner of confirming their story is perhaps the most disturbing demonstration of his own savage tendencies. He wordlessly shows them the severed head of a goblin and the pelt of a warg that he captured in the forest, who apparently provided the corroborating accounts of the events up in the mountains. We are left to fill in the rather chilling details for ourselves: Beorn's catching one goblin and one warg in the woods at night, his torturing or intimidating them into telling him everything they knew, his killing them and then dismembering and skinning them, and finally his bringing home the two grisly trophies to display outside his house. The narrator's only comment is drily understated: "Beorn was a fierce enemy" (123).

Beorn's blending of goodness and savagery is typical of his character; Beorn is a curious mixture of conflicting elements. It is not even perfectly clear what species he is. While introducing him, Gandalf explains that he has two forms, a huge and powerful human form and an even bigger and more powerful bear form. Gandalf himself is not at all certain what his real identity is; he could be a man who can turn into a bear, or he could be a bear who can turn into a man. Gandalf fancies that he is, at root, a man, but he is not really sure about this.* The important thing about Beorn is the fact that he is both at once: Man and Bear, human and beast. Even his name reflects this duality. *Beorn* is an Anglo-Saxon word that is often used to mean "man" or "warrior," but the word also means "bear" in that language. We should remember the conflict between

---

* In one of his letters, Tolkien states plainly that Beorn is a Man, but even this piece of evidence is not as clear as it might seem. In its context in the letter, Tolkien's statement is meant to clarify that Beorn is definitely not an Elf, rather than to settle the Bear/Man debate about Beorn's origins (*The Letters of J.R.R. Tolkien*, ed. Humphrey Carpenter, Houghton Mifflin, 1981, 178).

the eagles as predators and the woodmen as settlers and farmers, cultivating the land and trying to tame a small section of the Wild. Beorn, in himself, contains both sides of that conflict.

Much of what we are told about Beorn demonstrates this duality in his character. He lives alone, at least without human companionship, in communion only with animals. His bond with animals is so great that he does not hunt or eat wild beasts at all. And yet Beorn emphatically does not live a feral existence, scratching out a living with the beasts in their natural habitat. His home is very clearly a human house. In fact, the description of his hall and the drawing that Tolkien made of the inside of Beorn's house closely resemble the mead halls of the Anglo-Saxons, the homely and highly social gathering places of the Anglo-Saxon warrior clans. Indeed, Beorn even seems to have had a remarkably civilizing effect on his animal friends, for they wait on Beorn and his guests just like human servants. In his home as well as his person, Beorn brings together the world of beasts and the world of men.

When we get to know Beorn better, we can also see that his fierce personality is more complex than it might first appear. He is more alarmingly savage than the eagles are, and his pleasure in violence seems almost to rival the goblins' own. But in addition to being "a bad enemy" (127), he is also a good friend, and he is willing to do much more for Gandalf and his companions than the eagles were. Once he confirms that Gandalf and the dwarves are telling the truth, Beorn is immediately concerned with ensuring their safety and helping them however he can. There is more to his life than hatred of the goblins, as we come to see; his love for his animal friends is just as fundamental a reality in his world. Gandalf says that "he loves his animals as his children" (127), showing a tenderness and devotion at least the equal of his bloodthirstiness and violence. Both inform his character, as we are reminded when Gandalf warns them with another piece of ominous understatement that they cannot guess what would happen to them if they mistreated Beorn's ponies or tried to take them into Mirkwood. In his mingled savagery and faithfulness, his simultaneous human and bestial natures, Beorn is a true native of the Wild.

Bilbo's Nature: The Wild and the Civilized

In examining the characters of the eagles and the wargs in Chapter Six, we began to consider the nature of the Wild itself, and Chapter Seven gives us a lot more to think about. In particular, I would like to consider more what the term *Wild* seems to mean—what exactly Tolkien is saying about this region when he calls it "wild." The word *wild* has many different usages, but there are two major threads among them that I would emphasize: the sense of "uncontrolled" or "unrestrained" and the sense of "uncivilized" or "undomesticated." The Wild in *The Hobbit* is certainly wild in the first sense: all of the residents of the Wild, whether good or evil, are uncontrolled and prone to sudden, violent action. I believe, however, that the primary importance of the Wild within the themes of *The Hobbit* lies in the second sense of the word.

The Wild is uncivilized in the sense that human society and social customs have made few inroads there. The narrator makes a big deal of Beorn's lack of politeness, for instance. We are told that he is never very polite, and in fact he seems to disregard social niceties almost aggressively. When the wizard says, "I am Gandalf," Beorn replies rudely, "Never heard of him" (111). He is even ruder to poor Mr. Baggins, frowning down at him and saying quite slightingly, "And what's this little fellow?" as if he were Gandalf's pet. Gandalf and the dwarves' excessive politeness is quite funny in contrast to Beorn's bluntness. The elaborate bowing and hood-sweeping of Balin and Dwalin actually make Beorn laugh, and he roughly tells them to "sit down and stop wagging" (114). Gandalf's assurance that Bilbo is "a hobbit of good family and unimpeachable reputation" is certain to be as pointless and unnecessary as Bilbo's painful consciousness of his many missing waistcoat buttons (111).

But the Wild is not completely without social customs. Beorn's speech is rough, but his hospitality is excellent. His furniture is crude and the domestic staff is extremely unusual, but his food is good, the best meal Bilbo has had since leaving Elrond's house. The eagles apparently observe some rather elaborate courtesies among themselves, even though those customs are foreign to Bilbo and the dwarves. There is a polite thing to say among eagles when you say good-bye, we learn, and Gandalf, fortunately, knows the "correct reply" (106).*

---

* You may recall that the eagles' formal good-bye is "Farewell wherever you fare, till your eyries receive you at the journey's end!" The correct reply is "May the wind under your wings bear you where the sun sails and the moon walks" (106). These are quite elaborate ritual formulas, and their references to "eyries" and "wings" show that it is an internal formula—what eagles say to each other upon parting, not what they say to others. The implication is that they *don't* usually greet others, which makes their assistance of the dwarves even more significant and Gandalf's knowledge of the formula even more remarkable.

The social customs of the Wild are not exactly the same as those of civilized lands, but they do exist.

In fact, in some ways politeness is even more important in the Wild than in more polished societies. In the Wild, politeness might save your life. Back in Chapter Six, the narrator cautioned us, for example, that "you ought not to be rude to an eagle, when you are only the size of a hobbit, and are up in his eyrie at night!" (102). Balin and Dwalin try to appease Beorn's obvious disapproval by doing "their best to be frightfully polite," and when Beorn cuts through the conventional dwarves' greeting by telling them that he doesn't want their service, just their names, they don't dare to be offended (114). We even saw Thorin briefly try to butter up the Great Goblin back in Chapter Four for a similar reason, indulging in a little flattery about "truly hospitable mountains" (60). Beorn's rudeness to Thorin and Company shows, in part, that he does not fear them.

The primary contrast that Tolkien's treatment of the Wild invites, therefore, is not that between the wild and the civilized, but between the wild and the domestic. Even the title of this chapter, "Queer Lodgings," points to this tension. In this chapter, we see Bilbo and his friends lodged in two very different homes, but neither of them are Homely Homes. They are strange and uncanny, and uncomfortable in various ways.

As usual, it is Bilbo's Baggins perspective that repeatedly emphasizes this contrast. We see this most forcefully at the very opening of Chapter Seven, when Bilbo wakes up in the eagles' eyrie. When he awakes, he jumps up "to look at the time and to go and put his kettle on," only to discover that he is "not home at all" (105). There are, obviously, many ways in which an eagle's nest among the peaks of the Misty Mountains is different from Bilbo's hobbit-hole under the Hill. What strikes Bilbo most forcibly in this moment, however, is the absence of domestic comforts. He sits down and wishes "in vain for a wash and a brush," lamenting also that he will get neither "tea nor toast nor bacon for his breakfast" (105). As Dwalin warned him back in Chapter Two, he now has to do without his pocket-handkerchief and many other things (29).

Bilbo twice nearly gets in trouble for continuing to process his experience in the old, cultivated Baggins terms that are quite inappropriate to his current setting in the Wild. The first gaffe he makes is his comparison of the eagle who rescued him to a fork (and then, accidentally, a stork) and himself to a piece of bacon. Dori's urgent correction that "eagles aren't forks!" reminds Bilbo of his error. The homely simile comparing himself to bacon is perhaps unwise under the circumstances, as Bilbo probably doesn't want to invite the giant bird of prey who has brought him to its nest to associate him with breakfast meat. But far worse is Bilbo's implication that the eagle himself is merely an inanimate object, like a tool in someone else's hand. Bilbo's stumbling correction suggests that he had indeed momentarily forgotten that the eagle sitting right next to him is an intelligent, sentient being, perfectly able to understand his words. Bilbo cannot afford to slip into the assumptions he would have made at home about birds and beasts.

Bilbo's second and even more serious mistake comes when Gandalf is telling him about Beorn's remarkable ability to turn himself into a bear. Gandalf calls him "a skin-changer," meaning, as he goes on to explain, that Beorn can change his skin, altering his form (108). Bilbo, however, has no prior experience with this kind of thing. He thinks that Gandalf is saying that Beorn is a furrier, "a man that calls rabbits conies, when he doesn't turn their skins into squirrels" (108). Bilbo's prior experience not only misleads him, but misleads him disastrously, leading Gandalf to urge Bilbo not to "mention the word furrier again as long as you are within a hundred miles of his house, nor rug, cape, tippet, muff, nor any other such unfortunate word!" Bilbo's mistake here reminds us of something we observed back in Chapter Six: wildness is not necessarily evil, and civilization is not necessarily good. Beorn is strong and dangerous, but Gandalf is afraid he will be made truly savage if he overhears even a reference to the cultivated custom of killing wild animals and turning their skins into fashionable clothing. Bilbo's domesticated background couldn't possibly have done more to lead him wrong.

The Wild may be strange and frightening compared to the quiet, comfortable, and predictable world to which Bilbo is accustomed, but Tolkien at times emphasizes its loveliness also. As Bilbo is being hoisted out of the burning tree and carried off by the eagle, for instance, the narrator pauses to describe how Bilbo "looked down between his dangling toes and saw the dark lands opening wide underneath him, touched here and there with the light of the moon on a hill-side rock or a stream in the plains" (100). Similarly, when Bilbo takes off on the back of an eagle the following day, we get a description of morning in the country below him: "The morning was cool, and the mists were in the valleys and hollows and twined here and there about the peaks and pinnacles of the hills" (105). The Wild is rough and rugged, but it is grand and beautiful as well.

Bilbo, however, through whom we catch these glimpses of beauty, is not really very open to it. On both of the occasions cited above, in fact, he actually shuts his eyes to it. His brief conversation with the eagle during his second flight demonstrates the conflict in outlook between the tame little hobbit and the majestic denizen of the Wild. Perceiving the hobbit's fear, betrayed by Bilbo's frantic clutch on his back, the eagle notes encouragingly, "It is a fair morning with little wind. What is finer than flying?" (105). The eagle no doubt intends this as a purely rhetorical question, but Mr. Baggins has an answer that he would give if he dared: "A warm bath and late breakfast on the lawn afterwards." This moment could serve as a kind of encapsulation of Bilbo's entire situation at this point in his journey. A short time ago, the hobbit was riding uncomfortably on the back of a pony through the familiar lands near his home, wondering what people would think of him in his ill-fitting dwarf hood and worrying about the fact that he had no pocket-handkerchiefs and no spending money with him. Now, we see him astride the back of a giant eagle, soaring over the Misty Mountains and the Great River, near the eaves of Mirkwood, and preparing to descend into that wilderness with no food, no mount, and no path to follow. We can clearly see how far Bilbo has come as an adventurer by how well he is taking all of this. But his perspective has not undergone any kind of revolution. He is bearing up under the circumstances wonderfully well, but he can't enter into the eagle's enjoyment of the Wild that surrounds him. He is capable of sleeping on the hard rock of an eagle's eyrie "more soundly than ever he had done on his feather-bed in his own little hole at home" (103), but nevertheless his heart still yearns for the familiar and domestic pleasures of Bag-End.

There is one moment, however, that I believe points to the beginnings of a genuine change in Bilbo's values. Chapter Six ends with a sentence describing a dream Bilbo has; this is Bilbo's third and most perplexing dream yet. As I described back in Chapter Four, his first dreaming episode consists of the disturbing dreams he is said to have had at the end of Chapter One, after falling asleep listening to Thorin singing his dwarf song. The second dream is the remarkable vision in the goblin cave which foretells or describes what is actually happening in the room around him. How he has this dream or where it comes from may be a mystery, but its connection with the action of the chapter is clear enough. His third dream seems to be, like the first, a reflection of his internal state, but it is much less clear what it has to do with the events of Bilbo's waking life at the time.

When Bilbo goes to sleep on the rock floor of the eagles' eyrie, the narrator informs us that "all night he dreamed of his own house and wandered in his sleep into all his different rooms looking for something that he could not find nor remember what it looked like" (104). That Bilbo should be dreaming of Bag-End at this point is hardly surprising. Bilbo is in what must seem a most inhospitable place, despite the (relative) friendliness of the eagles. The eagles may have rescued and fed their guests, but their hospitality is quite uncomfortable and undomesticated. No one could call an eagle's mountaintop eyrie a Homely House! We might even expect Bilbo to dream fondly of his hobbit-hole while in such a situation.

What is so intriguing about this dream, however, is that it is *not* simply a dream of longing, a mental retreat to the world where one eats a comfortable second breakfast in an armchair, or where the tea-kettle is just beginning to sing. Bilbo dreams of home, but it is a dissatisfied dream; in his dream, he can't find what he is looking for in any of the rooms of his house.

He doesn't even know what it is that he can't find! Whatever it is, though, is not there in Bag-End.

I think that in this dream, we can see a hint of how Bilbo's adventurous life is beginning to change him. Although his Took side has gotten a great deal of exercise, his Baggins side has always been present, continually informing his perspective and his reactions. In this odd dream, we get the first suggestion that his Baggins side itself is being influenced and altered. He might seem as if he is not moved by his Wild surroundings, shutting his eyes to its sublimity and desiring only his safe and quiet world, but the dream suggests that his relationship with that domestic world is shifting. However much he may sometimes wish he could be magically whisked back to his home, he would not now be completely happy or satisfied if that wish somehow came true. Bilbo is seeking something that he cannot find at home in Bag-End, something that will only be found at the end of his journey.

Luck: The Wind of Destiny

In Chapter Seven, we see again a trend to which I first drew attention back in my analysis of Chapter Three: the tendency of this story to involve stunningly unlikely coincidences. If we back up a bit and take an eagle's view of the companions' path through the Wild, we will notice the remarkable luck that has accompanied them over and through the mountains. What is more, we can begin in Chapter Seven to perceive something new about the strokes of fortune that accompany Bilbo and his friends on their adventure: the intriguing interrelationship of good luck and bad luck.

Much of Bilbo's luck seems at first to be very bad luck, of course. When the party set out from Rivendell, we were told that, although there are many paths and many passes over the Misty Mountains, few of them actually work out, but luckily Gandalf and Elrond were around to guide them to "the right road to the right pass" (52). Unfortunately, they get diverted from this pass when they are captured by the goblins. As a result of this unexpected side trip, they come out of the mountains, as Gandalf explains, "too far to the North," leaving them with "some awkward country ahead" (90). Even if they can make their way east without ponies or food, they are facing disaster, for they are no longer anywhere near the "old forest road" through Mirkwood that they had been aiming for originally (125). Their journey now seems hopeless due to the misfortune of their capture by the goblins.

However, they learn later that their apparent bad luck has actually turned out to be good luck. Beorn tells them that the old forest road they had originally been aiming for would have likely led them to disaster. It is "now often used by the goblins, while the forest-road itself, he had heard, was overgrown and disused at the eastern end and led to impassable marshes where the paths had long been lost" (125). The detour that at first seemed to doom their journey to failure actually saves them from it.

But the luck of Bilbo and the dwarves has an impact on much more than just their own expedition; the lives of thousands and the political future of the entire region also seem to have turned on a single stroke of their fortune. In their flight from the pursuing goblins in Chapter Six, Bilbo and company are finally driven to take refuge in the trees by the pursuing wolves. It turns out, of course, that the glade next to which they have been treed just happens, by coincidence, to be the meeting place of the goblins and wargs. It also unfolds that, in a further stroke of luck, that very night there had been a plan for the wargs and goblins to meet there. What a colossal misfortune! Here are the dwarves trying desperately to escape their enemies, and instead they end up blundering into the very gathering place of those same enemies. Bilbo and the dwarves must surely be cursed!

However uncomfortable the situation might be for Bilbo and his companions, it is a remarkable blessing for the woodmen who live down in the valleys. The reason that the goblins and wargs had been planning to meet that night was to come together in force so that they could sweep down upon "some of the villages nearest the mountains" and exterminate them (95). All of the "brave" woodmen and their families "would have been killed except the few the goblins kept from the wolves and carried back as prisoners to their caves." The fortuitous presence of the dwarves and Gandalf and Bilbo in the mountains that evening, however, has ensured that the attack will not happen that night, and since the Great Goblin is now dead and the Chief Warg injured, the attack may not happen for quite some time. The goblins' attention is now focused on revenge against the dwarves rather than on the unsuspecting woodmen, and in addition, Beorn has now been alerted to their plans and may also take action to oppose them. Thanks to the dwarves' unusual string of misfortunes, the entire balance of power in the Wild may have been shifted and many lives may have been saved. It looks almost as if the dwarves' journey is part of a larger plan that is shaping the destiny of Middle-earth.

We can hear distant echoes of this theme of destiny even in a rather unlikely place: the song that the dwarves sing at night in Beorn's hall. While the dwarves feast with Beorn, he tells them tales of "the wild lands on this side of the mountains," and especially of "the terrible forest of Mirkwood" (118). This makes the dwarves uncomfortable, since it reminds them that they themselves have to think about passing through that dark forest soon. Left to themselves afterwards, they eventually start singing:

> *The wind was on the withered heath,*
> *but in the forest stirred no leaf:*
> *there shadows lay by night and day,*
> *and dark things silent crept beneath.*
>
> *The wind came down from mountains cold,*
> *and like a tide it roared and rolled;*
> *the branches groaned, the forest moaned,*
> *and leaves were laid upon the mould.*
>
> *The wind went on from West to East;*
> *all movement in the forest ceased,*
> *but shrill and harsh across the marsh*
> *its whistling voices were released.*
>
> *The grasses hissed, their tassels bent,*
> *the reeds were rattling—on it went*
> *o'er shaken pool under heavens cool*
> *where racing clouds were torn and rent.*
>
> *It passed the lonely Mountain bare*
> *and swept above the dragon's lair:*
> *there black and dark lay boulders stark*
> *and flying smoke was in the air.*
>   *(119)*

Before we even examine the content of the song, its poetic form and the circumstances of its singing give us some clear guidance on what to expect from it. If we look closely at the verses, we can notice that this song has the same meter and rhyme scheme as the more famous "Far over the misty mountains cold" song that the dwarves sang back in Chapter One (14–16). Notice the four-line stanzas with the rhyming words at lines one, two, and four and a separate internal rhyme in line three. The two songs sound exactly alike; most likely, they would have been sung to the same tune. Like the earlier song of the dwarves, this song is also sung in the darkness after a feast. Both times they are in a place of comfort and safety, preparing themselves for departure on a major leg of their long and dangerous journey. Given the similarities between the two songs, therefore, we might suspect that this song, like the first one, relates to the quest of the dwarves and their journey.

The words of the song don't immediately seem to confirm this suspicion. Where the earlier song spoke explicitly of their ancient home under the Mountain and of their setting out on their quest "ere break of day," this song is more lyrical, speaking only of wind blowing in various places. The dwarves do mention the "lonely Mountain" by name, but there seems little other connection between all this windy imagery and their journey.

If we pay close attention, however, we will see that this song actually tells an even more consistent story than the first song did. The song does not just give images of wind; it tells the story of a particular wind. The wind begins on the "withered heath" while a forest, filled with perpetual shadows, is still and unmoved. In the second verse, however, we get motion. The wind descends now from "mountains cold" and rips through the forest, tearing away leaves and making the trees toss and moan. In the third and fourth verses, the wind, moving "from West to East," whistles across a marsh, tearing even the "racing clouds" in its strength and speed. In the fifth verse, it sweeps over the "lonely Mountain bare," making the smoke from the "dragon's lair" fly before it. The action of the song might be impersonal, but it is really quite dramatic.

The song also gives us more than enough cues to allow us to recognize the particular regions it is describing. The forest covered in shadows beneath which dark things creep is plainly Mirkwood, which the dwarves were thinking about and dreading during the feast, before they started singing. Both Mirkwood and the Withered Heath to the north "where the great dragons bred" appear on Thror's map, as Thorin mentions back in Chapter One (20). The "mountains cold" are almost certainly the Misty Mountains, described with that same phrase in the dwarves' first song, and the marshes that the wind gets to by proceeding "from West to East" must be the "impassable marshes" Beorn mentions, on the western edge of Mirkwood and south of the Long Lake (125). From these wetlands, the wind arrives at the one location that is explicitly named: the "lonely Mountain" where the "dragon's lair" is. The song seems to be telling the story of the passage of a particular and mighty wind along the very path of the dwarves' journey and quest.

The dwarves' Wind song, therefore, invites us to read the passage of this mighty wind in parallel with the quest of the dwarves, especially when we remember its similarities in form and context to the dwarves' song about their journey in Chapter One. When we think about it this way, we can see in the Wind song a kind of heroic, fantasy version of the dwarves' quest. The story begins in the Withered Heath, where the dragons breed and from which Smaug came; his is the first move in this story, but it is not associated with any actual movement of the wind. The path of Thorin and Company down the Misty Mountains, through Mirkwood, and to the Mountain, by contrast, is depicted as a howling gale that sweeps away irresistibly all obstacles and dangers. It rolls down the mountains like a tide, tosses the great and shadowy forest which can only moan in feeble protest, and finally sweeps over Smaug's lurking-place, driving him before it like smoke before the wind. For dwarves who are nervous about the dangers that still lie before them on their journey, this song is certainly a confidence booster, inviting them to imagine their quest as an unstoppable, irresistible force, the winds of destiny carrying them home.

The song, however, doesn't end there. The very last verse suggests that the Lonely Mountain is not the endpoint of the mighty wind's journey:

> *It left the world and took its flight*
> *over the wide seas of the night.*
> *The moon set sail upon the gale,*
> *and stars were fanned to leaping light.*
> *(119)*

At the end of the song, the wind takes its flight into the heavens, and not only does it go to the heavens; it plays an important and fundamental role there. The same wind that roars down the path of the dwarves' quest to the Lonely Mountain, it turns out, also wafts the moon on its course through the night sky and fans the stars into life. The wind that the dwarves sing of, which always seemed much bigger than even the largest of earthly landmarks or obstacles, is actually a celestial wind that also orders the heavenly bodies along their courses and inspires the stars.

It is not clear how much the dwarves themselves are really thinking about the theological implications of their song. Certainly the image of the wind fanning the stars "to leaping light," like the breeze from a bellows into a forge, is a very dwarvish image. Perhaps they are seeing their return home as a part of the orderly craftsmanship of the universe and of history; it is hard to say.* But the song certainly serves to prompt us to put the journey of Bilbo and the dwarves into a wider context, which the events with the woodmen and the dwarves' fortuitous re-routing to the north have already invited us to see. The journey to the Lonely Mountain will not be anything like the effortless and irresistible progress of the wind in the song, but nevertheless we are invited to see it as part of a much greater story, one thread of a larger tapestry that is the history of Middle-earth.

---

* It is an interesting fact that the first draft of the dwarves' Wind song, though almost identical to the final version in other respects, does not contain the last stanza at all. Tolkien added that later when he revised the text. This suggests two things: that the last stanza does indeed add a new dimension to the song that it didn't have before (or emphasizes something that was only implied), and that this new dimension is something Tolkien was thinking about more in the latter stages of writing the book than he was at the beginning. It does seem that the references to luck and the implications that some destiny is taking a hand in the events of the story increase as the story goes along.

8

The Stinging Fly

Mirkwood: Darkness and Magic

At the beginning of Chapter Eight, the dwarves and Bilbo stand at the western edge of Mirkwood. Mirkwood has been an ominous name throughout the book so far. It appears on Thror's map, and Gandalf has just confirmed at the end of Chapter Seven that its southern regions are the "land of the Necromancer," the "black sorcerer" who captured and tortured Thorin's father (129). Beorn himself speaks with caution about the forest, warning them that in Mirkwood, the "wild things are dark, queer, and savage" (124). And remember that this is Beorn speaking—if the creatures of Mirkwood are "queer" and "savage" by *his* standards, the dwarves and Bilbo are right to consider the passage through Mirkwood "the most dangerous part of all the journey" (129).

Despite their fears, Bilbo and the dwarves are not set upon at once by unspeakable monsters. They march on for days through the dark and tangled forest in fear and suspense, surrounded by frightening evidence that they have drawn the interest of the forest's dark residents. Bilbo can hear "queer noises" along their path: "grunts, scufflings, and hurryings in the undergrowth, and among the leaves that lay piled endlessly thick in places on the forest-floor," but Bilbo never sees what is making the noises (130). At night they are surrounded by the unsettling gaze of strange and glowing eyes in the dark, "pairs of yellow or red or green eyes" staring, disappearing, and returning all night (131). Most unsettling to Bilbo are the "horrible pale bulbous sort of eyes"—insect eyes, Bilbo thinks, "only they are much too big." Bilbo and the dwarves are not attacked, but they are in constant danger and in continual suspense, walking by day and dozing by night through the "enormous uncanny darkness" of Mirkwood.

The darkness is the primary characteristic of this forest, as implied by its name. Mirkwood is thoroughly and oppressively dark. Night in Mirkwood is "not what you call pitch-dark, but really pitch: so black that you really could see nothing" (131). The shadows of Mirkwood seem to cling even to the living creatures that dwell there: the moths, the bats, and the squirrels that they see are all either dark-grey or jet black. The pervasive darkness of Mirkwood makes even innocent and harmless creatures, such as butterflies, seem ominous and vaguely threatening.

There is evidence, however, that Mirkwood is not naturally dark and black; it is a forest that has been twisted and corrupted. Notice, for instance, the description of the trees that form the gate around the opening of the path the dwarves are following. Those trees are so "strangled with ivy and hung with lichen" that they can't "bear more than a few blackened leaves" (130). The growth of the trees seems designed not to take in the sunlight or even to compete for it, but to choke it off completely. Near the edge of the forest, Bilbo occasionally finds "a slender beam of sun that had the luck to slip in through some opening in the leaves far above, and still more luck in not being caught in the tangled boughs and matted twigs beneath" (130). The plant life itself sounds malevolent, as if it were forming webs to snare the sunlight and ensure that the forest beneath is kept in sinister shadows.

The ultimate representatives of the darkness and corruption of the forest are the giant spiders. Bilbo thinks that the "nastiest things" he can see in the forest are "the cobwebs: dark dense cobwebs with threads extraordinarily thick" (130). The pale and bulbous eyes that Bilbo finds most disturbing in the black night of the forest almost certainly belong to them, as well. The spider colony that Bilbo eventually finds is a "place of dense black shadow . . . black even for that forest, like a patch of midnight that had never been cleared away" (144).* In all of northern Mirkwood, the spider colony looks like the very heart of the darkness, from which all light has been shut out.

But although the shadowy blackness of Mirkwood is its dominant feature, Bilbo and his companions also find themselves surrounded by an eeriness that has nothing to do with black-furred monsters or gigantic arachnids. In addition to its darkness and savagery, Mirkwood is also the home of some strange magic. The travelers encounter a magic stream full of uncanny-looking water (black, of course), which they must cross but which they must not touch. They hear the sounds of a great hunt coming to them through the trees north of the path, the distant blowing of horns and baying of hounds, but they never see any hunters. First a jet-black hart and then a pure white hind and her equally white fawns burst sud-

---

* The connection between enormous spiders and darkness has a long history in Tolkien's stories, and anyone who has read of Shelob's webs of shadow in *The Two Towers* or Ungoliant the Great's "dark nets of strangling gloom" in *The Silmarillion* will be familiar with it (*The Silmarillion*, 73).

denly upon them,* and although Thorin shoots the buck, they never find them or learn of their significance. They hear, drifting through the trees, the sounds of laughter and singing, and although it is "the laughter of fair voices," and the singing is beautiful, they hurry on faster, for it sounds "eerie and strange" (136). It is clear that when they crossed into Mirkwood, they did not just enter a land of danger and dread; they entered some kind of enchanted otherworld. Bilbo seems to have stumbled into the perilous realm of Faerie.

In his great essay "On Fairy-stories," Tolkien points out that fairy tales are not stories about fairies, but stories about humans who find their way into Faerie, the mysterious world of magic and wonder where fairies of all kinds dwell. Some people find Faerie at the top of a beanstalk and many find it deep in the forest, but all who end up there find themselves enmeshed in strange and often alarming events. It is full, as Tolkien said, of a "beauty that is an enchantment, and an ever-present peril; both joy and sorrow as sharp as swords."† To venture into Faerie is to encounter a world that operates by rules and customs strange to us, a world in which mortals may easily lose themselves. Tolkien calls Faerie "the Perilous Realm," not because the elves are hostile or belligerent, but because their world is so likely to overwhelm its human visitors, even if with beauty and delight.

All of this might sound strange to a modern reader. These days, the word *fairy* only makes us think of a tiny person with diaphanous wings and pixie dust: Tinkerbell is the modern icon for fairies. If you have read *The Lord of the Rings,* you might feel particularly resistant to associating Galadriel, Le-

---

* Tolkien is here using the older, Middle-English terms for deer: buck and doe, respectively.

† "On Fairy-stories," 33.

golas, or Glorfindel with sparkly little fairies. The words *elf* and *fairy*, however, are more or less synonymous, and when he was writing *The Hobbit*, Tolkien used the terms interchangeably for his Elves.* That doesn't mean, of course, that there is any pixie dust still floating around Elrond or the elves of his household. This idea of fairies as diminutive and cloying little sprites—what I call Tinkerbellism—is a purely modern phenomenon, and it is a sad cheapening, even a belittling, of the fairy-story tradition.

In the Middle Ages, fairies were neither tiny nor cute. In the classic poem *Sir Gawain and the Green Knight*, the Green Knight himself is a fairy. As soon as he rides into the court, King Arthur and his knights can see that he is obviously a fairy because he is completely green in clothes, skin, and hair—and because he is about seven feet tall and terrifyingly strong, carrying an enormous battle-ax. He inspires fear and awe in the Knights of the Round Table even before he picks up his own severed head off the floor, remounts his horse, and speaks out of the head he still holds at arm's length. We can see another very traditional kind of fairy encounter in the medieval poem "Lanval," when the Arthurian knight Sir Lanval is wandering in the deep forest, only to come upon an amazingly rich, bejeweled pavilion, wherein lies a woman of inhuman beauty who takes him in and loves him and blesses him with magical gifts, if Sir Lanval will promise never to speak of her or their love to anyone. When Sir Lanval's beloved presents herself at King Arthur's court at the end of the poem, that greatest and most glorious of all human courts looks shabby and dingy in comparison to her and her train, and her least handmaiden

---

* Remember, for instance, the narrator speaking in Chapter One of a rumor that a Took once took a "fairy wife" (4), which simply means "married an elf."

outshines Queen Guinevere's beauty itself like the sun eclipsing the night stars. *These* are the Elves of medieval fairy-story tradition, and it is from these characters that Tolkien's Elves take their inspiration.

The wonder, the beauty, and the power of enchantment that fairies have in this older tradition explain why Tolkien calls their world, the land of Faerie, the Perilous Realm. Humans who seek that land, or who stumble into it unawares, are always changed by it, and sometimes they do not return at all. Remember that Aragorn and Faramir both talk this way about Lothlorien in *The Lord of the Rings,* noting that most mortals who go there do not return, and none return unchanged. Lothlorien and its reputation among the mortals in the lands round about are very explicitly derived from this old tradition of Faerie.

Here in Chapter Eight of *The Hobbit,* we can also clearly see Tolkien painting a similar picture. When Bilbo and the dwarves enter Mirkwood, we expect them to face horrible monsters and terrible dangers right away—dangers, in fact, like the ones they have already been encountering. Instead, they find themselves in a kind of Faerie otherworld. The sounds that they hear, attached to no visible people—laughter and singing drifting through the trees and the sounds of a wild hunt—suggest that they have crossed into a magical realm in which they are blundering trespassers. There is an unknown magic at work in Mirkwood.

While in Mirkwood, they have several encounters that are straight out of traditional fairy stories. The first is the magical stream, a stream of eerie black water that they must cross, but which they must not touch or drink from. Beorn warns them that it "carries enchantment and a great drowsiness and forgetfulness" (124). When Bombur falls into the river, he does indeed fall into a deep sleep, and when he wakes, we discover that he has forgotten everything that has happened since Chapter One. But it turns out that there is more to the magic of the stream than a magical sleep and partial amnesia. While he sleeps, Bombur has vivid dreams about Elves in the forest. He sees lights ablaze, and a woodland king sitting at a great feast, accompanied by merry singing. Bombur sleeps because he has been enchanted; the magic of the stream has drawn him into a vision of Faerie. He does eventually wake from this vision, but when he does, he is changed, and he wants only to return to sleep so that he may find his dreams again. Bombur is the first member of the party to experience the magic of the elves of Mirkwood, and to learn how perilous it can be to cross the boundary of Faerie.

Days later, when the dwarves and the hobbit are out of food and near starvation, they see lights in the distance between the trees, and in their desperation for food they leave the path, creeping up to see a fire-lit clearing and a scene that looks exactly like the vision Bombur was shown in his dreams. This sight confirms that Bombur's dreams were not mere imagination brought on by hunger and unquiet sleep. While he was under the influence of the magic in the stream, he was given true glimpses of the Faerie world. But when the dwarves run forward into the clearing, the elves vanish (141). Bombur and his companions find, as many mortals in fairy stories have found, that it does little good to try to burst into Faerie by force, uninvited.

The second time the companions attempt to cross into the elf ring, Bilbo is pushed forward alone across the boundary. This time, the elves not only disappear again, but they cast Bilbo into an enchanted sleep. When he is found, by luck, and wakened with difficulty, we find that he, too, like Bombur, seems to have been having a magical vision of "a most gorgeous dinner" (142). The similarity between their two dreams appears to confirm that the spell Bombur had been under was elven magic; Bilbo's companions all conclude that "he has gone like Bombur." Notice that both Bilbo and Bombur are enchanted when they cross a boundary and that the enchantment they are placed under is one that has two effects. They are cut off from the rest of the world around them by means of a magical sleep, but their minds or spirits are brought by the enchantment into the world of the elves' merrymaking. Although both return to the mortal world by waking from sleep, neither wants to leave the feast of his dreams, and both try to return to them. It is perilous for mortals to cross the borders of Faerie.

The third time that the dwarves try to intrude on the elves, it is Thorin who steps into the clearing, and once more the one who crosses the boundary falls "like a stone enchanted" (153). This is the third intrusion into the elves' feasting, and readers of fairy tales won't need to be told that the third repetition of an action is significant and raises the stakes. This time, the elves go one step further. Thorin is not only put to sleep and drawn into visions of Faerie; he is swept away bodily by the power of the elves and brought before the throne of the Fairy King himself to answer for his actions. This, of course, is one of the traditional dangers to mortals who wander in Faerie without leave; they may be taken by the fairies and never permitted to return to mortal lands. Thorin and his companions, having entered the realm of the fairies and even dared to intrude on their private feasts, are ensnared there.

There are, therefore, two different elements operating in the description of the forest of Mirkwood: its sinister darkness and its eerie fairy magic. To enter Mirkwood is to enter the realm of the Elvenking, the enchanted land of Faerie. At the same time, to enter Mirkwood is to be immersed in a choking darkness that smothers life and light, and to be surrounded by black creatures, twisted and corrupted. We must not simply confound these two elements, however; they are at war with each other. The elves are "not wicked folk," we are told (154). They have not caused the darkness of the forest; they oppose it. The dwarves and Bilbo see their lights and their feasting as a kind of oasis in the wilderness of gloom and desolation in which they have been suffering. Even the lack of food is due in part to the corruption of the forest; whatever has made the animals of the forest black has apparently also tainted them, judging by the black squirrel that they manage to shoot and that proves "horrible to taste" (132). It is the good magic of the elves, who made the forest path that they are following, that seems to have kept the unseen owners of the eyes that watch them by night at bay, and that has prevented the giant spiders from stretching their webs across the path (130). The spiders, whose colony is the darkest and most horrible part of Mirkwood that Bilbo sees, are the bitter enemies of the elves, and they are the only living things that the Wood-elves "had no mercy upon" (156). In Mirkwood, travelers face the very different perils of dark corruption and of elven enchantment, but either one is extremely dangerous. Bilbo and the dwarves, of course, manage to run afoul of both.

Bilbo's Choices: The Second Turning Point

When Bilbo and the dwarves fail for the third time to enter the fire-lit circle of the elves' woodland feasting, they are scattered and cannot find one another again. Bilbo finds himself alone in the utter darkness of a Mirkwood night, cut off not only from his friends but from the path that was his only protection and his only hope of escape. He has been in some pretty awful predicaments before, but this, as the narrator confirms, certainly ranks as one of the most miserable (143).

We should, of course, remember the parallel situation in which Bilbo found himself at the beginning of Chapter Five, when he awoke alone in the darkness, lost in the tunnels of the goblins. That was a "turning point in his career," when he found his magic ring and when he drew on his own resources for the first time to succeed as an adventurer (65). Now, in Mirkwood, he faces a challenge even greater than before, which will compel him to take the next big leap forward in his development, if he is to survive.

Just as in Chapter Five, Bilbo's first response to finding himself alone in the dark is an impulse to a Bagginsish escapism. He thinks of his hobbit-hole, and he tries to lose himself in images of "bacon and eggs and toast and butter" (143). Once again, however, he finds better and more substantial comfort from a much more Tookish source: his sword. In the dark of the goblin tunnels, he drew his sword for the first time and discovered that it too is a magical elvish blade. In Chapter Eight, he draws his sword in earnest, and now he actually uses it, for this time when he wakes up he finds that he is not alone in the dark after all. A monstrous spider is busily wrapping its "abominable threads" around his legs, so that it can drag him away and eat him.

The unsheathing of the sword is a pivotal moment in Bilbo's encounter with the spider. When Bilbo first wakes up, his response is defensive; he beats at the spider desperately with his hands to try to get it off him. Then he remembers his sword and draws it, and the spider leaps back; apparently the sword makes almost as big an impression on spiders who come across it as it does on goblins. Now the tables are turned for Bilbo and he attacks. Bilbo strikes the spider directly in the eyes, which had so terrified him near the campfires on the path days before. Bilbo has taken an enormously important step forward. He is no longer merely fending off the darkness and trying to escape from it, as he did in the mountains. Now, he is striking back against the darkness and defeating it.

The first turning point in Bilbo's career doesn't actually seem to make all that much of an impression on him. He feels pleased with himself and is glad to show off a little to the dwarves at the beginning of Chapter Six, but his attitude and perspective have not noticeably changed. After the reunion with Gandalf and the dwarves, he thinks about little but how hungry he is; he is both fearful and complaining. His relationship with the dwarves is also unaltered, despite their greatly improved estimation of his worth and abilities. He is still the almost helpless little fellow who has to be carried around on people's backs and hoisted up trees. Even in Mirkwood up to this point, Bilbo doesn't accomplish much. Bilbo has become a real adventurer, but his role doesn't seem very different than it was when he was riding awkwardly through the land of his home feeling self-conscious in Dwalin's spare hood.

Bilbo's second turning point, "the killing of the giant spider, all alone by himself in the dark without the help of the wizard or the dwarves or of anyone else," affects him profoundly (144). Now he feels "a different person, and much fiercer and bolder in spite of an empty stomach." In the wake of his second turning point, he is at least as weak with hunger as he was the first time, but he doesn't complain now. Back in Bag-End, in a brief flash of desire, he wished the dwarves to

think him fierce. In the mountains, when he realizes his little sword is one of the legendary blades made by the ancient
elves of Gondolin, he takes heart in thinking that the goblins
might be made, theoretically, to think him fierce. Now, with
a gigantic spider dead at his feet and the blade of his sword
stained black with its foul blood, he genuinely feels fierce, and
for good reason. Bilbo is no longer just carrying a sword con-
cealed in his breeches; he has now taken up that sword and,
unlikely though it may seem, become a warrior.

Bilbo marks the occasion in a style very typical of Tolkien's
fiction: by the granting of a new name. He gives the name
to his sword, addressing it aloud as if it were his companion
there in the darkness, and he calls it Sting (144). Although
Bilbo has not taken a new name for himself, his name for his
sword tells us a lot about Bilbo's own sense of his identity in
this moment. The chapter is called "Flies and Spiders," and
Bilbo knows that his is the role of the fly. The narrator made
that explicit when he told us that when Bilbo first tried to
beat off the spider, it "was trying to poison him to keep him
quiet, as small spiders do to flies" (143). Bilbo's attack with his
sword was a sudden reversal, just as unlikely and unexpected
as a fly rising up and killing the spider that has ensnared it.
Bilbo still sees himself as a fly amidst the spiders, but he is no
longer soft and helpless. Bilbo may be a fly, but he is now a
fierce fly, and the spiders had better be on their guard.

Luck: Resolution Rewarded

When Bilbo passed his first turning point and escaped from
the mountains, he found himself confronted by a dilemma
that immediately challenged his new adventurous resolve. He

realized that his friends might still be trapped in the goblin tunnels. Having only just managed to escape, he feared that it would be his duty to attempt something far more difficult: single-handedly locating his friends, rescuing them, and leading them out again. Although Bilbo was spared on that occasion, discovering that the dwarves have managed to escape already with the help of Gandalf, he was nevertheless prepared to do what he had to do. In Chapter Eight, he is faced with exactly the same dilemma, and this time there is no escape from it. With his Sting in hand, the bold fly turns and sets out to seek the home of the spiders and to cut free the other captive flies from their webs.

This moment of Bilbo's resolution is a place where Tolkien's first draft of the story is of particular interest.* In the initial version, Bilbo shows great resourcefulness in locating the spiders' nest. The spider that Bilbo killed when he woke had left a trailing thread, the hobbit finds, and Bilbo follows the thread back toward the path and past it to the colony, winding the excess string into a ball as he goes. Bilbo not only uses the thread to guide him back to the spider colony where the dwarves have been taken, but he also leaves a trail behind him back to the path, after he crosses it, a trail that he can follow to safety, as Theseus does in the Labyrinth of Crete. Before the book went to publication, however, Tolkien rejected this idea, got rid of Bilbo's guiding thread, and deleted almost every reference to it.† What he replaced it with was simple luck.

When Bilbo decides to go rescue his friends from the spi-

---

* See Rateliff, 309 and following.
† I believe that there is one lingering reference to Bilbo's ball of thread which Tolkien neglected to remove and which remains even in the latest editions of the story. We will come across this reference later on, in Chapter Twelve.

ders, he makes as good a guess as he can at the direction and, by luck, "he guessed more or less right" (144). It might seem at first that Tolkien's decision to replace Bilbo's clever use of spider-thread with yet another instance of blind luck coming to Bilbo's aid would serve to take something away from Bilbo's character. Instead, what we can see is the next stage in Tolkien's development of the idea of luck in *The Hobbit*. We have noted before the many remarkable strokes of luck that have contributed to Bilbo's story, from the almost miraculous timing of Elrond's holding the map up in the moonlight to the leaping of a startled fish onto Bilbo's toes by Gollum's pool. There is a larger plan or higher destiny at work behind these strokes of fortune that have been following Bilbo's quest from the start.

Now, in Chapter Eight, we can see this luck as particularly associated with Bilbo himself. As Bilbo guesses the direction of the spiders' nest and fortuitously sets off in the right direction through the deep shadows of Mirkwood, the narrator remarks that Bilbo was "born with a good share" of luck (144). The dwarves later speak of luck as if it were an attribute of the hobbit himself. They observe that Bilbo has "some wits, as well as luck and a magic ring—and all three are very useful possessions" (153). In some sense, the luck does indeed seem to belong to the hobbit.

As the idea of luck becomes attached to Bilbo, however, we can see that it does not diminish his accomplishments or reduce the need for his courage and resourcefulness. His luck may guide him to the spiders' webs, but he must then do what needs to be done to save their prisoners. The remarkable good fortune that accompanies Bilbo on his quest doesn't solve all his problems or make everything easy for him. If Bilbo is an instrument of some destiny or fate, he still has a very active role to play in bringing that destiny to fruition.

Bilbo's Nature: Warrior and Hero

The Bilbo Baggins who invades the nest of giant spiders to rescue his friends might well be unrecognizable to his neighbors back at home. His completely predictable life is now far, far behind him. Now, we need to pause and get re-acquainted with this new Bilbo, transformed by his defeat of that first spider and accompanied by his newly named sword. Tolkien helps us in our re-introduction to Bilbo in the same way in which he helped us to discover the nature and character of almost everyone else in the book so far: through poetry and song. It is, of course, a point of interest in itself that the "prosy" Mr. Baggins marks his recent blossoming into an adventure hero by composing the first—but far from the last!—poem of his life.

Bilbo's first song focuses on name-calling and insults:

> *Old fat spider spinning in a tree!*
> *Old fat spider can't see me!*
> *Attercop! Attercop!*
> *Won't you stop,*
> *Stop your spinning and look for me?*

> *Old Tomnoddy, all big body,*
> *Old Tomnoddy can't spy me!*
> *Attercop! Attercop!*
> *Down you drop!*
> *You'll never catch me up your tree!*
> *(147)*

The narrator draws attention to the insults in the song, confidently remarking (in my second-favorite line in the book) that "no spider has ever liked being called Attercop, and Tom-noddy of course is insulting to anybody" (147). There is much more to this song than funny names, however. The one thing we can see most clearly about Bilbo in this song is his boldness. His most frequently repeated insult to the spiders is that they are fat. In other circumstances, that would indeed be a weakness, but this doesn't seem to be the case with these spider monsters. Their unnatural hugeness is exactly what makes them so scary! Their huge hairy legs and fat bellies, swollen with the blood of who knows how many victims, are horrifying. In his song, Bilbo turns that around completely, making them sound slow, fat, and useless — "all big body." Bilbo also twice mocks them for their spinning, and to similar effect. He makes the weaving of their clinging webs of gloom sound like a rather silly waste of time.

The narrator suggests that this song is "not very good perhaps," and truly it isn't very elegant or very beautiful, but the last two lines of the song are very clever (147). On the one hand, they can be taken as a suggestion. He is trying to goad them into coming down and chasing him, so he tells them to drop down, pointing out that they won't catch him while they are up in the tree. The last line has another meaning, however, which the reader can see even if the spiders (hopefully) can't. If the spiders do drop down and chase him, then he can sneak up the tree in safety and they will not, in fact, catch him up their tree. The dramatic irony of the line invites us to laugh at the spiders alongside Bilbo. But the penultimate line also has a double meaning, and a more stinging one. "Down you drop" is not merely a polite suggestion; it is also a description of what they have been doing when he hits them with rocks. As long as they stay in the trees, he will keep hitting them with rocks and making them "flop to the ground" (146). Bilbo is quite the uppity little fly.

The second song takes a similar approach to the first:

Lazy Lob and crazy Cob
are weaving webs to wind me.
I am far more sweet than other meat,
but still they cannot find me!

Here am I, naughty little fly;
you are fat and lazy.
You cannot trap me, though you try,
in your cobwebs crazy.
  (148)

Again Bilbo insults the spiders, calling them names and accusing them of being not only lazy, but helpless and impotent. He increases the stakes a bit by teasing them with his own sweetness and naughtiness, increasing their desire both to eat him and to punish him for his insulting disrespect. Both of these songs are made up, we are reminded, "on the spur of a very awkward moment," but although they might not be very beautiful as verse, they are extremely effective in stirring up the desired emotion in his listening audience: blind rage (147).

Like the first song, Bilbo's second poetic effort also contains wordplay and double meanings that are quite clever. Notice, for instance, the play that Bilbo makes on the word *crazy,* which he uses in both the first and the last lines of the song. Although the word is used almost exclusively to refer to insanity these days, the primary definition of *crazy* is, as Tolkien would know well, "full of cracks," "impaired," "damaged," or "frail."* In line one, Bilbo applies the word to the spiders' mental status as usual, implying that they are crackbrained. He then plays on this sense of the word in his taunts throughout the middle of the poem, harping on the fact that, for some reason, the spiders can't even locate the sweet, juicy, annoying little fly who is standing right in front of them, in the very middle of their own webs. Remember that the spiders would have no understanding of Bilbo's magic invisibility ring; Bilbo seems to be trying to get them to doubt either their own senses or their own sanity. In the last line, Bilbo applies the word *crazy* to their webs, suggesting that they are frail and flawed, mocking the tools with which the spiders are attempting to catch him. Bilbo punctuates this last insult by drawing his sword, slashing easily through a web that is indeed crazy and shoddily constructed, and going off singing into the distance.

In Bilbo's songs, we can hear a remarkable amount of nerve, as Bilbo dares not only to sneak up on these terrifying monsters, but to throw insults at them and provoke them into a frenzy. Remember that back in Bag-End, just hearing Thorin mention the possibility that some of them might never return from their journey was enough to make Bilbo burst out in a shriek and collapse into a quivering heap on the floor. Now, he has both the courage and the coolness to deliberately goad dozens or even hundreds of giant spiders into charging at him, so he can lead them on a chase through the dark and trackless forest. He can stand a little bit later in the middle of

---

* This definition is drawn from the *Oxford English Dictionary*, which is not only the most thorough and dependable dictionary in the world but also the dictionary that Tolkien himself helped to write before he got his first academic post.

"hundreds of angry spiders" surrounding him and his friends and not only keep from panicking but actually charge to the attack: "He darted backwards and forwards, slashing at spi-der-threads, hacking at their legs, and stabbing at their fat bodies if they came too near" (152). As with the first spider he kills, Bilbo's fierceness quite startles his monstrous enemies. As Bilbo scatters the spiders on the ground around Bombur, we are told that his "little sword was something new in the way of stings for them. How it darted to and fro" (150). Bil-bo's sword, whose new name expresses its master's new bold and dashing spirit, cheerfully reflects its master's courage, shining "with delight" as he stabs at the spiders. By the end of the fight, the spiders "had become mortally afraid of Sting, and dared not come very near" (152). It is the monsters, not Bilbo, who lose heart and run away.

There is certainly no one who would mistake Bilbo for a grocer now! When Gandalf had been recruiting a fourteenth member for the dwarves' party, he ended up settling for a bur-glar when ideally he would have preferred a warrior, or even a hero. In this moment, it appears that he ended up getting the complete package.

9

Burgling Faerie

"BARRELS OUT OF BOND"

Elves: The Woodland Realm

Chapter Nine takes place entirely within the domains of the Elvenking of Mirkwood. In Chapter Eight, we looked at the elven magic at work in the forest and the effect it has on Bombur, Bilbo, and the others, culminating in Thorin's enchantment and eventual abduction. It would hardly be fair, however, to consider the Wood-elves only as one of the dangers of Bilbo's journey. Even in the midst of Bilbo and the dwarves' most disturbing encounter with them—the appearing and vanishing feast in the trees by night—the description we get of the feasting elves shows that they are not sinister people. The elves are beautiful, decked equally in gems and in flowers: "Their gleaming hair was twined with flowers; green and white gems glinted on their collars and their belts" (142). Most reassuring of all, they are singing songs "filled with mirth" that are "loud and clear and fair." Our initial impression of them in the darkness of the forest is much more ominous, and they are a good deal more cautious and jumpy, but their song and their laughter should remind us of the kindly elves of Rivendell. Perilous they might be, but these elves too are fair, merry, and joyful.

Although the elves of Rivendell take great delight in the world around them, the description of the Wood-elves emphasizes more forcefully their connection with nature. Even the simple name they are given, the Wood-elves, points to the close relationship they have with their forest home. The description of the Elvenking illustrates this connection most clearly. He wears no crown of gold or silver. When the forest is in autumn, as now, he wears "a crown of berries and red leaves" (158); in springtime when trees are in blossom, he is adorned with a "crown of woodland flowers." He carries in his hand no jeweled scepter, but only a "carven staff of oak." The symbols of his authority reflect the life of his forest realm.

The elves of Mirkwood are closer to the earth than the elves of Rivendell; they are also less lofty and ancient. Elrond is noble, strong, wise, and kind, and he is connected with ancient heroic tales from "before the beginning of History" (48). The Elvenking may be lord of a magical land, but he does not seem nearly so ancient. He can only look back and compare himself to the "elf-lords of old" (155). The narrator clarifies that the Wood-elves are a different people from the "High Elves of the West" to whom Elrond and his people are related (154). In what amounts to a one-paragraph summary of *The Silmarillion,* still nowhere near publication when *The Hobbit* came out, we are told that the High Elves went to Faerie in the West, the true blessed realm across the sea, beyond the borders of the Wide World. The Wood-elves loved this world, lingering "in the twilight of our Sun and Moon" (154). Tolkien has only given a very brief glimpse of the history of the elves here, but it is enough for us to begin to see why the Wood-elves are tied more closely to their woodland realms, which they never forsook.

The Wood-elves remain elves, and therefore "Good People" (154), but the narrator admits that "if they have a fault it is distrust of strangers," and also that they are "more dangerous and less wise" than High Elves such as Elrond's people. If we compare the receptions that Bilbo and the dwarves receive in the two hidden elven realms they visit, we can see that the Wood-elves are more dangerous because they are less wise and learned than their cousins in Elrond's house. Remember that though the elves in Rivendell seem so merry as to be frivolous, they are also very knowing. Somehow, they already know everything about Bilbo and his companions and their quest. They tease them and laugh merrily at them, but they also stand ready to help them, though they seem to have nothing to gain from doing so. The Elvenking knows nothing about them or their purpose. He makes it clear that the Wood-elves simply misunderstood the approach of the dwarves in the dark the night before, believing that they were trying to attack his people "at their merrymaking" (155). If the Wood-elves knew more and showed more wisdom and less suspicion, there would be no reason to imprison Thorin or his followers.

Moreover, the Elvenking has one other weakness that will become very important later in the story. He loves treasure, and he wants to increase his own personal hoard. The desire for beautiful things themselves might not be a terrible thing. The Elvenking particularly loves "silver and white gems" (155), and remember that the elves at the woodland feast were adorned not only with flowers but with "green and white gems" (142). This seems perfectly fitting. The Wood-elves seem to revel in the beauties of the natural world; why shouldn't they relish the glittering gems from beneath the earth as well as the fragrant flowers from above it? The Elvenking, after all, lives in a cave, and he sits in majesty in a "great hall with pillars hewn out of the living stone" (158). The evidence that the Elvenking's love of treasure is a weakness that might prove dangerous comes from the narrator's explanation of *why* he wants more treasure. He was "ever eager for more" of it, we're told, "since he had not yet as great a treasure as other elf-lords of old" (155). The Elvenking wants to increase his hoard not just out of an appreciation for beautiful things, but out of a desire to increase his status and reputation—to establish his place among the Elven kings of ancient legend. In short, he is motivated by pride, a pride that might, perhaps, also influence his decision to hold Thorin and Company captive.

Despite their flaws, however, the Wood-elves are recognizably elves, Good People like the elves of Rivendell. The Wood-elves might grab Thorin and the rest and haul them off to their subterranean dwelling, but the narrator is at pains to make clear that this does not make the Wood-elves similar to the goblins. The Wood-elves "were not goblins, and were reasonably well-behaved even to their worst enemies, when they captured them" (156). The Wood-elves' songs, of course, also give us a poetic invitation to contrast these singers with the wicked goblins. Consider for a moment the little song the elven servants sing to the barrels as they drop them through the trapdoor into the river:

Roll—roll—roll—roll,
roll-roll-rolling down the hole!

Heave ho! Splash plump!
Down they go, down they bump!
(168)

This song isn't much, just a silly bit of merry rhyming. The verse recalls the goblins' first song in certain respects, however. Both are composed almost entirely of monosyllables, and both also feature sound words: "Splash plump!" here to imitate the barrels dropping into the water, like the "Swish, smack!" of the goblins imitating their whips (58). This very similarity, of course, also plainly points to the enormous difference between the two songs, and their singers. While the goblins are singing to relish their violent and cruel actions, the elves are expressing delight in the work that they are doing, even though it is only menial labor. Like the elves of Rivendell, the Wood-elves interact with their world through song and laughter, taking pleasure in everything around them.

But how are we to reconcile this image of the elves as the laughing opposites of the goblins, and the enemies of the evil spiders, with their implacable imprisonment of the dwarves? Tolkien's handling of the interactions between the elves and the dwarves is quite delicate. First, the narrator gives some background on the relations between elves and dwarves, explaining the grievances that lay between their peoples and carefully presenting both sides of the story. Then, with that as a model, the narrator shows us Thorin's interrogation by the Elvenking, allowing us to see both sides of the argument.

From the Elvenking's perspective, the elves were feasting in the forest when they were three times attacked by a band of desperate, vagabond dwarves. He has a long-standing distrust of dwarves, and now he is confronted by an unknown number of resolute dwarves who have tried to ambush them, while the elves were unarmed and keeping no watch. Now, having captured one of them, the Elvenking finds that he won't explain why he came into the forest or what he was planning to do. This sounds understandably suspicious, especially with the Elvenking keeping in mind the memories of that old war which saw an army of dwarves marching as an invading force into the woodland realm of a great elf-lord. His insistence on knowing what brought Thorin into the forest is more than curiosity; it is very reasonable caution.

At the same time, Thorin's indignation is just as easy to understand. He and his companions were traveling through the forest on business of their own, and with no more intention of disturbing the Wood-elves than they had had of inconveniencing the goblins of the Misty Mountains. When they began to come near to death by starvation, they ran to an elven feast in order to beg for food. In response, Thorin is cast into an enchanted sleep and then bound and dragged before the Elvenking as a prisoner. He knows his own innocence, and even a less dignified and touchy person than Thorin might feel some understandable outrage at the ungenerous treatment he has received.

We can see the same pattern again when Balin and the other dwarves are brought before the king. Balin, nearly dead of hunger and poison and hopelessly lost, suddenly finds that they seem to have been arrested and brought to trial. He asks, with justifiable exasperation, "What have we done, O king? . . . Is it a crime to be lost in the forest, to be hungry and thirsty, to be trapped by spiders?" (158). He also adds, with unwise but pardonable tartness: "Are the spiders your tame beasts or your pets, if killing them makes you angry?" The king, of course, already on edge at what begins to look like increasing evidence of a dwarvish conspiracy, is justifiably offended by this remark and sentences them to prison until he can get to the bottom of the situation.

Both dwarves and elves leave these encounters feeling that they are the injured and insulted party. We are brought to understand the tension between the two sides, and yet we can sympathize with both. The elves are not simply another one of the enemies that the dwarves must somehow contrive to escape. We are not really prompted to think ill of either side, but rather to perceive that the two groups could and should be friends, and that their conflict is based on a tragic misunderstanding, assisted by the pride of both sides. In this encounter, Tolkien has laid the foundation for the confrontation outside the Lonely Mountain several chapters down the road, where we will once more sympathize with both sides of the unfortunate dispute that breaks out there.

Bilbo's Nature: The Burden of Leadership

Bilbo's relationship with the dwarves has undergone some big changes by the time we get to Chapter Nine. The dwarves' initial attitude to Bilbo was summed up in Gloin's direct but unkind question back in Bag-End: "Will he do, do you think?" (18). The skepticism expressed in that question lingered for a long time; it is only after Bilbo's escape from the Misty Mountains and his sudden appearance in the midst of their camp in the beginning of Chapter Six that they began to look at him with new respect (88). Even after this, however, they still often find him merely a burden, as we can hear in Dori's complaint that he "can't always be carrying burglars on my back" (93). They may have come to accept him, but they still don't count on him for much. Although he is chosen to be the one who goes forward first into the elf ring on their second attempt to communicate with the nocturnal feasters, this is not because of any ability or skill that qualifies him for the task. He is selected only because he is so small and so obviously harmless that the elves couldn't possibly be afraid of him (141). The dwarves may have come to respect Bilbo much more than they did, but their estimation of him still has strict limits.

Bilbo's second turning point and his successful raid on the spider colony have permanently altered this situation, changing the dwarves' opinion of him radically. Once the dwarves have escaped from the spiders with Bilbo's help, they fully realize "that they would soon all have been dead, if it had not been for the hobbit" (152). We have seen that the customary dwarf greeting involves placing oneself "at the service" of the person to whom one is being introduced, but this is often, as it was in the case of the Great Goblin, "merely a polite nothing" (59). Beorn, too, recognizes the emptiness of the statement, observing that what they really mean is that they need *his* service (112). The dwarves now have incurred a real and undeniable debt to Bilbo, and they even formalize this with all the polite ritual that their weak and wobbly condition will allow. The dwarves thank Bilbo many times, and several of the dwarves, those who can stand, anyway, "got up and bowed right to the ground before him" (153). This elaborate bowing is like a kind of re-introduction to Bilbo, meeting him anew on equal terms, just as Balin did in the beginning of Chapter Six. Bilbo will never again, in the eyes of the dwarves at any rate, be merely "the little fellow bobbing and puffing on the mat" (18).

In fact, the dwarves now view Bilbo not only as an equal, but even as a leader. Once the dwarves are sufficiently recovered from their ordeal to begin asking what they are to do next, it is "from little Bilbo that they seemed to expect to get the answers" (152). Back in Chapter One, when Thorin turned to appeal to their "burglar-expert" for suggestions, he was being sarcastic, showing mere "mock-politeness" (21). In Mirkwood, the woozy and exhausted dwarves genuinely feel a "great respect" for Bilbo, and the narrator quickly assures us, "Indeed they really expected him to think of some wonderful plan for helping them, and were not merely grumbling" (152). At his departure from the company, Gandalf laughingly commented to Bilbo, "You have got to look after all these dwarves for me" (128). It now seems that Gandalf spoke the truth, as usual.

The dwarves have excellent reason to look to Bilbo for guidance. It was his cleverness and his courage, applied in equal measure, that freed them from the spiders' webs. Not only does he have the nerve to undertake the rescue and the resourcefulness to bring it off, but he shows the presence of mind to make new plans, communicate them to the dwarves, and carry them out even in the middle of a battle. Even more significantly, Bilbo cements his leadership status through his acts of self-sacrifice, putting himself in harm's way in order to save his friends' lives. In the final stages of the struggle with the spiders, Bilbo's self-sacrificial spirit is elevated to heroic status. His whole plan to save the dwarves is to draw off the spiders if he can, turning their rage against himself instead of his friends (151). He turns up again when things look bad once more, charging into the spiders and placing his own little body once again between his friends and the horrible monsters who want to eat them. "Go on! Go on!" Bilbo shouts.

"I will do the stinging!" (151). It is one of his finest moments in the book, punctuated by the narrator's simple affirmation: "And he did" (152). The dwarves have every reason to believe that they can rely on Bilbo and follow his lead.

The dwarves' dependence on Bilbo is not simply a product of Thorin's absence. Someone, of course, needs to step up and take command once Thorin disappears, but we should notice that the dwarves turn to Bilbo for leadership even before they realize that Thorin isn't there. Moreover, Bilbo's new responsibilities do not subside once Thorin is found again. In the Wood-elves' prison, Thorin asserts his authority in the message he has Bilbo deliver to the other dwarves, ordering them to wait on the word of "Thorin their chief" (161). But Thorin's own plan is simply to wait for "the remarkable Mr. Invisible Baggins (of whom he began to have a very high opinion indeed)" to "think of something clever" (162). Thorin in effect puts the weight of his own authority behind Bilbo.

Bilbo's initiative also receives the endorsement of an even higher authority: the luck that has guided their journey. When Bilbo sees the chief of the guards go off to drink with his friend the Elvenking's butler, Bilbo can tell that "luck was with him" (164). The narrator almost immediately lays great stress on this point, emphasizing that "luck of an unusual kind was with Bilbo" as the two elves drink themselves into unconsciousness. Once more, we can see the pattern that began to emerge in Chapter Eight: Bilbo's "peculiar" luck prepares the way for him, but he must use his own resourcefulness and courage to take advantage of the opportunity provided to him. He must formulate the plan and carry it through. Bilbo is not a passive beneficiary of good fortune, living some kind of charmed life. As he himself realizes, if his friends are going to be freed from the dungeons of the Elven-king, "it would have to be done by Mr. Baggins, alone and unaided" (161).

Burglar Bilbo: Job Approval and Dissatisfaction

Having established himself as a warrior and a hero during the fight with the spiders, in the dungeons of the Elvenking, Bilbo also finally comes into his own as a burglar. This label had not seemed to fit Bilbo very well at all when Gandalf first gave it to him in Chapter One, and the dwarves were openly dubious. By breaking his friends out of prison, however, Bilbo puts his abilities as a burglar beyond question. Stealing the guard's keys from his belt, silently unlocking the cells of all his companions, and then daringly replacing the keys on the snoozing guard's belt is a sequence worthy of any professional burglar. As Thorin remarks, "Gandalf spoke true, as usual! A pretty fine burglar you make, it seems, when the time comes" (165).

In fact, during the weeks he spends in the halls of the Wood-elves, Bilbo becomes a professional burglar in more than one sense. He is not only rendering the dwarves his "professional assistance," as he is contracted to do in the formal letter Thorin left on his mantelpiece in Bag-End (28); he is also earning his living by burglary on a day-to-day basis. In the caves of the elves, he is living a "sneaking sort of life," putting the power of his invisibility ring and his own knack for stealth to work in order to "pick up a living of some sort by stealing food from store or table when no one was at hand" (161). His burglary becomes quite casual and offhand, as we see when he sneaks away from the barrels on the river to find food among the riverside huts. We are told that he "no longer thought twice about picking up a supper uninvited if he got the chance" (171). In the halls of the Elvenking, Bilbo has become a subsistence burglar.

We might think that Bilbo would be rather pleased with his accomplishments. We have seen on several occasions that Bilbo cares very much what the dwarves think of him. As we saw in Chapter One, he takes uncharacteristic offense from the very beginning at overhearing that he looks more like a grocer than a burglar. In his first deployment in his professional capacity, his investigation of the trolls' campfire, the entire reason that he tries to pick William's pocket in the first place is that he "could not go straight back to Thorin and Company emptyhanded" (34). When he has his magic ring in hand, he sets out to impress the dwarves with his skills and competence, remaining smugly silent about his new magical advantage and basking in his employers' praise (88). We might reasonably expect, therefore, that by Chapter Nine, when surely his burglarious accomplishments would seem to have ensured him the rank of "really first-class and legendary burglar" (33), he would be feeling very satisfied with his career trajectory.

Instead, what we find is that he really hates the job. His life as a subsistence burglar is not glorious at all; it's miserable. He is "all alone, and always in hiding, never daring to take off his ring, hardly daring to sleep" (159). Instead of feeling satisfied, he feels trapped, remarking to himself, "I am like a burglar that can't get away, but must go on miserably burgling the same house day after day" (161). The prospect of having to remain in the caves indefinitely seems like a terrible fate. As the elves are rolling the dwarf-filled barrels into the river, he is filled with dread that he might be "utterly left behind and have to stay lurking as a permanent burglar in the elf-caves for ever" (168). "This," Bilbo concludes, "is the dreariest and dullest part of all this wretched, tiresome, uncomfortable adventure" (161).

Unsurprisingly, this thought brings him back once more to his recurrent wish: "I wish I was back in my hobbit-hole by my own warm fireside with the lamp shining!" (161). He has wished this many times before, but usually it was when he was lost or starving or in terrible danger. It is not the desire to escape danger that leads him to wish for home this time, however. Bilbo has now experienced adventure, and he has become an accomplished burglar. He has become fully acclimated to the adventurous and unpredictable world that intruded into his parlor and redirected his life. In his longing for Bag-End in Chapter Nine, we can see an expression of his simple preference for his old way of life over his new one. He has not ceased to be fundamentally Bagginsish in his perspective.

The fact that Bilbo prefers his old, quiet life doesn't mean that he hasn't changed at all. His wistful memories of his distant home and the comforts of his earlier life are now informed by his Tookish experiences. Most telling is the moment when he is stealing dinner among the riverside houses of the raft-elves and we are told that "he knew now only too well what it was to be really hungry, not merely politely interested in the dainties of a well-filled larder" (172). Bilbo's adventure has taught him, for the first time in his plump and comfortable life, what it is like to go without food for days on end, to be moments away from a terrible death. The experience has given him a whole new appreciation for the life that he had had without truly valuing it. His desire to return to his hobbit-hole is no longer simply escapism, an attempt to avoid or deny the harsh new reality surrounding him. Now, he recognizes Bag-End for what it really is: a paradise of warmth, light, rest, peace, and satisfaction. His Baggins nature, informed and seasoned by his Tookish experiences, has gained a new sharpness, maturity, and self-awareness.

As the elves are rolling the barrels into the river and Bilbo is preparing to leap into the icy water and out of the Elven-king's caves, the Wood-elves sing a song of benediction over their departing barrels. They don't realize, of course, that they have any living audience for their song. Bilbo knows that they aren't singing to him, and he is probably paying little attention in the midst of his anxiety. Nevertheless, the elves' song turns out to be remarkably relevant to the only sentient beings in earshot.

The song begins by ushering the barrels off on their journey:

> *Down the swift dark stream you go*
> *Back to lands you once did know!*
> *Leave the halls and caverns deep,*
> *Leave the northern mountains steep,*
> *Where the forest wide and dim*
> *Stoops in shadows grey and grim!*
> *(169)*

I don't know what the response of the barrels might be to these instructions, but if the dwarves can hear them, they would sound like sweet music indeed. "Leave the halls and caverns deep," where they have been locked away without cause and without hope of release? Leave the "forest wide and dim" and its "shadows grey and grim"? The elves wouldn't have to say that twice! Go "back to lands you once did know"?

Thorin has longed and labored toward that end for a hundred years now. In a strange piece of dramatic irony, the Wood-elves themselves become the first unknowing heralds of the end of Thorin's long journey and the return of the King under the Mountain.

The song then follows the progress of the barrels over the wetlands to the east:

> *Float beyond the world of trees*
> *Out into the whispering breeze,*
> *Past the rushes, past the reeds,*
> *Past the marsh's waving weeds,*
> *Through the mist that riseth white*
> *Up from mere and pool at night!*
> *Follow, follow stars that leap*
> *Up the heavens cold and steep;*
> *(169)*

Notice how similar this passage is to the dwarves' Wind song back in Chapter Seven. The barrels in the Wood-elves' song are accompanied by a "whispering breeze" rather than the roaring gale of the dwarves' verses, but they travel along the same route. The barrels, like the dwarves' wind, go past rushes and weeds and then over meres* and pools. Most remarkably, the barrels are then given the rather unexpected advice to "follow stars that leap / Up the heavens cold and steep." The barrels themselves are unlikely to follow these instructions in a literal sense, but we should be reminded of the dwarves' heavenly wind which, after ripping through the Long Lake and Lonely Mountain region, "left the world and took its flight /

---

* A *mere* is a pond, though the word can also mean "fen" or "marsh."

over the wide seas of the night" (119). The elves are no doubt being merely playful, but their words resonate. The barrels, and the dwarves inside them, will not literally ascend into the heavens, but it may be that they are being blown along by the celestial wind, which is bringing the dwarves to Lake-town and which will soon be stirring the smoke that rises from the dragon's lair.

The end of the song, however, turns with the barrels in their watercourse and heads in a new direction:

> *Turn when dawn comes over land,*
> *Over rapid, over sand,*
> *South away! and South away!*
> *Seek the sunlight and the day,*
> *Back to pasture, back to mead,*
> *Where the kine and oxen feed!*
> *Back to gardens on the hills*
> *Where the berry swells and fills*
> *Under sunlight, under day!*
> *South away! and South away!*
> *Down the swift dark stream you go*
> *Back to lands you once did know!*
> *(169)*

The last lines of the song anticipate a different homecoming, a return to lands of peace and plenty. It is a cultivated and civ-ilized world, a land of "pasture" and "mead" and "gardens on the hills." It is a land of warm sunlight, which looks down on plump berries, and probably on daisies in the grass, as well. The elves, of course, are thinking of the land "South away! and South away!": the regions from which many of their im-ported goods derive. But if Bilbo were paying attention, it might also sound like his own country, far away in the civilized West, on the other side of the Wild. The repeated refrain, "Back to lands you once did know," is rather a conspicuous one in the context of a book subtitled *There and Back Again,* after all.

The advice that the elves give to the barrels in this last section of the song is as unintentionally relevant to Bilbo as the first portions were to the dwarves. When a new dawn has come over the land to which he is traveling, he will indeed "turn" and "seek the sunlight," returning to "gardens on the hills." As Bilbo has realized anew during his miserable tour of duty as a full-time burglar in the Elvenking's halls, he wants nothing more than to return to the lands he once did know. The dwarves may be approaching the end of their journey, but Bilbo still has a very long way to go before he arrives at *his* destination.

10

The Return of the King

"A WARM WELCOME"

Luck: The Only Road That Is Any Good

As Bilbo is floating down the river out of Mirkwood, he catches his first glimpse of the Lonely Mountain looking "across the marshes to the forest," as if it had been waiting for them (174). The narrator's immediate emphasis is once more on the remarkable luck of Bilbo and his friends, as he remarks that they were "very fortunate ever to have seen it at all, even from this distance." By listening to the raft-men,* Bilbo learns that the "elf-road through the wood," the path that Bilbo and the dwarves had been following at the advice of Beorn, "now came to a doubtful and little used end at the eastern edge of the forest" (175). The path that they had been so sternly warned not to leave under any circumstances would have led them to likely disaster if they had followed the advice they had been given.

---

* The "raft-men" here are Wood-elves, not Men (humans). Tolkien often uses the word *men* generically, at times to refer to hobbits and elves as well as to specify humans as a race. The people whose conversation Bilbo is overhearing are certainly the same who later speak up to the Master of Lake-town and who are obviously elves, being called "the raft-men of the elves" and referring to the Elvenking as "our king" (181). In that same conversation, Thorin also refers to them as "the raft-men of the king."

In this news we can see the repetition of a now-familiar pattern. The dwarves' departure from the path and getting first lost in the forest and then imprisoned without hope in the dungeons of the elves seemed at the time like a complete disaster. But then, their waylaying by goblins in the mountains and re-routing first under the mountains and then through the air had also seemed like a serious misfortune at the time. Their first detour turned out, Beorn informed them, to be a good thing, since their original road would have been no good. The narrator emphasizes the extraordinary good fortune of their second detour even more forcibly. He tells us that "only the river offered any longer a safe way from the skirts of Mirkwood in the North to the mountain-shadowed plains beyond, and the river was guarded by the Wood-elves' king" (175). Not only did the imprisonment by the elves end up helping the dwarves and Bilbo, but it turns out to have been completely indispensable. "So you see," he insists, lest we overlook the implication, "Bilbo had come in the end by the only road that was any good." The only path that they could have taken to the Mountain went through the cellars of the Elvenking, which they could never have reached without first being captured, and without the "unusual kind" of luck that presented the opportunity for escape seized by a resolute and resourceful burglar (164).

That burglar himself fully recognizes the role luck has played in this last leg of their journey, and, despite the dangers and discomfort of their current position, he realizes that "he had been more lucky than he had guessed" (174). The wind of destiny from the dwarves' song does indeed seem to be blowing Thorin and his companions back toward the Mountain. It is heading up to the dragon's lair, but first it will pause to fan the flames of hope and anticipation in Lake-town.

The Homecoming Spoken of Old

The strange little town built out on the surface of the Long Lake on "huge piles made of forest trees" is still thriving, even "under the shadow of the distant dragon-mountain" (176). There was a time, however, when the town had been "wealthy and powerful" and had its place in "wars and deeds which were now only a legend." That had been when "Dale in the North was rich and prosperous," and when "dwarves dwelt in the Mountain" (175). Those days are now "remembered only as a shadowy tradition" and the Men of the Lake "remembered little" about it. They are not, however, allowed to forget it completely. Whenever the lake water sinks during a drought, they can still see along the shore of the Lake "the rotting piles of a greater town" (176), a reminder of the lost glory of their civilization.

Even before Thorin and his companions enter Lake-town, we can see that there is an internal division within the minds of its residents. They may not remember much about their history as such, but they do remember songs and legends. Some in the town "still sang old songs of the dwarf-kings of the Mountain, Thror and Thrain of the race of Durin, and of the coming of the Dragon, and the fall of the lords of Dale" (176). These songs sound like quite accurate history, based on what we have seen and heard throughout the book, but they are apparently not regarded as such by the Lake-men. Remember that dwarves live a long time, and although the fall of the Mountain kingdom happened within Thorin's own lifetime, it was actually over a hundred and fifty years before. Generations of the Lake dwellers have lived and died since Smaug laid waste to the Mountain and to Dale, and the events are now regarded as ancient legends.

Some of the songs remembered in Lake-town, however, look forward rather than back. These songs say "that Thror and Thrain would come back one day and gold would flow in rivers, through the mountain-gates, and all that land would be filled with new song and new laughter" (176). Lake-town retains not only a dim memory of a noble past, but also lingering hopes for a glorious future. The town has not entirely forgotten the old king, nor quite given up hope that he will return from exile.

Thorin's sudden arrival, therefore, hits the town like a lightning bolt, jolting both the memories of the past and the hopes for the future into new life. The Lake-men are not very vigilant, "not keeping very careful watch" despite the nearness of the dragon, for some of the people of the town "openly doubted the existence of any dragon in the mountain" (180). At Thorin's arrival, however, everything immediately changes. The imaginations of the people of Lake-town flare up in response. So complete and instantaneous is their acceptance of Thorin that "some of the more foolish ran out of the hut as if they expected the Mountain to go golden in the night and all the waters of the lake turn yellow right away" (180). The excitement spreads "like fire through all the town" (182), leading to "scenes of astonishing enthusiasm" (183). Crowds of people throng the dwarves' lodging "and sang songs all day, or cheered if any dwarf showed so much as his nose." The people of Lake-town seem to have turned back to faith in the old songs, which they had mostly forgotten or disbelieved, with amazing speed and thoroughness.

It is easy to give the Lake-men more credit for keeping the faith than they really deserve, however. Their tremendous excitement seems more like a new foolishness than a return to old wisdom. We need to be cautious and resistant even when

we hear the song that they sing. At first glance, we might assume that we are getting a transcription of one of those old
songs that prophesied the return of the dwarf-king, referred to
at the beginning of the chapter. If we read carefully, however,
we will see that this is not necessarily the case. Thorin's return
does indeed stimulate memories of the prophetic songs, and
"some began to sing snatches of old songs concerning the return of the King under the Mountain" (182). All those people seem to remember, however, are snatches—not the whole
song. "Others took up the song," we are told—that is, people other than those who remembered the isolated snatches.
It seems most likely, therefore, that the song that we hear is in
fact a new song, inspired by the overheard snatches of the old
songs, but expressing the recent and rather foolish excitement
more than any ancient insight.

The first two verses of the song focus on the dwarf-king
himself and the re-establishment of his kingdom:

> *The King beneath the mountains,*
> *The King of carven stone,*
> *The lord of silver fountains*
> *Shall come into his own!*

> *His crown shall be upholden,*
> *His harp shall be restrung,*
> *His halls shall echo golden*
> *To songs of yore re-sung.*
> *(182)*

The second verse, in particular, seems almost to echo the
dwarves' "Far over the misty mountains cold" song in Chapter
One, with its references to crowns, harps, echoes in dwarvish

halls, and songs sung underground. This echo, though obviously unintended by the singers, is fitting enough, since the current song speaks of the fulfillment of the dwarves' desired return and the restoration of the lost kingdom and treasures which the dwarves sang of so lovingly back in Bag-End.

However, the Lake-men's song betrays an important weakness in their thinking. Notice that almost the entire second stanza is in the passive voice—the song describes actions, but it gives no indication of who is doing the actions. Somehow, the king's harp will be restrung. Someone will re-sing the songs of yore. Most significantly, the king's crown will be "upholden"—but how, and by whom? These things are all apparently just going to happen. This grammatical quirk in that second stanza points directly at the unrecognized problem with all the celebration in Lake-town. No one has actually accomplished anything yet. The Mountain still needs to be reentered. The kingdom still needs to be re-established. And the dragon still needs to be disposed of. *Someone* has to do these things, but the Lake-men continue to party and sing as if they had already happened somehow.

The last two stanzas turn from the dwarf-king and discuss even more optimistically what will happen in the region round about:

> *The woods shall wave on mountains*
> *And grass beneath the sun;*
> *His wealth shall flow in fountains*
> *And the rivers golden run.*

> *The streams shall run in gladness,*
> *The lakes shall shine and burn,*

All sorrow fail and sadness
  At the Mountain-king's return!
    (182)

Once again we get an echo of the dwarves' first song. Where the dwarves sing of the pines "roaring on the height," buffeted by the wind of the incoming dragon's wings, the Lake-men sing of the new growth of trees and grass that shall cover the land now laid waste, waving cheerfully in a gentle breeze (15).

These last stanzas seem to match the almost mindless enthusiasm of the Lake-men even better than the disquietingly passive second verse does. Greenery will spring up in the desolation and on the sides of the Mountain itself. Wealth shall pour downstream, so that the river will run gold. Gladness shall abound; all sorrow and sadness shall cease. This fantasy of the heavenly utopia that will spontaneously emerge as soon as the dwarf-king shows up is certainly attractive, but it seems rather unlikely.

In the midst of all this sweetness and light, however, stands one ominous line: "The lakes shall shine and burn" (182). The discord of this one line is greatly intensified if we already know what is going to happen a few chapters later: the burning of Lake-town itself by Smaug. The reference to the lakes shining and burning could be connected with the rivers flowing with gold, of course—presumably the Lake-men are thinking of it that way. But this line stands out for two reasons: it is not cloyingly optimistic, and it foretells an event that will actually happen.

Remember that the narrator told us at the beginning that the song we are hearing began with remembered "snatches" of old songs, snatches that are taken up in the general excitement and spun into a full song. The song that we get seems to fit that description very well: it is a song full of wild effusiveness, but it contains a nugget or two that, though they can be swept up into the tone of the crowd on the quays of Lake-town, nevertheless don't completely fit with it. References later in the book suggest that "the rivers golden run" is one of these nuggets of old prophecy; I think "The lakes shall shine and burn" is very likely another. Although the Lake-men don't realize it, the old songs that they don't remember in full predict not only gladness but suffering: the destruction of their town itself. The return of the King under the Mountain will indeed bring prosperity and joy back to this region, and green grass will wave beneath the sun where there is now a rocky desert. But the gladness that is coming to the people of the Lake will only come through loss and hardship. Those who would take the old songs to indicate only a future of joy and bliss are misunderstanding them, and they have an unpleasant surprise coming to them.

Not everyone gets carried away by the excitement of the moment, however. The Master of Lake-town has a very different perspective on Thorin's arrival from most of his fellow citizens. The Master's interest is in practical matters. He does not "think much of old songs," instead "giving his mind to trade and tolls, to cargoes and gold" (182). The Master is a skeptic about the King under the Mountain, doubting "if any such person had ever existed" (181). His response to the situation in Lake-town is both pragmatic and cunning. He goes along with the "general clamour" out of necessity, even while completely disbelieving Thorin's claims (183). Yet, the Master prudently prepares for every eventuality, even what he considers the most unlikely chance: that Thorin is telling the truth. The Master of Lake-town intends to profit no matter what.

The Elvenking is also thinking in practical terms. He suspects that nothing will come of Thorin's quest, but if Thorin were to succeed in getting his hands on any treasure, the Elvenking figures to get a piece for himself. He declares, "No treasure will come back through Mirkwood without my having something to say in the matter" (184): the Elvenking too likes thinking about tolls and cargoes. His estimation of Thorin's plans and prospects is not based on general skepticism, as the Master's is, but instead on his rather low opinion of dwarves in general. He "did not believe in dwarves fighting and killing dragons like Smaug." The Elvenking does not suspect Thorin of being a mere fraud, but he doesn't think he can or will actually reclaim his kingdom from the dragon who conquered and still holds it.

The dragon, of course, is being overlooked by almost everyone else. Smaug is conspicuously absent from the song we are given, and even Thorin (who certainly hasn't forgotten him) seems to be trying to ignore him. The narrator tells us that Thorin looks and walks around Lake-town "as if his kingdom was already regained and Smaug chopped up into little pieces" (183). The Master has inspired some new songs for the people to sing outside the dwarves' windows, and they speak confidently of two things: "the sudden death of the dragon" and "cargoes of rich presents coming down the river to Lake-town." The dwarves are not particularly pleased by these new songs. No doubt the indication that the Lake-men will expect a share of the treasure explains most of their displeasure. But I suspect that some of it at least comes from the uncomfortable reminder that the dragon is still to be dealt with and is unlikely to suddenly drop dead on his own.

As the narrator points out, however, the Elvenking is "not quite right" in his assessment of Thorin and Company, and the Master is quite wrong (184). Both have underestimated what a dwarf will "dare and do for revenge or the recovery of his own" (185). When Thorin prepares to set out to re-conquer the Mountain, even the Master is "surprised and a little frightened" (184). The songs are indeed coming true; Thorin son of Thrain son of Thror is returning home.

Thorin himself undergoes a startling transformation in this chapter. At the beginning of the chapter he is at one of his lowest points. When Bilbo pulls him from his barrel, he is almost unrecognizable. He lies "groaning on the shore," and he has the "savage look" of "a dog that has been chained and forgotten in a kennel for a week" (178). He might expect to be treated with pity and charity by the Men of the town, though they seem likely to take him for a mere tramp in his "dirty and tattered sky-blue hood with its tarnished silver tassel." He undoubtedly looks out of place at the feast of the Master of the town, and probably even in the guard chamber. In any case, he seems destined to be a pathetic anticlimax as the returning king.

But when he appears to the Lake-men, something seems to come over him, overshadowing his ragged appearance in the eyes of the townspeople. When he boldly declares to the astonished guards that he is "Thorin son of Thrain son of Thror King under the Mountain," the narrator adds, "and he looked it, in spite of his torn clothes and draggled hood" (180). A very short time before, he "could hardly stand or stumble through the shallow water," but now his presence is so commanding that it inspires some of the guards to run outside and check to see if the Mountain has already turned golden in the night (178).

Thorin quite self-consciously steps into the nearly messianic role of returning king. "I return!" he proclaims as he steps into the Master's feast, knowing the sensation he would cause with this dramatic declaration (181). When the guards tell him to lay down his arms, he replies, "We have no need of weapons, who return at last to our own as spoken of old" (180). The return of the king is unstoppable by anyone or anything, he asserts, including the interference of the Elvenking. "Lock nor bar may hinder the homecoming spoken of old," Thorin declaims (181). This kind of speech is, no doubt, what encourages the cynical Master of Lake-town to believe that Thorin is simply a con artist, a fraud "who would sooner or later be discovered and be turned out" (184). Thorin, however, not only is the genuine grandson of Thror, but he believes, or at least wants to believe, that his return to his kingdom is ordained by fate. As he strides proudly around Lake-town amidst the singing and cheering crowds, it is easy to believe it along with him.

Bilbo's Nature: A Sober Perspective

Bilbo is the one person in Lake-town, other than the Master, who is resistant to the excitement buoying the spirits of Lake-men and dwarves alike. We might have expected that the hobbit would be delighted by the turn things have taken upon their arrival at the Lake. Although he has had interludes of safety and comfort before now in the homes of Elrond and Beorn, this experience would seem to be even more satisfactory. He has received a hero's welcome and is treated like a celebrity, given all the respect he could wish, along with the more substantial comforts of all the food and rest he could desire. If anything is going to convince him that adventures aren't always nasty and unpleasant, this would be it.

Yet, despite his festive surroundings, the hobbit seems to remain in the same gloom that he developed while lurking around the halls of the Elvenking. In the Wood-elves' stronghold, lonely and afraid and uncomfortable with being relied on by everyone, Bilbo was distancing himself from the adventurous life, regardless of his success in it. His circumstances have changed radically, but his attitude has not. In Lake-town the people are celebrating and the dwarves are thinking confident and stirring thoughts about their own destiny, but Bilbo remains "the only person thoroughly unhappy" (185). Even his physical state reflects his difference in perspective, his quite prosaic and mundane head cold striking a sour note in the midst of the glamour and romance of the dwarves' unlooked-for return from the wilderness.

Bilbo is neither a cynic nor a wet blanket. Although none of the old songs allude to him "even in the obscurest way" (183), he appreciates perhaps even more than Thorin the providential chain of events that has led to their improbable arrival at Lake-town. He was the one, after all, who learned about the worsening of the paths and roads by listening to the raft-elves, discovering that their passage through the forest was even "more lucky than he had guessed" (174). But unlike the dwarves, Bilbo has also "not forgotten the look of the Mountain, nor the thought of the dragon" (184). When he first sees the Mountain, Bilbo did not like the look of it (174), and his time in Lake-town has done nothing to change his mind. The Lake-men might be able to sing cheerfully in the passive voice, as if the kingdom of the dwarves would just somehow be re-established by someone. Thorin might be able to look so confidently forward to the fulfillment of the prophecies spoken of old that he can forget about the decidedly awkward presence of the dragon in his destined realm. Bilbo cannot, and in this he shows more wisdom than anyone else around him.

In Bilbo's sobriety at Lake-town, I believe we can see his Took and Baggins sides working together. On the one hand, his situation is about as outlandish as it can get. Having just broken his friends out of prison in a magical kingdom, he is planning to invade a dragon's lair in order to gain its hoard and re-establish a fabled kingdom as foretold in old songs. That program would no doubt be both appalling and incomprehensible to his respectable neighbors back at home. Bilbo is not only immersed in the adventurous, Tookish life; he is very competent within it. And yet, on the other hand, he continues to look at his situation from a distinctly prosy and businesslike Baggins perspective. Thorin, the dwarves, and the citizens of Lake-town are swept up in their hopeful and optimistic poetry just as Bilbo was briefly swept up in the dwarves' song back in Bag-End. Bilbo resists the excitement, remaining plain Mr. Baggins, a hobbit who is fully aware that he is preparing to assault the lair of a living dragon in cold prose. In Chapter Nine, we could see Bilbo's adventures seasoning his Baggins values. Now, we can see him applying his solid Baggins point of view to his adventure.

II

When the Thrush Knocks

The Desolation of the Dragon: A Land Devoured

For most of the book so far, the dwarves have been avoiding the thought of what lies in wait at the end of their journey. Their focus has been on the reward that awaits them, especially the vast wealth of Thror which they hope to reclaim. Bombur, you may recall, once referred to their journey as a "treasure hunt" (63). Under the influence of enthusiastic songs in Lake-town, they have been swept up into thinking about the re-establishment of the fabled dwarvish Kingdom Under the Mountain, the heritage of Thorin from his father and grandfather. What they have not thought about very much is the dragon.

In the wilderness around the Lonely Mountain, they are finally and inescapably confronted with the reality of the dragon in the Desolation that he has caused. The land they travel through becomes "bleak and barren, though once, as

Thorin told them, it had been green and fair" (187). The land, once filled with life and growth, is now "desolate and empty" (186). The glimpse of the Front Gate that Bilbo gets is also very evocative. Out of the gate "the waters of the Running River sprang; and out of it too there came a steam and a dark smoke" (189). The river, which gave life to the area, still flows from the Mountain, but its source is choked by the smoke of the dragon and even partially vaporized, turned into steam by the heat of Smaug. "They were come to the Desolation of the Dragon," the narrator states, "and they were come at the waning of the year" (187). There is no longer any way to ignore the thought of the terrible creature they must confront.

As a result, the dwarves' quest takes on a tone of much greater moral seriousness. The dragon is not just a very dangerous guardian of the treasure. He is an evil creature, and his domination of this land is a great evil that needs to be remedied. As Balin stands next to Bilbo under the "grey and silent cliffs" of the mountainside, he shares with the hobbit his own recollections, which contrast poignantly with their present surroundings: "The mountain's sides were green with woods and all the sheltered valley rich and pleasant in the days when the bells rang in that town" (187). There was a time when the mountain was green rather than grey, and when the valley was filled with music and merriment. Balin's memories of beauty and peace are both "sad and grim," for Smaug has not only murdered hundreds of people but strangled the life of an entire region. In the Desolation we begin to see that the true task that lies ahead of Thorin, Bilbo, and their friends is not the acquiring of a treasure, nor even revenge, but the healing of the land itself.

Dwarves: Hopeless and Adrift

As the dwarves advance across the Desolation with the Lonely Mountain "towering grim and tall before them" (186), the premature celebrations of Lake-town fade quickly into the distance behind them. In the waste north of the Lake "there was no laughter or song or sound of harps, and the pride and hopes which had stirred in their hearts at the singing of old songs by the lake died away to a plodding gloom." The men who bring them to the northern shores of the Lake haven't forgotten the old songs and still hope that they will come true, but all the same they find it "easier to believe in the Dragon and less easy to believe in Thorin in these wild parts." Everyone seems to recognize what no one wanted to consider back in the safety of Lake-town: the end of their journey, which is drawing rapidly closer, might be "a very horrible end" (187).

The dwarves' hope and high spirits have been thoroughly deflated by the Desolation of the Dragon, proving what we might have suspected even during the festivities back in Chapter Ten: the confidence of the dwarves was never very well founded. Upon arriving at the slopes of the Lonely Mountain, the goal they have been toiling and struggling for months to attain, they face a depressing irony: "they were at the end of their journey, but as far as ever, it seemed, from the end of their quest" (189). The narrator adds, almost superfluously, that "none of them had much spirit left." The dwarves show the same emotional volatility throughout the chapter. When they find the location of the secret door, their spirits rise "a little," but soon they sink back "into their boots" (192). The dwarves' confidence, which seemed so unshakable back in Lake-town, proves to have very shallow roots; when the dwarves are confronted with real obstacles, their confidence crumbles and they become "glummer and glummer."

Bilbo, on the other hand, proves as resistant to the dwarves' emotional lows as he was to their emotional highs. The same businesslike Baggins perspective, grounded in simple reality and not carried away by imagination, that kept Bilbo from getting swept up in the enthusiasm at Lake-town now prevents him from falling into the gloom that oppresses the dwarves as they approach the Mountain. The dwarves seem almost paralyzed by the thought that they are "alone in the perilous waste without hope of further help" (189), but Bilbo is more practical. He approaches the situation as a problem, almost as a riddle to be solved. He "would often borrow Thorin's map and gaze at it, pondering over the runes and the message of the moon-letters Elrond had read." The dwarves are too stubborn and determined to quit, but they are almost entirely impractical and at times seem to lack the ability to think for themselves. It is Bilbo who makes the dwarves "begin the dangerous search on the western slopes for the secret door." Despite the fact that their only idea about getting into the Mountain without alerting Smaug is finding the secret passage indicated on Thror's map, the dwarves apparently require the hobbit's prodding to begin looking for it. Bilbo's solid, down-to-earth perspective is practically the only thing moving the quest along at this point. In Mirkwood, Bilbo became the real leader of their group; now, on the slopes of the Mountain itself, the expedition is threatening to turn into a one-man show.

Even when Bilbo's own spirits drop and he is "no longer much brighter than the dwarves," his gloominess is different from theirs (192). Instead of wandering aimlessly about as the dwarves do, Bilbo turns back west and looks toward the homeward road. Bilbo is, as he explains to the dwarves, sitting on the doorstep and thinking, but he is not thinking about entering the Mountain; he is thinking instead about returning to his little Hill, far in the West. The dwarves celebrated their homecoming a little too soon back in Lake-town; now they have actually arrived at the Mountain, and they are at a loss. Bilbo has now reached the farthest point of his outward journey; the Mountain stands at the opposite pole from the Hill. He sits "with his back to the rock-face" and stares back toward what "lay beyond the blue distance, the quiet Western Land and the Hill and his hobbit-hole under it" (192). Bilbo is keenly aware of the contrast between the Mountain and the Hill, between his safe and cozy home and the desolate, dragon-haunted wilderness in which he must complete his seemingly impossible mission before he can even begin his homeward journey. The quiet life of Bilbo's hobbit-hole, however, is almost equally far removed from the optimistic visions harbored by the people of the Lake and (briefly) by the dwarves. Bilbo will not really fit in out here in the East, no matter what happens.

Bilbo's separation from the dwarves' reactions and moods is exacerbated by the very different relationship he has with this adventure. The dwarves are on a quest of great importance to them and their families. Bilbo is a hired professional, an unlikely mercenary. This difference between Bilbo's status and that of the rest of the dwarves has been clear ever since Chapter Two. When they see the trolls' fire winking through the trees, the dwarves say, "After all we have got a burglar with us" (32). What we can hear in that line is not only their reference to Bilbo's position as hired help, but also the "us"—Bilbo is *with* them, but he is not one of them. Despite the fact that Bilbo and the dwarves have become friends and gone through a great deal together, that division is never completely removed. Just at the beginning of Chapter Ten, when Thorin is groaning and grumbling on the beach of the Long Lake after climbing half-dead out of a barrel, Bilbo reminds him that this "silly adventure" is "yours after all and not mine" (178).

The separation between Bilbo and his companions is still visible on the slopes of the Lonely Mountain, but the dynamics have shifted dramatically from the early days. In Chapter Two, Bilbo was so uncertain of himself and eager to impress his new companions that he went off to the trolls' campfire without protest, though he had no idea what to do or what was expected of him. In Chapter Eleven the frustrated dwarves begin to talk about sending Bilbo through the Front Gate, since "he has got an invisible ring, and ought to be a specially excellent performer now" (193). This time Bilbo cares little for what they think of his skill, and he is alarmed and irritated at being singled out again for this kind of duty. He is still being sent on the dangerous missions, but his reaction is now one of weariness and irritation at having to save the dwarves yet *again*.

We can hear a similar shift in the dwarves' affectionate recollections of the Unexpected Party that lead them to call the grassy space outside the secret door "the doorstep." The dwarves are remembering "Bilbo's words long ago . . . when he said they could sit on the doorstep till they thought of something" (192). Bilbo made that comment near the end of the party when he was trying to get rid of them, and when he said it, he was only trying to cover the fact that he had nothing at all to say (25). Now that he has proved himself many times over, the dwarves look back on Bilbo's cluelessness with fondness. What is more, there is an ironic reversal in the circumstances. Now it is the dwarves who have no idea what to do or what to say, and Bilbo who is the only competent person around.

Luck: The Prophecy of the Moon-Letters

The dwarves do indeed look quite foolish compared to Bilbo during the hunt for the secret door. For one thing, they seem to have almost completely forgotten about the instructions or prophecy that Elrond read in the moon-letters on the map: "Stand by the grey stone when the thrush knocks . . . and the setting sun with the last light of Durin's Day will shine upon the key-hole" (50). Even after they find the location of the secret door, the dwarves disregard this miraculously discovered message. In Rivendell, Thorin was the one who explained to Elrond that Durin's Day was "the first day of the last moon of Autumn on the threshold of Winter" (51). Yet neither he nor any of the dwarves seem to remember Durin's Day when Thorin himself casually remarks on the mountainside that "tomorrow begins the last week of autumn" (192). Giving no thought to the runes, the dwarves merely try to hack at the door with mining tools, which is as useless as it is ill-advised.

As we discussed in Chapter Three, the message in the moon-letters contains some instructions, but mostly predictions. Perhaps the dwarves would have found it more satisfying and memorable if it had contained more detailed directions, but as it stands, the role of the door-opener is mostly

passive. On Durin's Day, the thrush will knock and the setting sun will shine on the key-hole. Even the one piece of instruction given, "stand by the grey stone," is not particularly
active. This message obviously does not suit the dwarves. Even
when the ray of light has magically revealed the key-hole, the
dwarves disregard it, rushing to the rock and pushing on the
door with their hands. Again and again, the dwarves show
that they just don't get it.

It is Bilbo, of course, who pays attention to the runes
and respects what they say. He is the one waiting patiently
by the grey stone, and since he has been thinking about the
moon-letters, he is also the one who notices the thrush cracking snails against the side of the rock and realizes that the
prophecy is being fulfilled. Notice that in the critical moment, as the sun goes down and the dwarves are "watching
impatiently" with wagging beards, it is the hobbit who obeys
the instructions in the message, "standing by the grey stone"
(194). When the dwarves are groaning in disappointment as
the sun runs into the bank of clouds on the horizon, Bilbo is
the one who keeps up his hope, continuing to stand almost
motionless next to the stone. Thorin, who only approaches
the rock-face when Bilbo calls for him, would not even have
thought to try the key that Gandalf had given him in the miraculous key-hole if it weren't for the hobbit. The other occasions on which Bilbo has saved the day might have been a
little more action-packed, but none are more important than
this one.

The moon-letters give us the sense that there is something
magical, something supernatural, about the opening of the secret door, and the event strongly confirms it. On the morning
of Durin's Day, Bilbo has "a queer feeling that he was waiting

for something" (193). This feeling seems to lead him to anticipate something good and potentially magical. "Perhaps the wizard will suddenly come back today," he thinks. Instead, Bilbo finds himself standing in the middle of events mysteriously foretold more than a century before: the knocking of the thrush followed by the last light of Durin's Day striking the rock wall. The unfolding of events leaves no possibility that this could have been completely natural. The "last light of Durin's Day" turns out to be a single ray that escapes from a "belt of reddened cloud," pointing "like a finger" at the keyhole with striking precision (194).

Even the thrush, whose involvement might otherwise have been explained by natural means, contributes to the preternatural feel of the moment. The old thrush, who has been watching the long-awaited event transpire with great interest, his "head cocked on one side," gives "a sudden trill" as the single ray of light strikes the rock wall, immediately before the loud crack, like a magical echo of the thrush's own snail-cracking, splits open the key-hole (194). The thrush's apparently natural late-afternoon meal of snails serves as the sign for the opening of the door, as foretold in the runes, and the bird apparently waits, watching from high above in order to serve as a herald of the moment of the prophecy's fulfillment. We should scarcely need to be told, as Thorin will reveal in the next chapter, that the thrushes of the Lonely Mountain are a "long-lived and magical race" (209). The strange good luck that has brought Bilbo and his friends to the Mountain by convoluted and unforeseen paths has apparently gotten them there just in time for a magical event spoken of over a century before.

The opening of the secret door brings Bilbo to the beginning of the very last stage of his quest. This knowledge brings no relief, however, for the narrator's description of the secret passage is nothing short of terrifying. "It seemed," he says, "as if darkness flowed out like a vapour from the hole in the mountain-side, and deep darkness in which nothing could be seen lay before their eyes, a yawning mouth leading in and down" (194). Bilbo is standing by the grey stone, watching darkness itself being exhaled from the door like the smoke and steam that so disturbed him when he saw it billowing out of the Front Gate. He stares at the passage, which resembles the mouth of the dragon himself gaping open to swallow him, knowing that he, Bilbo Baggins, will be the one who has to walk down into that darkness.

12

Bilbo Earns His Reward

Bilbo's Choices: The Third Turning Point

Bilbo's descent into the Mountain, seeking the lair of the dragon himself, is a crucial moment in Bilbo's life. He puts on his ring and creeps "noiselessly down, down, down into the dark" (196). Soon he is not only out of touch with his friends, but even out of reach of the light of day: "All sign of the door behind had faded away. He was altogether alone" (197). Alone in the darkness, Bilbo is in a situation distinctly similar to the two previous turning points of his career. The first time, he woke from unconsciousness to find himself alone in the dark tunnel of the goblin caves, just before his encounter with Gollum. The second time, he woke from sleep in the dark of Mirkwood to find a giant spider wrapping his legs in webbing. Now, once again, he is alone in the utter darkness, without friends, without help, and facing a deadly enemy.

The three turning points, taken together, form an interesting pattern. We can, for instance, see a progressive escalation of the danger and hopelessness of the situations. First, he was lost in the mountains in unknown tunnels filled with goblins, needing to escape from a desperate and furious Gollum on his own. Then he was lost in the even more hopelessly impenetrable darkness of Mirkwood, having not only to escape from the arachnoid hunters, but to seek out their lair and attack them in order to rescue his friends. The third time, he must go by himself to invade the lair of an enormous fire-breathing dragon who has destroyed whole kingdoms by himself. Fortunately for Bilbo, this is his final turning point!*

We should also notice that there has also been an escalation in Bilbo's own engagement with these moments. The first time, comparatively little is asked of Bilbo. His decision to step forward on his own is a huge moment, but his options are limited. The second time, he not only shows the presence of mind to save himself from immediate assault, he puts himself in great danger to save his friends. The third time, he doesn't fall asleep or get knocked out and wake up to find himself alone; this time, he deliberately turns his back on his friends and on the world of sunlight and steps down into the darkness. The narrator heavily emphasizes Bilbo's choice, noting that "going on from there was the bravest thing he ever did," and adding, "The tremendous things that happened afterwards were as nothing compared to it. He fought the real battle in the tunnel alone" (197). Bilbo has now taken the final step.

Even in this final moment of commitment to his Tookish life, however, we find that his mind is still full of very Baggins-like thoughts. Bilbo is not coolly acclimated to his life

---

* Just about the only thing I can think of that would be more dreadful and more impossible would be traveling alone with his servant into the guarded realm of the Dark Lord himself in order to seek the very center of his ancient might and throw the Ring of Power into the Cracks of Doom. Thankfully, he will get to leave that task to his nephew Frodo.

of high adventure any more now than he has been all along. His thoughts dwell instead on how the courageous action he is currently performing is silly and pointless. "I have absolutely no use for dragon-guarded treasures," he thinks to himself, "and the whole lot could stay here for ever, if only I could wake up and find this beastly tunnel was my own front-hall at home" (197). Even as Bilbo is taking the plunge and performing the bravest and most adventurous deed of his entire life, he affirms his Baggins values. His own front-hall and the treasures that lie at the end of it—his tea-kettle, armchair, fireplace, and pantry—are more precious to him than the enormous heap of gold and jewels lying at the end of the dark tunnel. He may have passed the final turning point of his career, but he still sees things in a fundamentally Baggins way.

It isn't that Bilbo hasn't changed, of course. Chapter Twelve is sprinkled with recollections of Chapter One, which invite us to take notice of just how far Bilbo has come. When the secret door opens, Thorin makes an impressive speech, in the style he reserves for "important occasions," all about how the time has come for Bilbo to "earn his Reward" (195). As he does so, we should recall Thorin's first impressive speech, made in the same style back in Bag-End, at the "solemn moment" when they were about to set out on their journey (17). On that occasion, Bilbo interrupted Thorin by collapsing onto the floor and shrieking in helpless terror. The mere mention of the fact that he might never return from the journey had reduced poor Mr. Baggins to hysterics. In his speech at the opening of Chapter Twelve, the danger Thorin is speaking of is much more immediate and concrete: he is announcing that it is time for Bilbo to trot down the corridor in front of them and face a live dragon alone. This time, the seasoned

Bilbo's response is merely irritation, and even impatience. He coolly parodies Thorin's style in his response, with his overly elaborate "O Thorin Thrain's son Oakenshield, may your beard grow ever longer" (195). Part of his irritation seems to be at Thorin's reference back to the original contract between them, after all they have been through together, but he also seems simply impatient to get started. "I think I will go and have a peep at once and get it over," he says flippantly.

Even Bilbo himself reflects on the changes he has undergone since leaving home. He notes, "Perhaps I have begun to trust my luck more than I used to in the old days" (195). The narrator emphasizes the comment by interrupting the dialogue to add, "he meant last spring before he left his own house, but it seemed centuries ago." Although the actual time that has passed is relatively brief, the extent of the change in Bilbo makes it seem a very long time.

As Bilbo sets off down the secret tunnel, the narrator again prompts us to reminisce, noting, "Already he was a very different hobbit from the one that had run out without a pocket-handkerchief from Bag-End long ago" (196). The recollection of the handkerchief invites us to place two images next to each other. One is the picture of Bilbo, quite flustered and completely unprepared, "running as fast as his furry feet could carry him down the lane" to meet the dwarves at the very start of their journey (29). The other is the image of Bilbo, "trembling with fear, but his little face . . . set and grim" as he creeps down into Smaug's lair, loosening his sword in its sheath (196). In these two contrasting images we can see more than just the stiffening of Bilbo's spine. Bilbo's whole relationship to his adventure has changed; it is no longer just something that is happening to him. On the earlier occasion, we are told that "to the end of his days, Bilbo could never remember how he found himself outside" and running down the lane like that (28). He is helplessly swept off onto the road, passive despite his breathless activity. In Chapter Twelve, he is making his own decision. Having accepted his role and knowing full well what it means, he is walking deliberately toward the dragon he knows to be lying only a short walk away.

We can also see in these two scenes a change in Bilbo's outlook on life. What troubles him at the beginning of Chapter Two is not going on the journey so much as going without the comforts and conveniences he assumes will be essential, such as money or a handkerchief. Now, in the secret tunnel into Smaug's lair, the narrator points out that our determined, collected, and professional burglar "had not had a pocket-handkerchief for ages," and yet he is surviving (196). The handkerchief is only a token, of course, for the many other things he has done and is doing without. Just as the experience of being really hungry has changed his perspective on food, so too his attitude toward the peace and comfort of his life back "in the old days" has been altered, but not reversed.

We can still hear Bilbo grumble about the adventure in which he finds himself: "You went and put your foot right in it that night of the party, and now you have got to pull it out and pay for it!" (197). Yet even these words show, though playfully, a choice to take action, a resolute will to see his adventure through, returning afterwards to his Baggins world with a whole new appreciation. Bilbo's last turning point moves him toward the final marriage of the two sides of his nature, the ultimate mingling of Took and Baggins, poetry and prose, that gives Bilbo the strength and the firm foundation that enable his remarkable accomplishments in this last phase of his story.

Bilbo's Nature: Riddles with Smaug

Bilbo's comfort with his identity as an adventurer even goes a little too far, once he is past his final turning point, requiring a rather strong corrective before he returns to the proper balance. For a time, Bilbo's newly won self-confidence gets him a little carried away. He offers to go and visit Smaug a second time, and as he approaches the dragon's lair, we are told that he "was inclined to feel a bit proud of himself as he drew near the lower door" (203). Bilbo seems to be letting himself believe that he is too much burglar for even Smaug to handle.

When Bilbo starts telling Smaug who he is, inventing riddling names for himself, we get a clearer picture of how he is imagining himself in that moment. He begins, simply enough, with oblique references to his travels and the geography he has covered: "I come from under the hill, and under the hills and over the hills my paths led" (204). He then quickly adds a more heroic and mysterious dimension, adding in a fragmentary afterthought, "And through the air. I am he that walks unseen." Bilbo implies that he is not just a traveler, but a magical creature, one who can fly and make himself invisible. Since the latter of these two is obviously quite literally true, his magical self-description seems credible, as Smaug confirms.

Bilbo's second round of names focuses on a particular portion of his adventures: "I am the clue-finder, the web-cutter, the stinging fly. I was chosen for the lucky number" (204). I believe that all four of these "lovely titles" (as Smaug sarcastically calls them) refer to the encounter with the spiders in Mirkwood, either directly or indirectly (205). "Web-cutter" and "stinging fly" are quite plain allusions to that episode, but we should think also about what they imply about Bilbo and his attitude toward Smaug himself. Those names don't simply recall the events in Mirkwood; they recall his status as the taunting, deadly fly, the sweet and juicy prey whom no trap could hold. Bilbo is not threatening the dragon, of course, but he does point out that other predators have found him more than they could handle.

"Clue-finder" is a bit of a puzzle, since it isn't clear what clue Bilbo is referring to. It might conceivably be a reference to Bilbo's figuring out the meaning of the message in the moon-letters. However, I suspect that Bilbo means something quite different here. The word *clue* originally meant a ball of string; the Greek hero Theseus famously found his way out of the Labyrinth in Crete by sneaking a clue of thread in with him. The use of the word *clue* in the Theseus story led to the modern sense of the word: something you follow to find the way out of a puzzling problem or situation. Bilbo is referring, I believe, to this older meaning of the word *clue;* he is probably referring to the ball of spider-thread that he used to find his way around Mirkwood. In Chapter Eight, I explained how, in the first draft of the book, Tolkien described Bilbo paying out and winding up a ball of spider-thread which he used to find his way to the spider colony and then back to the path, Theseus-style.* Tolkien later re-wrote that chapter and cut the ball of spider-thread out of the story, but Bilbo's naming himself "clue-finder" dates back to that first draft which included it, where it would fit very naturally with "web-cutter" and "stinging fly." I think Tolkien probably kept this riddling name in the published version even after he removed the actual clue-finding episode from the story because "clue" does still work, if taken in its modern sense.

---

* See Rateliff, 309.

After three names commemorating his heroics in the spider colony, therefore, Bilbo adds, "I was chosen for the lucky number" (204). Bilbo refers, of course, to his being added as the fourteenth member of the party in order to prevent bad luck, as Smaug himself plainly figures out. In the context of the Mirkwood references, Bilbo seems to imply that, contrary to Smaug's observation that "lucky numbers don't always come off," it did indeed turn out to be lucky that the dwarves brought Bilbo along (205).

All four of Bilbo's second set of names for himself, therefore, emphasize his accomplishments, his importance to the quest. Having established himself as a great traveler with mysterious powers in the first set of names, he now presents himself as the resourceful hero without whom his companions would never have survived. Bilbo is not exaggerating—this is all perfectly true!—but he is certainly painting a grandiose picture of himself.

The third set of names continues in the same vein: "I am he that buries his friends alive and drowns them and draws them alive again from the water" (205). He seems to have moved on from his spider rescue to his prison break here. His riddling comparison of what he did with the barrels to burial and drowning and then to resurrection makes his actions seem not only resourceful, but downright miraculous. Bilbo has not only rescued his friends; he has brought them back from the dead. Once again, he implies to the dragon that he is a magical figure of unknown powers, not to mention rather unpredictable behavior.

The end of the third set of names moves in a different direction, and in some ways it is a most surprising one. "I came from the end of a bag, but no bag went over me," he says (205). Once more, Bilbo alludes to a time when all the dwarves were captured and he himself escaped: the troll incident, when the dwarves were caught in sacks. The main point of this remark, however, is the pun between the bagging of the dwarves by the trolls and the name of Bilbo's own house, Bag-End, and the pun establishes a parallel between them, though perhaps unintentionally. Both halves of the "bag" comment emphasize his *not* being in a bag, and thus in riddling form denying his own name of Baggins. I am not suggesting that Bilbo subconsciously feels his Baggins life to be a prison; we have just seen Bilbo looking back to Bag-End with longing a few pages earlier. But in this moment, when he is constructing for himself in riddles a daring, powerful, important, and even magical identity, Bilbo is perhaps unconsciously distancing himself from his respectable hobbit world. This moment when he is engaging in suave repartee with the dragon is undoubtedly Bilbo's most fully Tookish moment in the entire book.

The fourth and last set of names Bilbo gives himself starts comparatively modestly, emphasizing his consequence only by association with the unusual people he has met in his journey, calling himself "the friend of bears and the guest of eagles." From here, however, he moves into his final cluster of names: "I am Ringwinner and Luckwearer; and I am Barrelrider." By this time, Bilbo is simply oozing confidence and assurance. "Luckwearer" he may be, but "Ringwinner" is at least straining the truth, and possibly twisting it.* His final name is his fatal slip, the one he will bitterly regret afterwards, when

---

* As I explained in Chapter Five, in the first edition of *The Hobbit,* Gollum does put the ring, the "present," up as a prize in their riddle-contest, and so Bilbo does win it in a sense, but even in the first edition the name is a stretch. In the later editions, when Gollum never dreams of handing over his precious treasure, the name implies outright self-deception.

the fateful word *barrel* leads to, or at least accelerates, the destruction of Lake-town.

It is clearly no coincidence that his slip comes when he is "beginning to be pleased with his riddling" (205). As he prepares to leave, he is once again feeling "rather pleased with the cleverness of his conversation with Smaug," confident in his self-constructed identity as the fortunate and heroic adventurer who can banter with dragons and even taunt them, as he does in his "parting shot" (208). Even before he begins to regret his reference to barrels, he is jarred out of his cocky new attitude by a sharp dose of terror and pain. As Bilbo is sprinting up the tunnel "in great pain and fear" with the dragon's fire searing the skin on the back of his head and his heels, he is shaken "into better sense." Bilbo's flirtation with audacity is over, and his more down-to-earth perspective reasserts itself.

Bilbo's flash of self-aggrandizement goes too far, overreaching his good sense. His comments before and after his conversation with the dragon, however, give us some insight into the proper relationship between the wild Tookish world Bilbo is surrounded by and the mundane Bagginsish world to which he longs to return. Speaking cheerily to the dwarves before setting off down the tunnel for the second time, Bilbo comments, "'Every worm has his weak spot,' as my father used to say, though I am sure it was not from personal experience" (203). If we pause and think about this remark for a moment, it begins to sound quite astonishing. Bungo Baggins, the pillar of dullness and predictability, had advice on dragons relevant to Bilbo's current situation? Bungo himself never went adventuring, certainly, and Bilbo is quite sure that this advice was not based on his father's own experience. But Bungo apparently had heard stories, and even his ultra-mundane life had been seasoned by wisdom drawn from tales and legends still remembered by the hobbits. Bilbo, we may remember, loved Gandalf's stories when he heard them in his youth, and he seems to have known something of trolls, wolves, and the story of the fall of Elven Gondolin. What is more, the sagacious Bungo is quite correct. Smaug, despite his insistence that Bilbo's information about dragons' underbellies is "antiquated," does indeed have his weak spot (208). Even the most sheltered Baggins, apparently, can be enriched by wisdom derived from adventures and old stories.

Immediately after he (barely) escapes Smaug's fire, Bilbo chides himself firmly: "Never laugh at live dragons, Bilbo you fool!" (209). The narrator informs us that this expression will, in later years, become "a favourite saying of his" and pass into a proverb. Bilbo may have briefly left behind his good sense and his well-grounded perspective, but at least he does learn from the experience. What is more, we see the birth of a new aphorism, yet another dragon proverb that future generations of hobbits will inherit. Bilbo's experiences from his journey, it seems, will do more than change and shape him personally, helping him to value his peaceful life more when he returns to it. His story will reach out to influence others, granting them a measure of the wisdom that Bilbo himself is gaining through his memorable, if often painful, experiences.

The Desolation of the Dragon: Emulating Smaug

When Bilbo is down in Smaug's lair posturing in riddles and allowing his self-image to get a bit inflated, he can take con-

solation in the fact that he is only the second-most vainglori-
ous and over-confident person in the room. Smaug is tremendously proud and thinks a very great deal of himself. When
Bilbo offers him flattery at first, claiming that he wants to
see "if you were truly as great as tales say," Smaug doesn't believe him and yet is "somewhat flattered" anyway (204). When
Bilbo praises his "waistcoat of fine diamonds," Smaug is "absurdly pleased" (208). His mind is full of the idea of his own
greatness, but he is deluding himself. Believing that he has
only gotten stronger with age, he is not even aware that he
is missing a scale underneath, nor does he suspect that Bilbo
is asking to see his belly "for reasons of his own." In his own
cockiness and self-assurance, Bilbo seems to have been mirror-
ing one of the shortcomings of the arrogant dragon himself.

In fact, drawing his enemies into thinking and acting like
him seems to be a big part of what Smaug does to people. A
dragon's outlook is apparently contagious. Bilbo, for example,
is not generally very prone to obsessive thoughts about gold.
Even as he is walking down the tunnel toward the dragon's
lair for the first time, he is remarking to himself that he has
"absolutely no use for dragon-guarded treasures" (197). The
actual sight of the dragon-hoard changes this, however. Bilbo
had "heard tell and sing of dragon-hoards before, but the
splendour, the lust, the glory of such treasure had never yet
come home to him" (198). Even Bilbo, whose recurring fantasies mostly involve his tea-kettle and armchair, finds his heart
"pierced with enchantment." The brief enthrallment that
Bilbo experienced under the influence of the dwarves' song
back in Chapter One was only a shadow of this. Then, a fire
in the distance made him remember dragons, and he snapped
out of it. This time, the enchantment of the "gold beyond

price and count" is so great that not even the living, breathing dragon himself scares him out of it! The theft of the cup is actually performed under the influence; he seizes it when he is "drawn almost against his will" to the mound of treasure. When faced with the mountain of dragon-gold, even Bilbo begins to think dragonish thoughts.

Bilbo is briefly stricken with a dragonish desire for the hoard when he sees it, and he unconsciously emulates Smaug's vanity during their conversation. There is another aspect of the dragon's character, however, that Smaug himself tries quite actively to infect Bilbo with: suspicion and distrust of others.

As we noted in Chapter Eleven, Bilbo remains separate from the dwarves. Thorin's impressive speech on the doorstep about the time having come for Bilbo to "perform the service for which he was included in our Company" (195) emphasizes the gap between them quite pointedly. The narrator confirms that "they had brought him to do a nasty job for them, and they did not mind the poor little fellow doing it if he would" (196). No matter how friendly Bilbo and the dwarves have become during their journey, Bilbo is still hired help.

Smaug seems to have a shrewd suspicion of Bilbo's situation, and he sets out to exploit it. Smaug advises Bilbo not to "have more to do with dwarves than you can help" (205). He professes a great expertise on dwarf character, and he sets out to foment division and distrust. His innocuous question of whether or not Bilbo "got a fair price for that cup last night" is an excellent illustration of his cunning (206). The answer is not nearly as important as Smaug's planting the question in Bilbo's mind. The more Smaug can get Bilbo to think of the dwarves as his employers—and employers who are leaving him to take all the risks for small reward—the greater the divide between them. From there, it is only a short step to en-couraging the suspicion that they might not only cheat him, but murder him once his job is done.

Smaug has a "wicked and a wily heart" (206). He lives alone, trusting no one, jealously guarding treasure that he can never use and brooding only on his ownership of it, as well as his strength and majesty. This outlook is what the narrator will later call the dragon-sickness, and it is highly infectious.

Poor Bilbo struggles not to fall under the dragon's influ-ence. His statement that "not gold alone brought us hither" is a declaration of solidarity. He later strengthens it, claiming that "gold was only an afterthought with us" (207). Notice that he is resisting two aspects of the dragon-sickness here, trying to "remain loyal to his friends" while also downplaying the importance of the treasure. For all his brave statements, however, Smaug's words fester. Even when the dwarves are trying to reassure him later, he finds himself wishing "that he could feel quite certain that the dwarves now were absolutely honest" (211). Smaug does indeed have "rather an overwhelm-ing personality" (207), and the dragon-sickness, once con-tracted, is hard to shake.

Dwarves: Decent Enough People

When Smaug tries to induce Bilbo to distrust the dwarves, his words are plausible enough that they make Bilbo feel taken aback (207). After all, the narrator's highest commendation of Thorin and Company, that they are "decent enough people," if "you don't expect too much" (196), is pretty faint praise. Bilbo already thought the same; when he asks who will accompany him down the tunnel the first time, "he did not expect a chorus of volunteers, so he was not disappointed" (195). Thorin and his companions are not, in fact, "bad lots," but even at the best of times they are "not heroes, but calculating folk with a great idea of the value of money" (196). Smaug's insinuations may be unfounded, but we have reason to fear that the dwarves will be vulnerable when they themselves come into contact with the dragon-sickness.

Even before that particular crisis arrives, however, the dwarves are continuing the poor showing that they made in Chapter Eleven. Once again, their primary problem is the kind of emotional and imaginative instability that they have been suffering from since Lake-town. When Bilbo brings them the golden cup from Smaug's hoard, the dwarves start "talking delightedly of the recovery of their treasure"—they celebrate as if the quest were achieved already (199). Minutes later, when Smaug awakes and they can hear the rumblings of his anger in the depths of the Mountain, they "forgot their joy and their confident boasts of a moment before and cowered down in fright." The dwarves swing from one extreme of emotion to another with little evidence of rational consideration. One minute, they are cheering as if victory is won; the next, they are absolutely paralyzed with despair. They lament that the dwarves left behind in the valley "will be slain, and all our ponies too, and all our stores lost" (200). "We can do nothing," they conclude hopelessly.

The dwarves' cowering and terrified reaction to Smaug's first attack leads the narrator to observe rather sententiously: "It does not do to leave a live dragon out of your calculations, if you live near him" (199). Although they have been talking about reclaiming their treasure and about bringing their "curses home to Smaug" ever since Chapter One (24), they never seem to have actually made any plans about how they might do so. Bilbo, too, feels "inclined to point out" that getting rid of Smaug "had always been a weak point in their plans" (202). Bilbo remains discreetly silent, though even if he had said as much aloud, it would have been an enormous understatement.

Tolkien doesn't allow us simply to dismiss the dwarves, however, by writing them off as complete idiots. Although they do continue to be foolish and changeable, we also see some positive moments that suggest that good things may still be expected from the dwarves. The first is the affection that Balin shows for Bilbo. His choice to accompany Bilbo partway down the tunnel and, even more, the charming effusiveness upon seeing Bilbo return safely that leads him to pick Bilbo up and carry him triumphantly out of the tunnel are both reminders that the dwarves really are Bilbo's friends, and that the attachment between them is mutual (199). The second instance is Thorin's first real moment of leadership. Although he has been the captain of the rest of the dwarves from the beginning, we have never seen him act with decision, courage, and self-sacrifice in a time of crisis, as we have seen both Bilbo and Gandalf do. In the midst of the dwarves' cowering paralysis at the sound of Smaug's irate approach, however, Thorin finally rises to the occasion. He takes command of the dwarves and moves them into action to save themselves and their comrades, but he also orders Bilbo, Fili, Kili, and Balin to go inside the tunnel, proclaiming, "the dragon shan't have all of us" (201). Thorin, it seems, is capable both of decisive action and of putting others before himself.

The dwarves have the capacity to change, to mature into

something more than the comic troupe that they have been through most of the book. In Chapter Twelve, we see the first glimmers of change, but a metamorphosis seems a long way off. Moreover, there is still the dragon to be dealt with. Even if the dwarves were to figure out a means to get rid of Smaug, they would still have to find the strength to resist becoming like dragons themselves.

Luck: Bilbo and the Thrush

Bilbo may get carried away in his conversation with Smaug, but it is hard to argue with him when he calls himself "Luck-wearer" (205). The dwarves also can't help but notice that the whole "lucky number" thing has indeed worked out rather well, and Thorin acknowledges that Bilbo is "possessed of good luck far exceeding the usual allowance" (195). Even Bilbo talks about the luck that has been with him throughout his journey as if it is indeed some attribute of his character.

Bilbo does not, however, lose sight of the bigger picture; he does not cease to recognize that the good luck that they have experienced on this journey is an external thing over which he really has no control. He points out, for instance, that their acquisition of the treasure "obviously depends entirely on some new turn of luck and the getting rid of Smaug" (203). Bilbo seems to suspect that there is something bigger going on here, and that his own actions are only a small part of it.

Bilbo goes a step further in this direction near the end of his speech with Smaug, shifting into a prophetic register. When he is trying to defend the dignity and integrity of the mission that has brought him and his friends to the Mountain against Smaug's demeaning accusations of petty theft, Bilbo proclaims, "We came over hill and under hill, by wave and wind, for *Revenge*" (207). In this statement, Bilbo reuses some of the same riddling terms that he used back in his descriptions of himself; it might seem that he is simply once again using riddling talk to puff himself and his companions up, making their arrival sound magical and weighty. Bilbo ends with a reference to wind, doubtless thinking of their eagle flight, but it should also prompt us to remember the Wind song that the dwarves sang in Chapter Seven. As Bilbo himself was realizing at the beginning of Chapter Ten, he and the dwarves really *have* been borne on the wings of destiny down the astonishingly unlikely path that they have followed from the Hill to the Mountain. There is no way that they could have found that path by mere chance. Smaug laughs at Bilbo's words, and his laugh is terrifying, but for all his bluster, the winds of fortune have indeed turned against him, as Bilbo's words (perhaps unconsciously) warn.

We are unlikely to scoff along with the dragon at Bilbo's portentous statement. The events at the end of Chapter Eleven, the fulfillment of the moon-letter prophecy, should have placed the involvement of destiny in this quest beyond doubt. Bilbo indirectly recalls the scene on the doorstep at the culmination of his meeting with the dragon. When Bilbo sees the bare patch on Smaug's breast, he says to himself, "Why, there is a large patch in the hollow of his left breast as bare as a snail out of its shell!" (208). The comparison of Smaug to a snail that has been broken out of its shell was certainly suggested to Bilbo by the activity of the thrush, whose knocking of snails against the grey stone was the signal for the magical opening of the door. The news of Smaug's snail-like vulnerability is also overheard by the thrush, who will be the messenger that enables the slaying of the dragon in Chapter Fourteen. The old thrush of "magical race," therefore, is bound up with the death of the dragon from beginning to end.

The thrush is a symbol of the harmony of the old days, when dwarves and men were at peace and even the wise and goodly birds were "tame to the hands" of Thorin's father and grandfather (209). The thrushes used to be sent as messengers between Dale and Lake-town, and in carrying the news of the dragon's weakness, the thrush will be fulfilling its ancient role, bringing about a rebirth of the old peace in these troubled later days. In the context of the whole story of the thrush as it unfolds before us in Chapter Twelve, we see that the reference to the knocking of the thrush, opening a hole in the armor of the snail that its beak will penetrate, serves as a cryptic metaphor for Smaug's downfall itself. In a sense, the moon-letters contain not only the prediction of how the dragon's lair will be entered, but an oblique foreshadowing of how the dragon will be destroyed.

Uttering prophecies of doom, even unawares, might seem a bit out of character for Mr. Bilbo Baggins, but if we read carefully we will notice that Bilbo has actually been having quite a few prophetic turns of late. Remember that the morning of Durin's Day in Chapter Eleven begins with Bilbo's mysterious sense "that he was waiting for something" (193), though he doesn't know exactly what. On the evening after his chat with Smaug, he is again unsettled, warning the dwarves, "I feel it in my bones that this place will be attacked again" (210). He admits that what he is feeling is simply fear (entirely prudent fear), confessing, "I fear that dragon in my marrow" (212), but he also declares firmly and unequivocally that "Smaug will be coming out at any minute now, and our only hope is to get well in the tunnel and shut the door" (211). The dwarves are moved by the foresight that has come over Bilbo here, for "something in his voice gave the dwarves an uncomfortable feeling" (212). Against their better judgment, they lock themselves in the tunnel, barely soon enough to save themselves, for Bilbo's prediction is exactly correct and his timing is precise.

In fact, Bilbo had already foreseen this moment, in a sense, during his riddling talk to Smaug. In his third set of names, Bilbo says, "I am he that buries his friends alive and drowns them and draws them alive again from the water" (205). When Bilbo speaks of burying his friends alive, he is no doubt thinking of packing them up in their barrels, suggesting a gruesome parallel between the barrels and coffins. By the end of the chapter, however, we see that Bilbo has indeed buried his friends, and himself, alive in a much more real and thoroughgoing way. They are now buried in the Mountain at Bilbo's insistence, and trapped as they are in a tunnel whose "only way out led through the dragon's lair" (211), the Mountain seems likely to be their tomb.

When the door closes behind Thorin and the tunnel-mouth is smashed by the dragon, the journey to the Lonely Mountain is officially ended. The dwarves have been here on the Mountain for days, of course, but they have always held themselves back, fearing to re-enter their lost halls in earnest and preferring to send Bilbo in to scout things out. Bilbo's foresight and Smaug's stealthy attack have finally compelled them to take the very last step of their journey. In anxiety and great fear, cowering in the dark and dreading sudden death, Thorin has finally re-entered his ancient home. The King under the Mountain has returned.

13

A Burglar Indeed

The Dwarves' Homecoming

For several chapters, the dwarves have been swinging rather wildly between sublime optimism and nearly catatonic despair. We start Chapter Thirteen with the dwarves in a depressive phase, groaning, "This is the end. We shall die here" (214). Once again, as has often happened, Bilbo is out of step with the dwarves. Bilbo's emotional response to the situation is at once more mystical and more down-to-earth. He suddenly feels "a strange lightening of the heart, as if a heavy weight had gone from under his waistcoat." This seems to be another of Bilbo's mysterious and semi-prophetic insights, for we have every reason to think that the rush of hope Bilbo feels at this moment coincides with Smaug's death at Lake-town (though we as readers don't learn about this until Chapter Fourteen). Bilbo doesn't understand what has happened, but somehow he senses the destruction of the dragon and takes heart.

Bilbo's hope, however, is not based exclusively on this subconscious spiritual perception. That is also derived from his application of a couple more of his father's sayings. Bungo certainly couldn't have anticipated that his words of wisdom, "While there's life there's hope!" and "Third time pays for all" (214), would be applied by his son when he was trapped in a dragon's lair, but they do turn out to suit the situation. Once more, in this final stage of Bilbo's adventure, we can see him seamlessly combining the magical and the mundane, the worlds of Took and Baggins. The combination gives him a huge advantage over his friends, the dwarves.

The difference between Bilbo and his companions is again painfully apparent when they come to the exploration of the great hall. All of them have been feeling increasing fear and suspense in the continued silence and darkness. They can't be sure that Smaug isn't just trying to lure them to their deaths, and they hardly dare to hope that he might actually be gone. Bilbo's response to the tension is boldness, even recklessness. He finally cries out a shrill challenge to the dragon: "Stop playing hide-and-seek! Give me a light, and then eat me, if you can catch me!" (215). Bilbo is not just slipping into over-confidence again here; he is being bravely resolute. He knows that he would be helpless against Smaug; he has no illusions about that. In the end, however, he would rather die in the light, throwing insults and defiance at his enemy, than cower in the dark. Bilbo is the stinging fly once again.

The dwarves, on the other hand, opt for cowering. They are still huddling just where Bilbo left them. Rather than helping Bilbo or joining him in standing up to the enemy they say they want to take vengeance on, they desperately try to shush him. Thorin attempts to cloak his cowardice in formal language, carefully explaining that Mr. Baggins is "still officially their expert burglar and investigator" (216). He can use his own judgment in his professional capacity, and meanwhile

Thorin and the dwarves will fearlessly "wait in the tunnel for his report." When Bilbo's courage finally fails him, Thorin, concluding that the dragon must be absent after all, decides that it is safe to go fetch the hobbit they have been allowing to act as dragon bait. Balin's comment that "it is about our turn to help" seems to express both shame and gentle reproof of Thorin for his rather questionable leadership (218). Balin's willingness somewhat redeems the dwarves, but they are clearly as far behind Bilbo in pluck as they are in wisdom.

Once the dwarves see the treasure, however, they quickly swing back from fearful despair to shortsighted jubilance. Most of the dwarves are overcome by simple-minded greed, stuffing their pockets with gems, which will do them no manner of good. The narrator also warns us that the heart of a dwarf can often be made fierce by gold. Nevertheless, we can also see that there is something rather beautiful happening here. The love of the dwarves for the work of their fathers is not simply possessive or miserly. They hold up the "old treasures" to the torchlight, "caressing and fingering them" (218). They aren't simply indulging in private greed, either; they share their delight with each other, speaking aloud and crying out to one another. In a simple overflowing of merriment, Fili and Kili take up golden harps—just like the "harps of gold" in their original song (15)—and strike them, filling the hall "with a melody that had long been silent" (219). The dwarves have returned to their ancient home, and the halls that have heard nothing but silence or the rumbling of the dragon are brought to life with music and harmony.

Even Bilbo gets swept up in this moment. Thorin gives Bilbo his coat of *mithril* mail with its belt of pearls and crystals. Remember how much Bilbo loved the fine brass buttons on his waistcoat, and how much he regretted losing them at the goblins' back door. Now he shines and glitters splendidly indeed, and he wishes for a mirror in which to examine himself. "I feel magnificent," he thinks (219).

Bilbo's innocent-seeming pleasure in his beautiful new coat might inspire caution, though. Understandable as it is, it should remind us of Smaug's absurd vanity about his appearance. In the moment when Bilbo is flattering Smaug into showing him his underbelly again, Bilbo declares, "What magnificence to possess a waistcoat of fine diamonds!" (208). Bilbo, his own belly now glittering with white gems, uses the same word to describe himself. But Bilbo has learned his lesson and is not going to be carried away into self-aggrandizement again. He tempers his admiration of his new finery with the recognition that "they would laugh on the Hill at home!" (219). Yet again, his memories from home keep him grounded.

Bilbo soon turns and attempts to encourage the dwarves to keep a sense of proportion as well, even in the moment of their reunion with their treasure. His own mind turns to more immediate practicalities, and he thinks that he "would give a good many of these precious goblets" for "a drink of something cheering out of one of Beorn's wooden bowls" (219). He speaks up, puncturing the dwarves' excitement in his attempt to bring them back to pressing realities: "What next? . . . This treasure is not yet won back. We are not looking for gold yet, but for a way of escape" (219). Notice that there are different levels on which Bilbo is appealing to his companions here. One is simply a reminder that they are getting distracted. A few minutes ago, they were in despair because they were trapped in the Mountain, apparently facing the choice between starving to death in the tunnel and being killed by the dragon waiting at the bottom of it. Now, they have found an unexpected and unexplained chance to escape from this deathtrap, and they are squandering it playing with jewels and harps.

He is also delivering a more grim reminder. The dwarves have, it seems, given in to the temptation to see this moment, the moment when they have arrived at their "long-forgotten gold," as an end in itself, a fulfillment of the quest that they sang about back in Bag-End (15). Once again, the dwarves are leaving a live dragon out of their calculations. Until Smaug is destroyed, they have not in any meaningful sense won their "harps and gold from him." Arming themselves with the legendary work of their forefathers may seem more practical than stuffing their pockets with gems, but even that is an illusion. Bilbo's question is pointed, but apt: "What good has any armour ever been before against Smaug the Dreadful?" (219). The fathers and grandfathers of the dwarves were quite likely wearing those very suits of armor and wielding the very weapons the dwarves have now taken up on the day the dragon came and killed them all. The dwarves are, so far as any of them know, no closer to the completion of their quest than they were when they were hiding in the dark of the tunnel.

Although the dwarves may not have accomplished very much, their own perspective has radically changed. At the beginning of the chapter, Thorin himself is feeling suffocated in the oppressive closeness of the dark tunnel, and he declares, "I must feel the wind on my face soon or die" (214). Once Thorin has the long-lost wealth of his people in his hands again, the situation is altogether different. Thorin is no longer a vagabond dwarf, as the elven raft-men labeled him. Now "royal indeed did Thorin look, clad in a coat of gold-plated rings, with a silver-hafted axe in a belt crusted with scarlet stones"

(219). It certainly does look as if the King under the Mountain has returned.

The title of the chapter, "Not at Home," touches on this central irony and conflict. Bilbo is the one to use the words "not at home," and when he says it, he is referring to the unexpected absence of the dragon (215). He is using strikingly homey language, of course, as if they had called on Smaug to fulfill a teatime engagement, but the prevailing assumption underlying Bilbo's words is that these halls are the home of the dragon. Bilbo and the dwarves are merely visitors—indeed, they are uninvited guests, even trespassers.

Thorin, on the other hand, now feels that *he* has returned home, and throughout the rest of the chapter, Bilbo is continually attempting to remind Thorin that he is "not at home," but rather in the lair of the dragon. Thorin starts referring to the darkened halls as "my palace." As they are walking through a "ruined chamber" filled with charred benches, rotting tables, and scattered skulls and bones, Thorin announces that they have arrived at Thror's great "hall of feasting and of council" (220). Bilbo, by contrast, refers to the place as a "nasty, clockless, timeless hole." When Thorin laughingly defends it, replying, "Don't call my palace a nasty hole! You wait till it has been cleaned and redecorated!" (222), Bilbo again attempts to puncture his enthusiasm and his fine visions by reminding him, "That won't be till Smaug's dead." Thorin may think of the mountain halls as his palace, but Bilbo reminds him of their current owner when he calls the Front Gate of Thorin's kingdom "Smaug's front doorstep" (221). Bilbo steadfastly refuses to leave the dragon out of *his* calculations.

Bilbo, of course, is most emphatically "not at home." Neither the hall of the dwarf-king nor the lair of the dragon seems very homelike to him. As we saw in Chapter Eleven, Bilbo is very conscious of the distance between the Mountain and the Hill, as well as the differences between this nasty, dirty, deadly hole with its dust and echoing darkness and unburied skulls and bones and his neat, safe, quiet hobbit-hole back home. The dwarves may be tantalizingly close to their long-awaited homecoming, but Bilbo is only approaching the end of his outward journey. He is even now as far from Bag-End as he will ever get.

Burglar Bilbo: The Arkenstone Heist

Bilbo never really does fit in with the dwarves. He is their companion—they even look to him for leadership—but he remains separate, sharing their experiences but not their perspective. When the narrator tells us in Chapter Twelve that Bilbo "had become the real leader in their adventure," he adds, "he had begun to have ideas and plans of his own" (203). In Chapter Sixteen, we will see that Bilbo's ideas will not always be ideas that the dwarves will like very much.

The entrance into Smaug's lair marks the culmination of Bilbo's career as a burglar, as Thorin reminds him in his impressive speech on the doorstep at the beginning of Chapter Twelve. When Bilbo sneaks down the tunnel to Smaug's lair, he is acutely conscious of how important the moment is for his career. Bilbo has accomplished a lot as a burglar, but his thought process in the Lonely Mountain makes it apparent that even after the spiders and the elven prison, he still feels the need to prove himself to the dwarves. When he steals the golden cup from Smaug's hoard, right under the nose of the sleeping dragon, Bilbo reflects triumphantly on what this will do for his professional standing. "I've done it!" he says to himself. "This will show them. 'More like a grocer than a burglar' indeed! Well, we'll hear no more of that" (199). And Bilbo gets just the response he had been hoping for. The dwarves "praised him and patted him on the back and put themselves and all their families for generations to come at his service." By any estimate, Bilbo is a "really first-class and legendary burglar" (33). He has accomplished the mission for which he was hired, and all is well.

The awkward truth is that Bilbo's glorious theft of the cup is actually quite pointless. It may be an impressive piece of burglary, and his employers certainly appreciate it, but it accomplishes nothing. As Smaug maliciously points out, the cup is "not much use on the mountain-side" (206). Indeed, the fruitlessness of Bilbo's fulfillment of his professional appointment calls into question the dwarves' entire strategy.

What, exactly, did they want a burglar for? A burglar's job is to sneak into houses and steal treasure. Smaug assumes that thieving is the dwarves' whole goal; he believes they plan to "steal the gold bit by bit" (206). Was that, in fact, what the dwarves had originally been thinking, prior to the singing of old songs in Lake-town? It seems possible, considering how little they have thought about how they can kill the dragon, which would have to be the starting point of any other plan. If that was their idea, however, it was a very bad one, as both Bilbo and Smaug see very clearly. Bilbo points out that if they wanted the whole hoard of Thror burgled, they "ought to have brought five hundred burglars not one" (202). Smaug makes the further point that even if they succeeded in this unlikely task, they would have made no real progress, for they could still have no profit from the treasure until they had gotten it safely out of the Desolation surrounding the Mountain.

The dwarves freely admit that they had given no thought to "delivery" or "cartage" or "armed guards and tolls" (206). Obviously, what they really need, and what their desire for vengeance demands, is the slaying of the dragon. For that job, their little burglar is quite useless: "Getting rid of dragons is not at all in my line," Bilbo protests (203).*

The shocking lack of advance planning on the part of the dwarves is perhaps something that we are prepared to believe of them. They have shown themselves so foolish and impulsive that it seems quite credible that they would have overlooked so basic a flaw in their plans. We must remember, however, that this was not their plan originally, but Gandalf's. Coming up empty in his search for a potential dragon-slayer, Gandalf had "settled on burglary" (21), selecting Mr. Baggins for the post. Events have already shown, of course, that bringing Bilbo along on the journey was a good idea. It would seem likely, therefore, that Gandalf's suggestion to bring a burglar was a good one and that there is in fact some burglarious deed that will need to be accomplished before the end.

In Chapter Thirteen, we come at last to Bilbo's final act of burglary. Instead of striking a blow against the dragon or recovering some precious thing for his friends, Bilbo's last theft is, in essence, from the dwarves themselves. Bilbo will crown

---

* It is a remarkable fact that in his original conception of *The Hobbit*, Tolkien did indeed plan to make Bilbo the dragon-slayer, unlikely though it may seem. Bilbo was to have crawled onto Smaug's belly and driven Sting so far into the dragon that it entirely disappeared, at which point Bilbo would have had to jump into a huge golden cup in order to avoid being drowned in the dragon's blood, which would have swept Bilbo in his cup out of the hall in a river while Smaug thrashed and destroyed the hall around him in his death-throes. Tolkien changed his idea about this very early on, however, and replaced it with the more plausible protestation that Bilbo gives here in the published text. See Rateliff, 496.

his career by stealing one of the most valuable objects in Middle-earth: the Arkenstone of Thrain.

When the dwarves have talked about the treasure of their ancestors, their emphasis has primarily been on their respect for the craftsmanship of old, on the works wrought by their fathers. The Arkenstone was "cut and fashioned by the dwarves" (217), but it cannot really be said to be their highest achievement of craftsmanship. Remember in the dwarves' first song all the references to infusing light into gems. The dwarf smiths caught light "to hide in gems on hilt of sword," and they strung "the flowering stars" on necklaces and hung "the dragon-fire" on crowns and "meshed the light of moon and sun" in twisted wire (15). The Arkenstone seems to have been the model that inspired all these efforts. Thorin's love for the Arkenstone is not a reflection of his reverence for the craftsmanship of his forefathers; it is a love for a beauty and wonder outside and beyond the skill of the dwarves, discovered by them at the roots of the Mountain.

The Arkenstone is the Heart of the Mountain, and to love it is to love the beauty of the natural world itself. Thorin explains that the Arkenstone is "like a globe with a thousand facets; it shone like silver in the firelight, like water in the sun, like snow under the stars, like rain upon the Moon!" (212). The loveliness of all the earth, reflected in so much dwarvish artistry, shines within it. The Arkenstone seems to be tied up with the dwarf kingdom itself in a deep and symbolic sense. Just as the land has withered since the Mountain was usurped by the dragon, so all was right and harmonious when a Dwarf King ruled under the Mountain, the Arkenstone in his hands.

When Bilbo enters the empty treasure-hall on his third trip, the reddish glow of the dragon is gone. What replaces it is "a pale white glint," the shining of the Arkenstone that twinkles in the darkness like a star and draws Bilbo directly to it (215). The Arkenstone's light may be very different from the dragon light, but Bilbo's attraction to the stone is distinctly dragonish. He is enthralled by the gem, and he doesn't even seem to pick it up of his own free will, for his arm "went towards it drawn by its enchantment" (217). Bilbo's heart is drawn to it as strongly as his hand, and as impressed as he had been by the mound of gold when he first saw it, he now declares, "I think I would choose this, if they took all the rest!" Bilbo has claimed his Reward.

It is quite clear that Bilbo knows full well that he is doing something wrong. As he thrusts the gem into "his deepest pocket," he closes his eyes, as if he himself doesn't want to witness what he is doing (217). He recognizes that he has a moral obligation to tell the dwarves about the Arkenstone, for he has already heard Thorin speaking of how precious the stone is to him, but he puts off this confession until some point in the indeterminate future. When Bilbo thinks to himself, "Now I am a burglar indeed," he is acknowledging that he has just crossed a line. If he goes on and keeps this thing for himself, he really will be a thief.

We must not allow our knowledge of what Bilbo is going to do with the Arkenstone in Chapter Sixteen to influence us too much, at this point. When he puts the gem in his pocket, Bilbo anticipates that "trouble would yet come of it" (217). It very much looks as if the story could be headed for a tragic turn. Just as the dragon is off getting killed, the dragon-sickness seems to be setting in among Bilbo and his companions. Could the story of their journey together end in murder and back-stabbing and a bright gem clasped in bloody hands? At the end of Chapter Thirteen, that seems like a very real possibility.

There is one solid reason to hope that Bilbo's theft of the Arkenstone will not end in disaster. As Bilbo has been engaged in his official capacity as burglar in Chapters Twelve and Thirteen, sneaking into the Mountain and stealing treasure, Tolkien has taken repeated steps to affirm that Bilbo is no criminal. When Bilbo steals the golden cup, the narrator informs us that Smaug "shifted into other dreams of greed and violence, lying there in his stolen hall while the little hobbit toiled back up the long tunnel" (199). In the very moment that Bilbo steals something valuable for the first time, we are given a strong reminder that the person Bilbo is stealing the cup from is not its rightful owner, but a violent, greedy plunderer who himself stole the hall and everything in it. The rightful owner, in fact, is waiting at the top of the tunnel. Bilbo is not stealing treasure; he is simply repossessing it, reclaiming stolen property in the name of justice.

Smaug, in his conversation with Bilbo, calls him "a thief and a liar," but Bilbo is no thief and actually tells him no lies (204).* Burglary might be a shady career, generally speaking, but Bilbo maintains his moral integrity. Despite the career path that was chosen for him, Bilbo's general honesty and forthrightness give us reason to hope that perhaps the theft of the Arkenstone will turn to good and not to evil.

---

* Actually, Bilbo does tell Smaug one lie, when he exclaims that Smaug's obviously flawed belly-armor is "Perfect!" and "Flawless!" (208). This one untruth, however, doesn't seem to undermine his honesty very much.

14

The Meeting of Opposites

Smaug's Hydrophobia

When Smaug descends on Lake-town in wrath and flame, the fight seems like a terrible mismatch. The wooden buildings of the town with their roofs of thatch stand defenseless against the blazing fire of the dragon. "All had been drenched with water before he came," we are assured, and yet "fire leaped from thatched roofs and wooden beam-ends" until "flames unquenchable sprang high into the night" (227). The people of the Lake are as helpless to escape the destroyer as their homes. As they try to flee in boats, the narrator tells us of Smaug's plans to prepare a welcome for them on the shores: "Soon he would set all the shoreland woods ablaze and wither every field and pasture."

The warriors of Lake-town put up a hearty resistance; in fact, they are the only people who "had dared to give battle to him for many an age" (227). But all their valor is in vain. The dragon can dive unheeding "straight through the arrow-storm, reckless in his rage," for "no arrow hindered Smaug or hurt him more than a fly from the marshes." He once boasted to Bilbo, "I kill where I wish and none dare resist" (207), and it seems to be only too true. The despair and destruction of Lake-town are mere entertainment for Smaug, the "Chiefest and Greatest of Calamities" (204). He is "enjoying the sport of town-baiting more than he had enjoyed anything for years," and he is looking forward to following it up with a casual game of refugee-hunting later on (228). When, with a sweep of his tail, he smashes the roof of the Great House, the hall where the dwarves were so recently feasted amidst the singing of old songs, Smaug does indeed look like "the real King under the Mountain" (213).

But this view of the event, quite understandably held by the screaming, weeping people of Lake-town, is not the only possible view. The title of the chapter, "Fire and Water," prompts us to look at the fight between Smaug and Lake-town from an entirely different perspective. If the fight between the dragon and the town on the Lake is like the elemental conflict between fire and water, the end is indeed a foregone conclusion, and Smaug cannot possibly hope to win.

Even before Smaug crashes down in ruin, we are given glimpses of his weakness that point to the dragon's comparative helplessness. When Smaug approaches Lake-town, his very first move is an attempt to land on the bridge connecting the town to the shore, but he finds that "the bridge was gone, and his enemies were on an island in deep water" (226). I believe that we are supposed to understand that Smaug is "foiled" by this tactic because the bridge was the only open space big enough and strong enough for him to land on safely; now his only other option would be an awkward perch on top of a house. Smaug is afraid of the water. He knows that if "he plunged into it, a vapour and a steam would arise enough to cover all the land with a mist for days" — in short, a direct conflict between fire and water would begin, and end, with predictable results. This is why Smaug's plan is to burn the townspeople's buildings and drive them to take refuge in boats and eventually on the dry land, where he fears nothing. But the lake is "mightier than he"; he knows perfectly well that "it would quench him."

Smaug is killed by an arrow, of course, and yet the spectacle of his destruction is again given to us in elemental terms. He spouts fire into the air as he shrieks out his death cry, and then he falls onto the town, splintering it "to sparks and gledes," as if he himself were extinguishing the flames consuming the town by scattering the fuel (229). Then, with a tremendous cloud of steam, "the lake roared in" and Smaug the Mighty is swallowed up with only "a hiss, a gushing whirl, and then silence." Water conquers fire.

The descriptions of the fight and of Smaug's downfall invite us to see his attack on Lake-town not only as a mighty dragon mercilessly crushing a defenseless town, but also as an upstart flame daring to assault a massive body of water. When we see the battle as a conflict between Fire and Water, the outcome—which at first seems miraculous—looks inevitable. The prophecies of the old songs might not have come true quite as the people of Lake-town expected, but the wider, elemental view of the events at Esgaroth encourages us to hold out hope.

The Awakening of Lake-town

In Chapter Ten, we looked at the divided views of the people of Lake-town. Most of the people were, like the dwarves, swept up into a wild and largely irrational enthusiasm. Forgetting the dragon, they boisterously sang songs about sudden floods of riches and the spontaneous end of all grief and suffering. The other voice in the town was that of the Master, whose cold practicality remained skeptical, seeking instead to manipulate events for his political and financial benefit. Neither side was correct in its response to the unexpected return of the wet and bedraggled King under the Mountain, and Chapter Ten ended with both Master and people confidently continuing in their skewed perspectives. The crisis that would test their beliefs by fire had not yet come.

On the last night of Esgaroth, both perspectives are still plainly on display. The comments we overhear from the common people of Lake-town are as foolish as anything we have heard from dwarf, man, or hobbit in the book so far. When the light from Smaug's fire in his attack on the dwarves' camp is seen in the town, it suggests to them only the forging of gold by the King under the Mountain. Anyone who stopped to think about that idea even for a moment would see how silly it is. Even assuming Thorin had somehow taken up his kingly residence in the Mountain once more, why would his forging of gold be visible as an actual glow on the mountainside? The suggestion that the golden light visible on the northern end of the Lake is wealth flowing from the Gates of the King is even more absurd. Even if Thorin were sending boatloads of gold to the town somehow (though they know he has no boats), they would not flood the darkness with bursts of golden light. As another chorus of "The King beneath the Mountain" breaks out on the quay, one is tempted to conclude that the average Lake-dweller is not equipped with an overabundance of intellect (226). It would be more accurate, however, to say that they are not really bringing their reason into play at all. The people of Lake-town have responded to Thorin's arrival by immersing themselves in a fantasy that is only tangentially connected to the old prophecies that they dimly remember, and it is almost completely detached from the world around them.

These people receive a harsh awakening from their pretty dreams that night. When the light they believe to be a magical tide of wealth resolves itself into searing bursts of dragon-flame, they begin to think that the "prophecies had gone rather wrong" (226). In fact, the dragon's attack neither proves nor disproves the prophecies. What it does is reduce the irrational fantasies that the people had built upon them to ash. The result is a swift reversal of sentiment. In the midst of the town's destruction, the "old songs of mirth to come" are exchanged for "mourning and weeping" over present grief and pain (227). The townspeople who had stood waiting for the opportunity to cheer the dwarves now curse them. When their homes are destroyed, their illusions are demolished as well, and they are left to face a new reality on the dark, cold shores of the Lake.

The practicality of the Master proves more versatile, and thus more durable. Despite a brief twinge of fear and uncertainty at the end, he disbelieved the songs about Thorin's arrival. However, he took advantage by helping in the composition of new songs that would turn the enthusiasm of dwarves and townspeople alike to his profit.

When that pleasant vision dies a sizzling death in the waters of the Lake, the people of the town blame the Master for his poor leadership, for leaving "the town so soon, while some were still willing to defend it" (229). This is actually a high-water mark for Lake-town rationality; the Master is not to blame for the dragon's attack, but he is genuinely culpable for giving up and abandoning the town in the midst of its greatest crisis. The Master responds to this sensible reaction of the townsfolk by building a new irrational fantasy on the smoldering ruins of the old one. By expanding on the disappointment of the initial "pleasant fancies" about the dwarves (230), he establishes an unpleasant one in its place: that "the dwarves had stirred the dragon up against them deliberately" (231). The Master holds himself aloof from all of these wild ideas, but being without belief, he can more easily direct or even manufacture them. The Master is invested in nothing, but he can exploit anything.

In Lake-town, there is only one voice that avoids both poles, that indulges in neither self-deceiving imagination nor self-serving manipulation. That voice, of course, is the grim voice of Bard the Bowman. Bard is the one who will ground the people of Lake-town in hard reality while also bringing them forward to the fulfillment of the prophecies of old.

Bard's voice is first and foremost the voice of gloom. Before we learn his name, he is only a "grim-voiced fellow," a discordant voice in the midst of an upsurge of outrageous optimism (226). In Chapter Thirteen, Bilbo is compelled to be a continual wet blanket, damping down the spirits of the over-exuberant Thorin who wants to proclaim the Mountain his own before the dragon has been accounted for. The grim voice of Bard plays a similar role at the beginning of Chapter Fourteen, puncturing the ridiculous moonshine of his fellow citizens with the reminder that the dragon is the "only king under the Mountain we have ever known" (225). When they see the lights approaching and the people start singing, Bard declares, "The dragon is coming or I am a fool!" (226). Bard, it turns out, is no fool.

The voice of Bard is also a voice of leadership. His warning cry to the Master almost coincides with the warning trumpets; it is as if Bard's voice *is* the warning trumpets that "were suddenly sounded, and echoed along the rocky shores" (226). He submits to the sovereignty of the Master, but his own voice rings with authority as he shouts, "Cut the bridges! To arms! To arms!" The men of Lake-town hear it, and it is only the grim voice of Bard, now named for the first time, who gives the men the courage to give battle to Smaug. The company of archers of which Bard is the captain are the very last "that held their ground among the burning houses" (228). More than ever, Bard is now "grim-voiced and grim-faced," but he resolves to follow his own urging and "fight to the last arrow" (227).

At the climax of the battle, we learn that Bard's voice is also the voice of legend. In the middle of the fight, the narrator pauses to tell us that Bard is the direct heir of Girion, Lord of Dale, descendant of the child smuggled out of the ruined town, like a lost heir of kings in a fairy tale.* As Bard prepares to shoot his final arrow, the thrush appears. This is the moment at which many lines of destiny are converging. The magical thrush, symbol of the old peace of the Mountain kingdom, instrument of the moon-letter prophecy, and the foreshadowing of the death of the dragon, brings to Bard, heir of Girion, the news he learned from Bilbo, the Luck-

---

* Such fairy tales are apparently told in Bilbo's world as well as our own. Remember that among the stories that Gandalf used to tell and that Bilbo loved to hear as a child were the ones about "the unexpected luck of widows' sons" (7).

wearer, the Chosen and Selected Burglar. Because the dwarves and the hobbit were standing by the grey stone on Durin's Day, the secret door was opened. Because Bilbo entered the tunnel and faced the dragon and escaped, the thrush knows of Smaug's weak spot. Because Bard is of the blood of Dale, he can understand the thrush's speech. Because Bard is brave and steadfast, he stands alone amidst the burning ruins of his town, ready to shoot his very last arrow. Because the Black Arrow did indeed come from the forges of the true King under the Mountain, it flies true. The shaft of fate strikes home and sinks into the heart of the dragon, "barb, shaft and feather" (228). Lake-town is saved, but also destroyed.

In the aftermath of the battle, Bard's voice is also the voice of reason. His entrance into the camp of his miserable fellow townspeople is extremely dramatic. They have just been praising his courage and "his last mighty shot," pledging that they would make him king if he had survived (229). Then, "in the very midst of their talk," Bard emerges from the shadows, and the people of Lake-town find that a second king of legend has stepped out of the darkness to stand wet and bedraggled before them. Like Thorin, Bard has a sense of the importance of the moment, and he declares himself: "I am Bard, of the line of Girion; I am the slayer of the dragon!" (230). Knowing the people of Lake-town, we might now expect enthusiasm of record proportions to break out.

But Bard steers a middle course, neither resisting the fulfillment of prophecy as the Master would do, nor allowing the imaginations of the people to run wild. He does not seek to profit from the people's adulation, continuing to act as the servant of the Master. But he also does not turn away from the kingship that the night's turn of fortune has now laid open to him. The people vehemently reject the Master's suggestion that the wise course would be to turn from their talk of kingships and instead "hope to rebuild our town, and enjoy again in time its peace and riches" (230), but Bard refuses to be rash and try to re-create the old kingdom overnight. With Bard there to resist both the machinations of the Master and the precipitousness of the people, Lake-town is prepared to embrace the real fulfillment of the old songs. In the sorrow and pain on the shores of the Lake, there are no more illusions about the evaporation of all griefs. They may indeed build a bright future and re-establish the kingdoms of old, but the road to that destination passes through their present suffering. Their one consolation is that the hopes of "recompense for all their harm" from the fabled treasure of the Mountain, which had been so fanciful, are now perfectly rational (231). The dragon has now been permanently removed from the equation.

The Writing of *The Hobbit:*
The Shadow of Grief

Chapter Fourteen is in some ways the climax of the book's action, the apparent consummation of all the strokes of luck and fortune. The chapter is still far from the conclusion of the story's action, but the death of the dragon and the destruction of Lake-town usher in an important and noticeable shift in the tone of the narrative.

The story has never shied away from terrifying or gruesome things. Back in Chapter One, I talked about how Tolkien presented frightening or sorrowful things but tended to soften their impact on his juvenile audience with comedy. This pattern is consistent through all of Bilbo's dangers, and we are always invited to mix laughter in with our experience of bears' houses, spiders' webs, and dragons' lairs.

After the ruin of Lake-town, however, we are given no such padding of the emotional blow. The narrator lists among the things that the townspeople have to be thankful for the fact that "three quarters of the people of the town had at least escaped alive" (229). That's a sobering figure, for it introduces us to the reality that fully a quarter of the people in the town had died either by fire or by drowning during the dragon's attack. In case the solemnity of the situation is lost on us in that one reference, the narrator expands on the sufferings of the people, which are only just beginning as their town sinks beneath the surface of the Lake. The excitement about the dwarf gold now lying up for grabs, as they believe, is severely dampened by the hardships of the people, which multiply as the days pass. "Many took ill of wet and cold and sorrow that night, and afterwards died," we are told, "and in the days that followed there was much sickness and great hunger" (231). The story is moving on to happy endings, but sorrow will always be near to it now. The joy of the good resolution will be tempered, as it always is in Tolkien's fiction, with the reality of human suffering. The narrator's voice, once so playful, now turns as grim as the voice of Bard himself.

15

To Sit on a Heap of Gold and Starve

"THE GATHERING OF THE CLOUDS"

The Desolation of the Dragon: The Adventure Continues

The death of the dragon at Bard's hand seems to be a wholly satisfactory conclusion to the story. Bilbo and the dwarves have been on a long journey to reclaim their treasure and, if possible, bring their "curses home to Smaug" (24). Now, with a great deal of help and far more than the usual allowance of luck, they have achieved their goal. The dragon is dead and the treasure regained. The Kingdom beneath the Mountain can now be re-established. As a bonus, events have turned up an heir to Girion of Dale, and he has satisfied the demands of justice by slaying the destroyer of his ancestral land and people himself. Surely the "happily ever after" part of this particular fairy tale must be imminent, and we will soon see Thorin restored to the seat of Thror in majesty and hear the merry bells ringing in the town of Dale once more. We have all kinds of reasons to imagine, with Bilbo, that "the adventure was, properly speaking, over with the death of the dragon" (237). If we believe this, however, we will find ourselves, like Bilbo, very much mistaken.

The transition into the next phase of the story is provided by Roäc the raven. Roäc stands at a crossing of the ways, in several senses. For one thing, the raven's speech to Thorin brings together the memories of the past with a vision for the future. The old bird, bald and blind, aged and decrepit, is like an embodiment of the memory of the old days of peace and plenty, which have nearly been forgotten in the desert waste. While all the rest of Thror's subjects have been scattered or killed and their descendants grown forgetful, the ravens "remember still the king that was of old" (235). Like the thrush, they are living memorials of a time when dwarf, man, elf, and beast were living in harmony.

Roäc offers advice to Thorin for the future. What the ravens desire is a return to the concord of old. "We would see peace once more among dwarves and men and elves after the long desolation," he explains (236). He gives very sound and practical advice toward this noble end, urging Thorin to trust in "him that shot the dragon with his bow." Roäc even provides further explanation: since Bard is "of the race of Dale, of the line of Girion," it stands to reason that cooperation with him would be Thorin's first step in re-establishing the thriving joint kingdom of Mountain and Dale.

Roäc also provides news of the present, and this news will bring Thorin to his first major decision as king, a decision that will play a big part in defining the course of his kingship and the nature of his kingdom. The raven acknowledges that some of his news will be "tidings of joy to you, and some you will not think so good" (235). The good news, of course, is that Smaug is dead. The not-so-good news is of the gathering of several armies now converging on the Mountain from Lake and Wood. As the chapter title recognizes, a storm is building. War is possible, but peace is preferable, with restoration of the friendship and allegiances of old the most desired end of all. Roäc has given his news and his counsel; now Thorin must choose a path.

Thorin's response to Roäc is swift and decisive. He bursts into anger, vowing, "none of our gold shall thieves take or the violent carry off while we are alive" (236). Thorin considers himself under attack already, and without even a single attempt to talk to the people approaching the Mountain, he immediately begins preparing for war.

The new dwarf-king has some justification for his actions, of course. Roäc did warn him that an army of elves is on the march, and Thorin and the Elvenking are not exactly on friendly terms at this point. The raven has even relayed the ill will toward the dwarves held by many of the refugees of Lake-town, thanks to the Master's instigation. However, Roäc also gives Thorin good reasons to believe that peace can still be maintained, despite appearances. The elves are not violent and cruel people, and there is only the wishful thinking of the carrion birds to suggest that they are interested in battle. The men of the Lake are not marching under the unscrupulous direction of the Machiavellian Master, whom Roäc obviously, and very rightly, distrusts. They are led by Bard, whom the raven affirms to be grim, but true. The people approaching the Mountain are not dragons or goblins, but Good People, even some of the very people who have already befriended and assisted Thorin and his companions. The situation is volatile and intricate, but war is far from certain; all might still be well.

Thorin does not appear to give these complexities a moment's thought. The narrator cautioned us earlier that "when the heart of a dwarf, even the most respectable, is wakened by gold and by jewels, he grows suddenly bold, and he may become fierce" (218). All Thorin can see is a threat to his gold, and upon seeing that, he is instantly ready to take on all comers. He has taken the delicate web of facts and advice that the wise Roäc has laid before him and hacked through it with an axe. Roäc's politely neutral response that he "will not say if this counsel be good or bad" shows plainly that the restoration of the old Kingdom under the Mountain in the wake of the dragon's death is already going awry (237).

The rising tension around the Mountain, however, cannot be attributed solely to Thorin's belligerent possessiveness. Both the Wood-elves and the Lake-men also bear their own portion of responsibility. Remember that one of the major faults of the Elvenking is his desire to increase his own glory and reputation by the enlargement of his personal treasure hoard (155). The elves have no claim on the treasure; but when the king hears of the death of Smaug, he immediately sets off with his army, simply as a profiteer. The advance of the Elvenking's army is shadowed by flocks of crows, who are "gathered thick above him" (232). The elven army has drawn the attention not only of carrion birds, but of singularly unsavory ones. It is possible that some of the very same "nasty suspicious-looking creatures" that used to linger around Smaug's Front Gate have now attached themselves to the elven-host (235). The elves are still Good People, as they show when they turn aside to help the people of the Lake. But in their march on the Mountain, they have much more in common with the crows overhead than they might like to admit. The army of the Wood is descending on the Mountain simply as scavengers, seeking to gorge themselves on the remains of the misery of others.

Bard, as well, fails to emerge spotless from careful scrutiny. He may be coming to the Mountain in peace, but his decisions as leader of the approaching army certainly invite misinterpretation. Bard believes that Thorin and the dwarves are probably dead, so when armed scouts arrive at the gate and find there the defenses the dwarves have recently built, "very great was their surprise" (238). They are not left in doubt about who has fortified the entrance, either. Thorin identifies himself loudly and asks what is certainly a sensible question under the circumstances: "Who are you . . . that come as if in war to the gates of Thorin son of Thrain?" (239). It isn't quite clear why they are armed for war, but Bard's response to this challenge is telling. Rather than coming to greet Thorin as a friend, he immediately moves the camp of his army "to the east of the river, right between the arms of the Mountain." Without a greeting and before making any attempt to talk, Bard places his forces in a more advantageous position for besieging Thorin's defenses. He may say the next day that he and the dwarf-king are "not yet foes," but his actions are indistinguishable from those of an opposing general in the field (241). His actions could easily be interpreted as an aggressive move, even by someone less paranoid and touchy than Thorin.

Thorin's own mindset is clearly articulated in the song that the dwarves sing to please him on the night before the parley. This song is "much like the song they had sung long before in Bilbo's little hobbit-hole," at least in form:

Under the Mountain dark and tall
The King has come unto his hall!
His foe is dead, the Worm of Dread,
And ever so his foes shall fall.

The sword is sharp, the spear is long,
The arrow swift, the Gate is strong;
The heart is bold that looks on gold;
The dwarves no more shall suffer wrong.

The dwarves of yore made mighty spells,
While hammers fell like ringing bells
In places deep, where dark things sleep,
In hollow halls beneath the fells.

On silver necklaces they strung
The light of stars, on crowns they hung
The dragon-fire, from twisted wire
The melody of harps they wrung.

The mountain throne once more is freed!
O! wandering folk, the summons heed!
Come haste! Come haste! across the waste!
The king of friend and kin has need.

Now call we over mountains cold,
'Come back into the caverns old!'
Here at the Gates the king awaits,
His hands are rich with gems and gold.

The king is come unto his hall
Under the Mountain dark and tall.

The Worm of Dread is slain and dead,
And ever so our foes shall fall!
(239–40)

The original song described their halls and the beauty of their lost treasures, told the story of their loss, and looked forward to the beginning of the journey to recover them. The new song also looks forward to action, but it is a war to defend the halls of their newly restored king. Bilbo is right to think the song warlike; the stanza about harps and song has been squeezed into a single line in order to make room for a full stanza in praise of weaponry and declaring their resolution to "suffer wrong" no more. The stanza about necklaces and crowns is largely incorporated from the original, but it is now given a wholly different force. Before, the description of the wondrous works of the ancient dwarves was a lament and an expression of reverence. Now, the same words are used as a spur to violence, a rallying cry to battle. Thorin is characterized as the "king of friend and kin," a generous lord of a mighty people, but apparently the definition of "friend" has become rather narrow.

Perhaps the most overtly threatening lines in the whole song are the repeated refrain at the end of the first and last stanza: "And ever so his foes shall fall!" In this line, the dwarves confidently predict that all of their enemies will suffer the same fate as the dragon. The dwarves' poetical chest-thumping seems to have over-reached itself here, falling into unintended irony. Both verses implicitly claim credit for the death of the dragon, even though everyone present knows perfectly well that no dwarf had even the most indirect involvement with the slaying of Smaug. They are saying that the dwarves' enemies will always suffer the same fate as the dragon, but that would actually translate to "death at the hands of our allies, guided by fate, assisted by the local fauna, and enabled by the information obtained by our friend the hobbit." In short, the slaying of Smaug was a community effort by those who have been the dwarves' well-wishers. Sadly, those also turn out to be the very people these lines are intended to threaten.

There is also a second irony that further undermines the dwarves' new song, this one concerning the gate of the Mountain. The song depicts the king waiting at the gates for his loyal kin with his hands full of gold and gems, associating the gate with welcome and with the outpouring of the king's generosity. This conception is very much in line with the previous ideas we have seen connected to the gate. When Smaug was alive, the Front Gate was a place of dread, a steaming hole from which the dragon might emerge in wrath at any moment. In the old days, however, the Gate of Thror was the open boundary between the two realms of the Mountain and Dale. The gate is given special significance by the fact that the River Running flows out of it from its subterranean wellspring. Figuratively, the life and well-being of the whole region flowed from the open gate of the King under the Mountain. The prophetic songs of Lake-town also emphasize this, anticipating the time when the river that emerges from those gates will run with gold from the underground kingdom. The dwarves have a more restricted conception of the outflowing of the royal generosity, but their image in the song clearly harmonizes with this older idea.

The dwarves overlooked something in their song, however. Thorin's kingdom has no gate at all. Where the gate of the King under the Mountain used to be, Thorin has built a solid stone wall with no door. This former site of union, of outflowing enrichment to the lands about, has been bricked up by the new king. Thorin's immovable gate is the perfect symbol of Thorin's kingdom so far, and it falls well short of anyone's hopes for the restoration of the kingdom of old.

The following day, that blank wall stands between Thorin and his neighbors as they begin their official parley. When Bard comes to speak about the treasure, he gives three different reasons why Thorin should surrender some of the gold. First, since Bard himself killed the dragon, he deserves a share of its gold. Surely if anyone has earned a reward (to use Thorin's language), it is Bard. Second, Bard points out that the treasure Smaug had collected is not only the treasure of Thorin's father and grandfather, but also the wealth of the Men of Dale. As the heir of Girion, Bard is pointing out that Thorin is laying claim to some treasure that isn't his at all. Bilbo considers these claims to be obviously sound, and he (wrongly) assumes that Thorin will have to "admit what justice was in them" (241).

In his third claim, Bard goes beyond mere justice and appeals to Thorin's charity, honor, and compassion. Thorin's heated rejection of this last claim is jarring. He calls Bard's appeal to gratitude and generosity his "worst cause" and complains that he put it "last and in the chief place" (241). Thorin replies only with legalism, arguing that since the treasure did not rightfully belong to Smaug, damages for Smaug's actions should not be drawn from it. This response, of course, completely dismisses the fellow feeling, the empathy for his neighbors, to which Bard was appealing. In this third appeal lies an invitation to Thorin to step forward and re-establish the Kingdom under the Mountain in its glory of old, when it was a source of blessing, prosperity, and protection to all of the surrounding peoples. Thorin has the opportunity to open the Gate of the King once more and help to bring about the renewal of the lands, just as the old songs foretold. Thorin refuses this invitation with indignation. The gate is shut.

The dragon may be dead, but his spirit lives. The narrator warns us of the "power that gold has upon which a dragon has long brooded," and its effect on "dwarvish hearts" (241). The dragon-sickness remains, and Thorin has an acute case of it. This dragon-sickness is more than simple acquisitiveness. Smaug was not merely greedy; he was arrogant and thoroughly self-absorbed, as Thorin is becoming, locked behind his stone wall with his hoard. The spirit of division and distrust that Smaug attempted to plant in Bilbo is also a major symptom of this illness, and that spirit is clouding the judgment of more than just Thorin. The Elvenking's armed profiteering, Bard's pre-emptive siege, the dwarves' bellicose song—all bear the taint of the dragon-sickness. As Bilbo says, "The whole place still stinks of dragon" (243). Even after Smaug has been destroyed, the Desolation of the Dragon continues to spread, and it now threatens to bring the region around the Lonely Mountain to a final and complete ruin.

16

A Leap in the Dark

"A THIEF IN THE NIGHT"

The Desolation of the Dragon: The Stalemate Continues

The passing of the days brings no change to the siege of the Lonely Mountain, other than the steady worsening of Thorin's condition. The divisiveness and self-absorption characteristic of the dragon-sickness now shows itself further in Thorin's threats against his own companions. Not even the bonds of kinship or friendship can outweigh his claim on the Arkenstone. On the other side, Bard and the Elvenking implacably continue their campaign against the Mountain, posting rings of sentries lest the dwarves try to sneak out for supplies. Winter is coming, but no one seems to be getting into a "softer mood to parley" (245).

Roäc the raven attempts to talk some sense into Thorin. There is an irony, of course, in being rebuked by a raven for acquisitiveness, given the famous desire of ravens for "bright things" which they "hide in their dwellings" (235). Even the raven seems to find Thorin's obsession incomprehensible. In their first conversation, Roäc merely laid all the facts before

Thorin and left him to choose, reserving judgment even when Thorin responded with rashness and anger. Now Roäc is more direct. "I do not call this counsel good," he states flatly, patiently trying to show Thorin that his belligerence and his refusal to treat with his neighbors is creating a no-win situation (244). The raven asks pointedly, "How shall you be fed without the friendship and goodwill of the lands about you?" The question should remind us of Thorin's own explanation of how in former days the dwarves of the Mountain never "bothered to grow or find" food for themselves, because of the close relationship between Mountain and Dale (22). Roäc, who wanted very much to see the old peace return, seems to have little reason to hope for it.

Bilbo's Choices: An Offer

Into this deadlock steps Mr. Baggins. While the dwarf lord, the Elvenking, and the dragon-slayer stare implacably at each other across the waste, entrenched in their obstinate insistence on their rights and claims, Bilbo Baggins of Bag-End is preparing to show all of them the way out of this mess. Once before, standing fearfully in the darkness as Gollum crouched before him, Bilbo made a life-altering choice. He chose mercy over ruthlessness and put compassion above his own best interest. Now, in the Desolation of the Dragon, he is going to repeat that choice publicly, showing all these great people the only cure for the dragon-sickness.

As we build toward Bilbo's finest moment, Tolkien seems to go out of his way to remind us of how small a person Bilbo is. When the elf sentries hear him, they refer to him as "that queer little creature that is said to be their servant" (246).

Bilbo objects to the "servant" remark and obviously does not like being seen as a person of such little consequence. When he introduces himself to these same elves, he calls himself "companion of Thorin." Yet, though Bilbo might not like it, even the narrator insists on his smallness, when he informs us that "the beginnings of a plan had come into his little head" (244). Bilbo might have earned a place among the great people, but although he now wears his silver mail and his magical sword with ease, they still look a bit odd on him. He is a study in contrasts to Bard and the Elvenking, who sit "gazing curiously at him," for "a hobbit in elvish armour, partly wrapped in an old blanket, was something new to them" (247). Bilbo is acclimated enough to this world of high adventure to be able to approach these great captains, but he is also sufficiently out of place to be able to help them.

In Bard's reaction to Bilbo's news about Dain, we can see that the dragon-sickness is at work in the camp just as it is in the Mountain. "Why do you tell us this?" Bard demands, "grimly" as ever. "Are you betraying your friends, or are you threatening us?" (248). Bilbo protests about how "hasty" and "suspicious" Bard is; the dragon-slayer is certainly showing the kind of distrust that would have pleased the dragon himself. Thorin may have a "stiff neck," as Bombur admits (245), but Bard is equally unyielding in his resolve to starve Thorin on his pile of gold. When Bard condemns Thorin as a fool, Bilbo has to point out that Bard's own camping in the waste with winter coming shows little more sense.

Bilbo approaches Bard and the Elvenking with calm reason, much as Roäc does in his attempts to convince Thorin. In fact, Bilbo puts on "his best business manner," a very Baggins-like tone, which he first showed back in Bag-End (247). As Roäc's failure to get Thorin to see sense has proven, however, it takes more than reason to reach someone deep in the dragon-sickness. Roäc has nothing more to give, other than his own loyalty and obedience, which he continues to give in despair. Bilbo, of course, has more to offer.

Bilbo alone acts against the draconian spirit dominating both sides of the conflict. When Bilbo yields the Arkenstone to Bard, we must remember what this gesture costs him. Bilbo took the stone in the first place because he fell deeply under its enchantment, and he adds to that the conscious choice to keep it for himself. "I think I would choose this," he thought, "if they took all the rest!" (217). Even as Bilbo surrenders it, we can see his continuing desire for it in his "glance of longing" and in the "shudder" with which he hands it over (248). Bilbo is not only giving away the "marvellous stone," he is also renouncing his own right to any reward or compensation for his long journey and his great labors. We know he has not forgotten his rights because he still carries Thorin's contract letter in his pocket, lest those rights be challenged at some point. Bilbo is not immune to the dragon-sickness, but he alone has overcome it. In the midst of a stalemate caused by people insisting on their rights, Bilbo has given up everything.

Why does Bilbo do it? His own answer is quite simple: he wants "to avoid trouble for all concerned" (248). This is a self-effacing answer, one that tries to minimize the significance of his action and to downplay the seriousness of the situation. It would be more dramatic but no less true if he were to say, "I am trying to avert a war and establish a new alliance between nations." Like Roäc, Bilbo too would see the ancient harmony return to these lands.

But Bilbo is also thinking of other things that are simpler and more personal, but nevertheless profound. Bilbo implies in his conversation with Bombur at the beginning of the chapter that his desire for "the feel of grass at my toes" is even stronger than Thorin's desire for his treasure (245). After his great sacrifice, his dreams that night are not haunted by visions of glittering gems. He dreams instead of eggs and bacon, showing clearly what is worth more than a river of gold to *him*. I suggested back in Chapter Five that in the riddles he told to Gollum, Bilbo was in a sense acting as the spokesperson for light, warmth, vitality, conviviality, and order. Now, surrounded by the reek of the dragon, Bilbo again stands firm in support of the truly important things: tea-kettles, smoke-rings, and bacon.

Bilbo also shows the premium he places on loyalty and friendship by insisting on returning to the dwarves. The Elvenking's warning against it is prudent, and by going back to the Mountain, Bilbo places not only his reward but even his own safety in jeopardy. But Bilbo won't even consider staying. When Bard asks if Bilbo is betraying his friends or threatening them, he is trying to figure out which side Bilbo is on. If Bilbo were to bring the Arkenstone to Bard and remain in the camp, his action *would* be a betrayal. Bilbo doesn't want to switch sides. Instead, he is trying to build a bridge between them, to bring down the wall that Thorin has built and Bard has besieged, even at the risk of his own life.

Burglar Bilbo: An Honest Burglar

When Bilbo hides the Arkenstone in his pocket, he says that he has become a burglar indeed. The taking of the gem was the last and greatest piece of burglary he ever performed, and as I discussed back in Chapter Thirteen, it could have led to a tragic ending. Thorin's threats of vengeance at the beginning of this chapter show clearly the path that the story could well have gone down. Bilbo resists being corrupted by the greedy and possessive feelings that led him to take the jewel for himself, and in doing so, he changes the entire story, turning the Arkenstone from a bone of contention into an instrument of healing. In a strange paradox, Bilbo's career as a burglar culminates not in stealing treasure, but in giving it away.

Now at last we can see why the dwarves needed a burglar in their company. When it actually came to it, a burglar was not all that much help in obtaining their treasure; a bowman was what they really needed for that. Bilbo was quite handy to have around at many points on their journey, but the one task he turned out to be uniquely qualified for was connected not with the recovery of their treasure, but with the recovery of themselves. Bard slays the dragon, but it is little Bilbo who works to make the prophecies of peace and prosperity come true.

Not even Gandalf could have foreseen that his chosen burglar would play this particular role in the adventure he arranged. Yet when Gandalf meets Bilbo again at the end of Chapter Sixteen, we can see that the wizard recognizes the full significance of Bilbo's actions and fully endorses them. His comment that "there is always more about you than anyone expects!" presumably is meant to include himself, and it acts as an admission that he had no idea of the unlikely turn events have taken (249). Gandalf's hearty "Well done!" is Bilbo's greatest reward. He has more than lived up to Gandalf's recommendation.

Throughout the book, Bilbo has been trying to prove himself as a burglar. In the end, he admits, "personally, I never really felt like one" (248). Although he accepted the position, he was never comfortable with the idea of being a thief. Gollum called him one (quite unfairly) and so did Smaug, but that label never really fit. His own conscience has recently been niggling at him about his concealment of the Arkenstone from Thorin, and his discomfort when Bard asks him how the stone is his to give betrays his guilt. When he took it, Bilbo used Thorin's pledge to let him pick his own fourteenth share as a rationalization, though even then he knew "that the picking and choosing had not really been meant to include this marvellous gem" (217). Now his self-justification is turned to self-sacrifice, and he is "willing to let it stand against all" his claim (248). Bilbo has proven himself an excellent burglar, but he has remained "an honest one . . . more or less."

Standing at the end of Bilbo's career arc, we can see a remarkable thing. As Bilbo has been changed by his experiences, he has come to fit more and more neatly the "Burglar" label that Gandalf so improbably placed on him in Chapter One. In the process, however, he has not been fundamentally changed; rather, he has transformed the role of burglar itself to fit the values of his Baggins world, taking the job in a quite unexpected direction. The description "honest burglar" sounds like an oxymoron, but it fits Bilbo. An honest burglar may be something new, but then so is a respectable Baggins wearing elvish armor, or a thief sneaking out by night in order to give away the wealth of nations.

17

The Sudden Turn

The Desolation of the Dragon: The Downward Spiral

The morning after Bilbo's act of quiet heroism, Thorin is still wrapped in his arrogance. Hearing that "matters were changed" in the camp (250), he assumes that his own strategy, the summoning of Dain from the Iron Hills, has finally had the effect that he planned and driven his enemies to capitulate. He speaks with great haughtiness to the messenger from the camp: "Bid them come few in number and weaponless, and I will hear." Thorin sounds for all the world like a great king or potentate condescending to allow his petitioners to appear before him.

When the Arkenstone is revealed, Thorin can think and speak of nothing but himself and what is due to him. "That stone was my father's, and is mine," he insists, entirely focused on *his* right to the heirloom of *his* house (251). "Why should I purchase my own?" he asks in outrage. In his surprise and anger, Thorin overlooks the fact that he has demanded that Bard do that very thing. "Your own we will give back in return for our own," says the heir of Girion, whose inheritance makes up a part of the hoard on which Thorin is squatting so possessively. Once again Bard puts forward a just claim to part of the treasure, but now the tables are turned, leaving Thorin to become a just petitioner for his inheritance, as well.

Bilbo now comes to the inevitable moment dictated by his return to the dwarves the night before, openly confessing his delivery of the Arkenstone. Thorin insults him and threatens to kill him, and although Bilbo bristles at the insults, he still tries to appeal to the dwarf. He appeals to Thorin by their friendship, and by the gratitude that Thorin has so often expressed. He appeals to Thorin by the dwarf's own sworn word, urging him to abide by the promise he made that Bilbo might choose his own fourteenth share. Bilbo says pointedly, "I have been told that dwarves are sometimes politer in word than in deed" (251). It was Smaug himself who told Bilbo that, of course, as Thorin should well remember. When Bilbo originally related the dragon's words to Thorin, the dwarf lord assured him that it was not true. Thorin then told Bilbo that he could pick and choose his own fourteenth share in order to convince the hobbit that Smaug's insinuations were unjustified. In recalling this exchange to Thorin now, Bilbo cleverly challenges the captain of the dwarves and would-be king to prove the dragon wrong.

But Thorin is beyond any appeal. Smaug tried to manipulate Bilbo into suspiciously reinterpreting the dwarves' actions and intentions. Bilbo resisted, but even without the dragon present to manipulate him, Thorin now sees everything and everyone around him through the distortion of his own pride and treasure-lust. Bard and the Elvenking are thieves; Bilbo's attempt to bring Thorin to see reason makes him a traitor. When Gandalf reveals himself, he only proves that they are all "in league" (251), all working together in a vast and ornate conspiracy against Thorin. The dwarf lord completes his utter rejection of Bilbo's appeals by repudiating his friendship and repenting of his previous gratitude by saying that the *mithril* coat Bilbo wears is too good for him (252). Some of the other dwarves may feel the same way as Thorin, but "more than one," we are told, "in their hearts felt shame and pity" at Bilbo's going. They feel pity for Bilbo in his mistreatment and shame for their leader's ungracious and even maniacal actions. It begins to look as if Thorin is completely unredeemable.

When Thorin agrees to an exchange of treasure, he only thinks of it as paying a ransom, a way to "redeem the Arkenstone, the treasure of my house" (252). Though Bard has reminded him of his own just claims on the treasure, Thorin has simply ignored them. The kings of old would have given matchless gifts to the valiant warrior who slew a dragon that was marauding their country. Neither Thror nor Thrain would ever have robbed the house of Girion and laid claim to the treasures of Dale. The King beneath the Mountain would have certainly shown mercy to his neighbors by the Lake if their town had been destroyed and they were left weeping and shivering with their families on the lakeshore in wintertime. But Thorin is so far gone that he seems not even to remember that he has brushed these claims aside. Gandalf is certainly right that he is "not making a very splendid figure as King under the Mountain."

Events begin to spin out of control, and the dragon-sickness on almost all sides threatens to become fatal. Dain and his warriors arrive, and "the knowledge that the Arkenstone was in the hands of the besiegers burned in their thoughts," so they resolve to attack without hesitation (255). Bard is eager to seize the tactical advantage the dwarves leave him and win the battle that he has obviously been ready to fight from the beginning. Thorin falls into sharp practice in his bargaining, trying to get out of paying over any gems, which is contrary to the original deal with Bilbo that he claims to be honoring. He then descends further into outright bad faith, "pondering whether by the help of Dain he might not recapture the Arkenstone and withhold the share of the reward" (252). Only the Elvenking repents, hoping to avoid "unhappy blows" (255). He at least can see now what he has gotten entangled in, and he seeks to delay "this war for gold" (254).

But the Elvenking's forbearance comes too late. Men and dwarves are already charging toward each other with weapons in hand. The first arrows of the battle that will permanently end the old peace among Mountain, Wood, and Dale have already been fired. Bilbo's noble attempt to bring about a cure has apparently failed. It appears that if the dragon-sickness is going to be treated, stronger medicine will be needed.

Eucatastrophe

The antidote to dragon-sickness, restoring peace among elves, men, and dwarves, arrives in a quite unexpected form: an army of goblins and wargs from the Misty Mountains. A battle breaks out, but not the battle that had been on the cusp of beginning. The intervention of the goblins instantly transforms selfishness and rage into solidarity and goodwill. The dwarves and men who had been in the very midst of an attack not only stop their charge and lower their weapons; they immediately start collaborating. Dain, the leader of the frenzied dwarvish assault, quickly joins Bard and the Elvenking to plan their defense. Bard rallies troops to defend the Mountain that he has been besieging for days. The armies of elves, dwarves, and men, working in harmony, combine to rout their mutual enemies in the valley. "The Goblins were the foes of all," the narrator explains, "and at their coming all other quarrels were forgotten" (256). Nothing else in Middle-earth could possibly have brought about such a miraculous shift. The dragon-like attitudes of a moment before have been swept away like smoke before the wind.

In the battle, we get a firsthand glimpse of an event that evokes the ancient legends we first encountered in Rivendell. The fall of elven Gondolin is recalled in the deadly wrath of the elves against the goblins. Their "cold and bitter" hatred makes the swords and spears of the elven-host shine "in the gloom with a gleam of chill flame," like Orcrist, Glamdring, and Bilbo's Sting (257). When the dwarves of the Iron Hills attack, they cry "Moria!" (258), remembering the fierce war between Thorin's clan and the goblins, which was retold in tales up and down the Misty Mountains. By telling us from the start that the battle that day "was called the Battle of Five Armies" (256), the narrator informs us that the battle we are seeing will become a prominent part of the history of those times. The old legends from ancient days, it seems, live on.

Of all the events in the tale of that day, however, the greatest is the healing of Thorin Oakenshield. Poor Thorin was fenced in the dark and stinking Mountain "like a robber in his hold" (241), blinded and consumed by the pride and greed that had led him to cast aside friendship, compassion, and finally even his own honor. In the midst of the battle, when the defenders are surrounded and all seems lost, Thorin throws down the stone wall that he has built and opens the Gates of the King once more. Gold does indeed flow from the gate, in the form of the King in shining armor, gleaming in the gloom "like gold in a dying fire" (259). "To me!" he cries, not only to his kinsfolk, but to the "Elves and Men" whom he was calling thieves just hours before. The haughty dwarf who seemed to care about nothing outside himself now throws himself into danger, leading the charge to save them and calling them to follow him.

And they come. All the dwarves, of course, come rushing to their lord and kinsman, but "many of the Lake-men" and "many of the spearmen of the elves" also run to his side, joining the last great charge of the King under the Mountain (259). Now, it would seem, the old songs are really coming true. Whatever happens in this desperate attack, Thorin Oakenshield has been saved.

Unfortunately, it appears that the day has not. Thorin's great charge stalls, and the Mountain is overrun by goblins, "victory now vanished from hope" (258). Back in the tunnels under the Misty Mountains, Bilbo had been encouraged to think that he was connected to the old legends, finding that he had a sword from fallen Gondolin itself. He now has a front-row seat at the making of one of those legends, but he finds it "very uncomfortable, not to say distressing" (260). Defeat may be glorious in songs, but he doesn't think much of the prose version.

Bilbo's luck, however, doesn't quite fail him. The moment when Bilbo looks up and sees the eagles in the West is twice foreshadowed in *The Hobbit.** The narrator says that "the clouds were torn by the wind, and a red sunset slashed the West" (260). The tearing of the clouds around the Lonely Mountain by the wind is specifically stated in the dwarves' Wind song, in which "racing clouds were torn and rent" by the wind of destiny which also guides the moon in its course and sets the stars aglow (119). The setting sun gleaming through the clouds also closely parallels the magical sun ray that reached through the bank of clouds in the west on Durin's Day and pointed to the key-hole of the secret door, just as the moon-letters foretold. The providence that has guided Bilbo and his companions and planned this soon-to-be-legendary story is not quite done with them yet, it seems.

The sudden rescue and happy ending that the eagles bring to the Battle of Five Armies is an iconic moment. Tolkien himself called this kind of "sudden joyous 'turn'" near the end of a story a "eucatastrophe": a good or happy catastrophe. In his great essay "On Fairy-stories," Tolkien described

---

* There might also be a third. He sees the eagles when "seeing the sudden gleam in the gloom Bilbo looked round" (260). This makes the third time that Tolkien has used that alliterative pair, "gleam" and "gloom," during the description of the battle, and the instances are quite similar and build on one another. First the elven spears and swords "shone in the gloom with a gleam of chill flame" (257), then we are told of Thorin: "In the gloom the great dwarf gleamed like gold" (259). Tolkien was extremely sensitive to the sound and even the etymology of the words he used; I find it hard to believe that such a remarkable repetition would have happened by accident and slipped by him in every revision. Moreover, Tolkien admired alliteration as a poetic device very much, and he often manipulated alliteration both in his poetry and his prose to create particular effects. I think it is very likely, therefore, that Tolkien's repetition of this word pair is deliberate, meant to draw a link between these three lights in the darkness that offer hope in the battle, culminating in the final eucatastrophe.

this kind of event as a "sudden and miraculous grace: never to be counted on to recur."* The unlooked-for arrival of the eagles in the nick of time is the classic example of eucatastrophe in all of Tolkien's fiction. The battle as Bilbo sees it ends with an image that I think beautifully captures the spirit of eucatastrophe: the "many wondering eyes" of the beleaguered warriors in the valley, looking up in sudden hope of deliverance, "though as yet nothing could be seen" (260).

In the Battle of Five Armies we see the final enactment of another theme that has recurred several times during this story: the striking tendency of apparent bad luck to turn out to be good luck. The Battle of Five Armies itself is the most extraordinary example of this pattern. A surprise assault by the assembled armies of all the goblins of the Misty Mountains and their warg allies would count as an enormous misfortune for anyone. In this instance, however, we cannot escape the fact that it was also a stroke of almost miraculous good luck. If the goblins had not appeared just when they did, blood would have been spilled between the dwarves of the Mountain and the men of Dale. No matter what had happened in that fight, irreparable damage with far-reaching effects would have occurred. A victory by the goblins would have been preferable to that, for even if the allied peoples had gone down fighting the goblins together, the legacy of the battle would still be one of unity, and the survivors would still have had a shared enemy. In the big picture, the real battle was already won as soon as the elves, dwarves, and men started to fight on the same side, rather than against each other. The onset of the Battle of Five Armies, terrible as it was, is actually a bigger

---

* "On Fairy-Stories," 86.

and more important eucatastrophe than the intervention of the eagles.

The Writing of *The Hobbit:*
The Hobbit Grows Up

The Hobbit, as we can see, has gotten very serious in the last few chapters. The quest of the dwarves and their inept hobbit burglar for dragon-gold that we saw in the first couple of chapters was a little cartoonish at times, but it has grown up since then. The destruction of Lake-town and the reminder that many of its people would die of sickness and hunger in the coming winter were sobering enough. The dark corruption of dragonish desires that has lain like a fog over the Mountain and its environs ever since has been even more oppressive. In the battle, the playful tone so prevalent in the first two-thirds of the book subsides amidst the horror of the slaughtered soldiers littering the ground, with vampire bats fixed on the corpses, lapping up the blood of the dead. When Thorin and Company charge out of the Front Gate, they look nothing like the comic troupe who fell in a heap on Bilbo's doormat in Bag-End. We have arrived at a world of grim realities.

The fairy-tale ending of the Battle of Five Armies does nothing to undermine these realities. Yes, the eagles arrive in time to rescue everyone, but Tolkien has avoided an overly simplistic and rose-tinted conclusion time and again in these last few chapters. Smaug died in Chapter Fourteen; it would have been simple to have that climactic event followed by the joyous re-establishment of the dwarvish kingdom and of Dale, and everyone living Happily Ever After. Instead, the whole region nearly goes up in flames as the desire for the dragon-gold almost destroys even the remnants of that ancient kingdom.

Next we have Bilbo's heroic and noble self-sacrifice in surrendering the Arkenstone, taking a brave but humble stand against the greed and mistrust that are running rampant around him. It would have been easy to have had his plan succeed; Thorin and Bard alike could have apologetically followed his excellent example and then sworn eternal friendship, living Happily Ever After. Tolkien could even have attached a nice sententious moral to the end of that story, like a Victorian nursery tale. Even within the battle itself, Thorin's heroic charge, which looks for all the world like a happy ending that has been waiting to happen, fails.

Life in Middle-earth, which after all is only an Old English name for the world we live in, is not usually that tidy and sterilized. Instead, Tolkien gives us reconciliation that comes in the face of war and loss, amidst sorrow and pain. Along the path to the happy ending lie the bodies of "many men and many dwarves, and many a fair elf that should have lived yet long ages merrily in the wood" (259). Bilbo, Gandalf, and many of their allies are indeed spared by an unexpected and miraculous grace, but victory comes through suffering, and it is often accompanied by great grief, as Bilbo will soon discover.

18

Snow After Fire

"THE RETURN JOURNEY"

The Desolation of the Dragon: Convalescence

Bilbo's attempt to "buy peace and quiet" turns out to be a failure (263). His intentions were good, and taken by itself the act of self-sacrifice involved was very admirable. In placing the good of others above his own gain and his private desire for the Arkenstone, Bilbo was working in direct opposition to the dragon-sickness affecting everyone else. In retrospect, however, Bilbo feels that he "made a great mess of that business with the stone." When greed and suspicion were the factors threatening the peace in the first place, trying to use Thorin's obsessive desire for the Arkenstone to bring about reconciliation was not likely to succeed. It is hard to imagine how Bilbo's plan could have led to harmony and goodwill; all it did was increase the stakes.

In the end, the only thing that could shake everyone out of the dragon-like mindset was a crisis that forced them to a renewed perspective on matters. The attack of the goblins reminded them of what they had in common, as well as of what they stood to lose if they did not cooperate. A heap of treasure might be a great thing, but there are other things that are more important.

In Thorin's dying apology to Bilbo, he admits that even he has come to see things differently. "Since I leave now all gold and silver," he tells Bilbo, "and go where it is of little worth, I wish to part in friendship from you" (262). Thorin's words suggest that his rejection of gold is due only to his imminent death, but I believe that it is also self-deprecation on Thorin's part, a recognition of his shame at how horribly he acted. His choices during the battle, however, show that his change of heart did not happen on his deathbed. Thorin's throwing down of the wall was a symbolically important moment. It demolished the barrier not only between Thorin and his allies, but between Thorin and the rest of the world. No more would Thorin allow himself to be cut off from everyone else by his paranoid possessiveness.

Thorin's rallying cry is another reversal, and an even more poetic one. Behind his wall, Thorin could think about nothing but himself and his own rights. When he throws the wall down, he once again puts himself at the center of attention, calling to everyone to run to him. In his charge, however, his self-absorption is turned to self-sacrifice.

Thorin's change of heart has already been demonstrated; the personal reconciliation with Bilbo is the truly important part of their last exchange. Thorin had generally been haughty and superior toward Bilbo, at least until the prison break in Mirkwood. His final benediction, however, offers Bilbo not only friendship, but great respect. "There is more in you of good than you know, child of the kindly West," he says (263). His statement beautifully reverses their relationship. Now Thorin assures Bilbo that he esteems Bilbo more highly than

Bilbo does himself. Bilbo's own feelings, of course, are made abundantly clear by his tears.

The recovery from dragon-sickness is now as widespread as the disease itself had become. When Dain becomes king in Thorin's place, he quickly starts living up to the old ideal of the King under the Mountain. Remember that when Roäc tells Thorin that he wishes to see the old peace return, he admits that that "may cost you dear in gold" (236). Roäc refers here not to bribes or purchases, but to gifts. Dain immediately gives away large amounts of treasure both to reward his friends and to cement the support of his allies. He crowns the chief of the eagles with gold and swears friendship with them forever. He wins the support of the followers and kinsmen of Thorin in large part, it is suggested, because he "dealt his treasure well" (265). That is a king's proper use of gold. Dragons gather treasure into a sterile pile and sit on it, allowing it to benefit no one, not even themselves. Thorin's willingness to "sit on a heap of gold and starve" exactly follows the draconic model (247). Instead, a king should be standing at the gates, his hands "rich with gems and gold" (240), a line from the dwarves' new song, which now, with Dain on the throne, is quite accurate.

The elves of Mirkwood return home in a very different spirit from when they set out. The Elvenking does not get the vastly increased hoard that he was hoping for, but the elves receive something far more substantial: "The dragon was dead, and the goblins overthrown, and their hearts could look forward after winter to a spring of joy" (266). The army that marched away to satisfy greed, followed avidly by flocks of jeering crows, returns with song and gladness to an unanticipated peace and security.

The Elvenking's own words at his departure turn out to

be quite ironic. "It is an ill wind . . . that blows no one any good," he had said, and it was a comment that showed him in an unflattering light (232). He had been referring to the probable death of Thorin and expressing his own intention to seize the opportunity that the deaths of both Thorin and Smaug afforded him to enrich himself with their wealth. As it turned out, providence was going to take advantage of him, instead. If he hadn't marched out with his army, he and his forces would not have been available when the goblins attacked. But it turned out that his greedy and overly aggressive decision to march in force toward the Lonely Mountain was not so ill a wind, and "now the northern world would be merrier for many a long day" (266).

From our vantage point after the Battle of Five Armies, when the treasure is being wisely used by Dain and Bard to save lives and establish alliances, the original plan of the party that met in Bag-End in Chapter One seems ridiculous. The idea that the fourteen of them would split the entire hoard, the wealth and livelihood of two entire nations, into fourteen equal shares is simplistic and naive almost to the point of childishness. Despite the more mature perspective he later attains, Bilbo originally buys into this scheme. He is so intent upon it, in fact, that he apparently carried his contract letter around with him during the entire journey to ensure that he would get what was due to him in the end.

Bilbo's experiences have now taught him new wisdom. His encounter with the dragon-sickness and the devastation that it nearly caused has made him look at money in a new way. He realizes now that he could not possibly have gotten his treasure home "without war and murder all along the way" (266). He has already forfeited his wealth in order to avert a war; he doesn't want to cause any new ones! When he refers to "war and murder," though, I believe he is thinking of more than just protecting his treasure on the road through the Wild. I think it is likely that he is also thinking of his neighbors back at home. The last few days have shown him quite forcibly how a big pile of gold can shatter peace and motivate desperate actions. His neighbors at home are very different from Thorin and the Elvenking, but Chapter Nineteen will show us that Bilbo is almost certainly correct to believe that they would not be completely immune to the dragon-sickness.

Bilbo's Nature: Reconciliation

Bilbo, at last, is beginning his homeward journey. The challenges and stresses of his quest are over, and the growth of his character has almost reached its endpoint. In Chapter Eighteen, we see that he has earned the admiration of kings and rulers, and yet he desires his own quiet home with no less eagerness. In the company of elf kings and dwarf lords, he probably no longer looks that odd in his shining armor, but nothing can prevent his leaving this grand world behind.

There are a few brief exchanges Bilbo has in Chapter Eighteen that show us how his sense of his own identity is resolving itself as his adventures come to an end. One is his farewell to the Elvenking. Before they go their separate ways, Bilbo awkwardly offers the Elvenking a gift, "stammering and standing on one foot" (267). Bilbo says that he is offering a "return" for the Elvenking's "hospitality," compensation for having "drunk much of your wine and eaten much of your bread." Bilbo is not just proffering payment, however; if that were his intent, he has plenty of gold or silver with which he could cover the cost of his food and drink at fair market value. Instead, he gives the Elvenking a valuable gift: "a necklace of silver and pearls that Dain had given him at their parting." In a situation where recompense did not seem required and certainly was not expected, Bilbo not only pays the Elvenking but gives him a token of respect which he himself had only just received. This might all seem a bit puzzling, at first glance.

Bilbo offers the necklace not primarily as compensation, but as a show of respect. Bilbo's relationship with the Elvenking did not start off smoothly; as Bilbo is indirectly recalling, he began the association by invisibly infiltrating the Elvenking's secret stronghold and later setting free his prisoners. Bilbo recalls his rather uncomfortable status with the king of the elves when he goes to parley with him in Chapter Sixteen. "I know your king well by sight," he admits to the elf sentries, "though perhaps he doesn't know me to look at" (246). Bilbo has worked against the Elvenking, and although they are now allies, Bilbo wants to make amends. We should notice that Bilbo's gift happens to be exactly the kind of treasure that the Elvenking likes best—he has a weakness for "silver and white gems," remember (155). Bilbo's gift is not only rich; it is thoughtful.

His show of respect to the Elvenking does not translate to an act of disrespect toward Dain, either. To a modern reader, Bilbo's giving away a special token of honor he has just received might seem discourteous. In context, however, I don't think it is. As Dain himself has shown, the proper use of treasure is giving it away. Bilbo is giving a kingly gift, both to a king and as a king would do. The gesture is recognized and accepted by the Elvenking. He names Bilbo "elf-friend and blessed," formalizing the bond that Bilbo's gift (and, more importantly, the intention behind it) has established (267).

In Bilbo's gift to the Elvenking we also see his final reconciliation with his burglar identity. In Chapter Sixteen, Bilbo admitted that although the label of Burglar had been put on him, he had never felt like one (248). He then established a new, paradoxical model for his profession: the honest burglar. Interestingly, Thorin addresses him in a very similar way from his deathbed, calling Bilbo "good thief" (262). In his last conversation with the Elvenking, Bilbo is at peace and comfortable with his new identity. He does not protest against being a burglar, or repent having acted as one. But "even a burglar has his feelings" (267), and Bilbo's feelings have guided him to a happy resolution of the tension between his adventurous job title and his honest, good-hearted nature.

The Elvenking addresses Bilbo as "Bilbo the Magnificent," a title that conveys an enormous compliment, and one that echoes some of Bilbo's own earlier language significantly. The word *magnificent* has several senses, two of which are particularly relevant here. One sense of the word refers to appearances, meaning "splendid," "sumptuously decorated," or "characterized by display of wealth or ceremonial pomp."* In this sense, the word refers only to superficial things, and Bilbo has lately used the word twice in this way. When Smaug is being absurdly vain about his bejeweled underside, Bilbo calls him "Your Magnificence," with just a hint of sarcasm (208). When Bilbo's own belly is glittering with his new *mithril* coat, he says, "I feel magnificent," with more than a hint of self-deprecation, since he goes on to add, "but I expect I look

---

* Definitions of *magnificent* are taken from the *Oxford English Dictionary.*

rather absurd" (219). But there is also an older and more solemn sense of the word, in which it was used to mean "glorious" or "exalted," referring not to appearances but to a person's character. A person showing "magnificence" in this sense was enacting all the virtues thought most fitting for a king or a noble to show. Bilbo mocks Smaug's superficiality with the term and then takes it good-humoredly to himself, but when the Elvenking applies it, the term is transformed, recognizing the worthiness of Bilbo's character and the generosity and graciousness of his actions.

On his deathbed, Thorin also acknowledges Bilbo's real worth, stating that he has "some courage and some wisdom, blended in measure. If more of us valued food and cheer and song above hoarded gold, it would be a merrier world" (263). Bilbo's priorities certainly have been praiseworthy, as was most clearly demonstrated in his surrendering of the Arkenstone. When Thorin charged out of his gate in the battle, laying himself open to attack and his hoard open to plunder, he embraced Bilbo's priorities, in a fashion. Thorin's statement, however, calls to mind the contrast that has been apparent in the last eight chapters, but which has quietly run through the whole book: the contrast between the Mountain, standing alone in its desert waste, and the Hill, waiting back in the "kindly West."

Thorin had always been focused on the Mountain and on the gold within it. Bilbo has always been looking back toward the Hill and his own fireside within it. Notice the change that has taken place along the way. At first, Bilbo's longing for Bag-End was escapist: he was looking back over his shoulder, wishing he could be whisked out of this nasty adventure and returned to his land of "safe and comfortable things" (52). At some point, however, that changed. His longing for Bag-End didn't grow less, but it ceased to be about turning back. The Hill was no longer the starting point he wished he had never left; it had become the endpoint that he was striving to reach. Bilbo's love of "food and cheer" no longer leads him to reject adventure, as it did in Chapter One. Of late, it has given him the resolve to complete it. His experiences along the way have enriched Bilbo's enjoyment as well. Not only does he love "food and cheer" even more keenly than before, he has developed a taste for "song," which hadn't previously been part of his life at Bag-End.

This new mingling of characteristics is the other thing that Thorin praises: the blending of "courage" with "wisdom" in his character. Since we have been following the interplay between Bilbo's Took and Baggins elements from the beginning, the existence of contrasting factors in Bilbo's character is no surprise. What Thorin perceives in Bilbo, here at the end of his quest, is the fact that they are now "blended in measure." "Courage" and "wisdom" are appropriate descriptors of his Took and Baggins sides, respectively—but only when they are properly combined. In isolation, neither side steers him in the right direction. By itself, his Tookishness comes out as rashness and arrogance. Left to itself, his Baggins side led him into laziness and timidity. In Chapter One, Bilbo was either putting his "foot in it," under the influence of his Took side (18), or quivering like a jelly on his hearth-rug when his internal Baggins was in charge. But blended together in measure, his different but complementary perspectives lend him both courage and wisdom. At the end of his journey, we see that neither the Took nor the Baggins side has won. They have been reconciled.

The ease with which Bilbo now inhabits both worlds, which came together so suddenly and disturbingly back in

Chapter One, is delightfully illustrated in his farewell to his surviving dwarf companions. On saying good-bye, Bilbo and his friends exchange invitations. "If ever you visit us again, when our halls are made fair once more," they say, "then the feast shall indeed be splendid!" (266). Bilbo is now at home in this world, a guest of honor at a rich banquet in the glittering, restored halls of the new King under the Mountain. "If ever you are passing my way," Bilbo responds, "don't wait to knock! Tea is at four; but any of you are welcome any time!" Bilbo may have a standing invitation to that high and noble world, but if you are looking for him, you will find him having tea and cakes back at his hobbit-hole. There is a very noticeable difference in his domestic life, though. Bilbo is now actually hoping for unexpected parties. If uninvited dwarves show up at his door again, at any time, they will be welcome—they needn't even knock. The Hill and the Mountain may stand at the opposite poles of Bilbo's journey, but they are no longer incompatible in his outlook.

Luck: The Big Picture

On his way home, Bilbo travels with Beorn and spends several months at his house. "Yule-tide was warm and merry there," and when Bilbo leaves, he leaves "with regret, for the flowers of the gardens of Beorn were in springtime no less marvellous than in high summer" (268). This stay at Beorn's house is another reminder of Bilbo's new outlook. On the outward road, Beorn's house was comfortable but "queer"—unsettling and dangerous. Bilbo paid more attention to the deadly bear guardians of the hall than the safety that they provided, and he spent as much time worrying about the huge, fierce bees as he did admiring the spectacular flowers. Beorn and his house alike were always half human and half beast, half Homely and half Wild. On the homeward road, Bilbo is completely at peace there.

Of course, Beorn too is changing. Beorn's story is a fascinating one, and it is especially tantalizing since every bit of it happens off-stage and only comes to us through rumors and synopses. Gandalf believes that Beorn originally came from the mountains, for he once overheard Beorn say while "watching the moon sinking towards the Misty Mountains" that "the day will come when they will perish and I shall go back!" (109). We are led to understand that the presence of the goblins has prevented his desired return, fueling his bitter hatred of them. Beorn's dramatic arrival at the Battle of Five Armies, therefore, is a climax in his own story as well as the story of the Lonely Mountain. When Beorn, "grown almost to giant-size in his wrath," bursts upon the goblin armies like a natural disaster, scattering the bodyguard of Bolg and crushing the goblin king himself, Beorn not only ends the battle, he removes the goblin threat from the Misty Mountains (264). Instead of returning there in bear's shape, however, Beorn apparently changes his mind and goes the other direction, calling the woodmen to join him "from far and wide" (268). He becomes "a great chief afterwards in those regions and ruled a wide land between the mountains and the wood." Why did Beorn turn from his reclusive home among the animals and his longing to return to the mountains and establish himself instead at the heart of a new human realm? We never find out, but I think a whole novel could have been written on the story of Beorn.

The glimpses of that story that we are given, however, show us one of the many distant repercussions of Bilbo's treasure hunt. The hobbit's haphazard journey through the Wild ended up touching off many separate avalanches. His chance meetings with the eagles, Beorn, the Wood-elves, and the Lake-men all lead up to the great nexus of the Battle of Five Armies, as each of these separate stories is woven together into the increasingly far-reaching tale that began as a little adventure arranged by Gandalf. Afterwards, all of these people, their fortunes blessed as a result of their involvement, establish new and peaceful realms that now stretch from the crags of the Misty Mountains to the Long Lake. In consequence of the strange vicissitudes of Bilbo's journey, the entire northern world has blossomed into a new and merrier age. Order, prosperity, and harmony have broken out wherever Bilbo has gone. All in all, it has been a remarkable run of luck.

In the end, Bilbo has gained a much greater appreciation for the larger world on which he has had such an impact and of which his own little home is such a small part. He first processes this not exactly in a song, but in highly poetic language, as he is climbing the Misty Mountains on the way home. On the outward journey, he looked back from the slopes of the mountains and could only think that somewhere far away, where "things were blue and faint," lay his "little hobbit-hole" (52). He thought little of the wide world all around it. On the way home, when he turns and looks back east over the Wild, he takes in the whole country, seeing Mirkwood stretched out below him and the Lonely Mountain tipped with snow in the far distance. "So comes snow after fire," Bilbo observes, "and even dragons have their ending!" (268). The opposition of snow and fire might remind us of the way in which Tolkien invited us, through the title of Chapter Fourteen, to see the fight between Smaug and Esgaroth as an elemental clash between Fire and Water whose end is inevitable. Bilbo's perspective here is even wider, and by opposing fire with snow, Bilbo is seeing the whole story in which he has been involved as part of a huge and unavoidable process, like the changing of the seasons. Smaug may have believed that he was unconquerable and that he would rule Mountain and Lake for age after age, but he was wrong. "Even dragons have their ending," just as summer heat is cooled by winter and spring comes again after. Bilbo's story, and the story of Thorin's family and their turns of fortune, and the story of the long and legendary career of Smaug the Mighty, all take their place in the much larger tale that rolls across lands and down through the ages, as the moon sails by overhead and the stars glow over all, like embers in the night sky.

19

Under Cloud and Under Star

"THE LAST STAGE"

And Elves Are Yet Singing

On Bilbo's outward journey, the valley of Rivendell served as an important boundary. Elrond's house was the Last Homely House, sitting on the border between lands of safety and ease (if you are willing to ignore a few trolls) and the Wild. Once Bilbo left Rivendell, his real dangers and adventures began. Elrond's house was also where Bilbo first came into contact with the great tales and legends, and the identification of the swords from Gondolin drew Bilbo's own story into those tales themselves. In more than one sense, Rivendell is where Bilbo's adventure became serious.

Now, on the way home, Rivendell is the place where Bilbo transitions out of the world of high adventure. He has come now not to the Last, but to the First Homely House. From this side, Rivendell no longer looks like the boundary between safety and danger; now it seems more like the boundary between Great and Small. Bilbo has returned from the lands where grand events decided the destiny of realms and is on his way back to the land of little problems and petty concerns. The elves of Rivendell and their songs play an important role in Bilbo's re-emergence out of great tales and back into the mundane world.

The elves greet Bilbo's return to Rivendell in the same way they greeted his first arrival: with a joyful and lighthearted song, a reprise of their original "Tra-la-la-lally" song:

> *The dragon is withered,*
> *His bones are now crumbled;*
> *His armour is shivered,*
> *His splendour is humbled!*
> *Though sword shall be rusted,*
> *And throne and crown perish*
> *With strength that men trusted*
> *And wealth that they cherish,*
> *Here grass is still growing,*
> *And leaves are yet swinging,*
> *The white water flowing,*
> *And elves are yet singing*
> > *Come! Tra-la-la-lally!*
> > *Come back to the valley!*
> > *(269)*

The first stanza appears distinctly relevant to Bilbo's adventure, since it begins with a celebration of the destruction of the dragon. Instead of moving on to address Bilbo more specifically, the song goes in the opposite direction, shifting to general principles. The first four lines emphasize in particular that the dragon fell and is now "withered" despite the great strength of his armor. The death of the dragon is an example of splendor humbled. The second four lines extrapolate outward, pointing out that everything that seems strong will fail.

Swords, thrones, strength, and wealth—all shall perish like the dragon and be brought low.

In the last four lines before the refrain, the elves point to the natural objects around them in four simple statements in the present progressive tense, emphasizing their continuous action. The grass, the leaves, the river, and the elves themselves are all here. These statements of fact, some lifted directly from the first song, no longer sound like bizarre non sequiturs, though. The context provided by the earlier lines makes their significance clearer. The things "that men trusted"—war, power, strength, wealth—are all ephemeral things and will always fail in the end. The small things—the leaves and grass and silly elf songs—will endure, for they are ever renewed.

In the second stanza, the elves return to the theme of treasure, for treasure was the goal of the journey that took Bilbo away from Rivendell before:

> *The stars are far brighter*
> *Than gems without measure,*
> *The moon is far whiter*
> *Than silver in treasure;*
> *The fire is more shining*
> *On hearth in the gloaming*
> *Than gold won by mining,*
> *So why go a-roaming?*
> *O! Tra-la-la-lally*
> *Come back to the Valley.*
> *(269–70)*

The elves point out that the night around them contains far more beauty than any hoard could. Since the stars, the moon, and the elves' fire all surpass the shining brightness of riches, then "why go a-roaming?" The elves' forest glade by the river is not only more lasting and permanent than anything in human society, but it is also more lovely and desirable than its greatest marvels.

The third stanza finally addresses the travelers directly:

> *O! Where are you going,*
> *So late in returning?*
> *The river is flowing,*
> *The stars are all burning!*
> *O! Whither so laden,*
> *So sad and so dreary?*
> *Here elf and elf-maiden*
> *Now welcome the weary*
>   *With Tra-la-la-lally*
>   *Come back to the Valley,*
>   *Tra-la-la-lally*
>   *Fa-la-la-lally*
>   *Fa-la!*
>   *(270)*

This last verse sounds most like the original song in Chapter Three, with its unnecessary questions and random observations. Again, though, this version of the song provides clearer context. The elves seem to chide Bilbo and Gandalf for taking so long in coming back. Do they realize how much river-flowing and star-burning they have missed while they were off fiddling around with comparatively inconsequential things, such as wars, crowns, and the fate of nations? The elves seek to correct their priorities. The singers also note, with apparent disapproval, that Bilbo is returning laden down with gold and silver. They refer to this only as a burden, which they associate not only with physical weight but with sadness and dreari-ness. Fortunately for Bilbo, he can now forget his troubles amidst a steady stream of "Tra-la-la-lally" and "Fa-la."

One important difference between this song and the orig-inal "Tra-la-la-lally" song is the repeated refrain. Each verse ends with a command: "Come back to the Valley." Given the overall focus of the song, the elves' message is clear: they are making an appeal to Bilbo to turn away from the concerns and triumphs of the world outside and to renew his perspec-tive. "Here elf and elf-maiden / Now welcome the weary," they sing. The spirit of Rivendell is the *real* cure of dragon-sickness, its opposite pole. Here there is joy and complete rest.

The elves' philosophy about the relative importance of hu-man affairs and singing under the stars may lead us to won-der if the elves might not be a little too detached from worldly concerns. Their song makes it sound almost as if nothing in the outside world matters at all to them. In Chapter Eigh-teen, we looked at some of the profound changes for good that have come about as a result of Bilbo's journey. Now the elves of Rivendell imply that it would have been better for him to stay and sing "tra-la-la-lally" instead. I do think that there is a case to be made for this critique. If the fault of the Wood-elves was "distrust of strangers" (154), the fault of the High Elves of Rivendell may well be too much isolation from the outside world.

We can't go too far in this condemnation, though. For one thing, their actions somewhat belie their words. When the elves escort Gandalf and Bilbo into Rivendell, the narrator says that there are "many eager ears that evening to hear the tale of their adventures" (270). The elves obviously care a little more about what is going on in the world outside than their song suggests. More importantly, we need to remember the immortal perspective of the elves. They can speak so lightly of the failure of mortal kingdoms and institutions because they have seen them fail many times before in their thousands of years of life. Peace descending on all the kingdoms of the North of Middle-earth might seem like a big deal—it is!—but the elves have seen the coming and going of many such periods of peace and plenty, and they will see many more. In Chapter Eighteen, Bilbo had a brief insight into the turning of the ages, seeing that snow comes "after fire, and even dragons have their ending" (268). For the elves, this inexorable cycle is more clearly visible.

In the midst of the storytelling, Bilbo falls asleep in a corner, but he wakes again in the middle of the night. He is in a bed, and what has wakened him, ironically, is a group of elves singing him a lullaby under his window:

> *Sing all ye joyful, now sing all together!*
> *The wind's in the tree-top, the wind's in the heather;*
> *The stars are in blossom, the moon is in flower,*
> *And bright are the windows of Night in her tower.*
>
> *Dance all ye joyful, now dance all together!*
> *Soft is the grass, and let foot be like feather!*
> *The river is silver, the shadows are fleeting;*
> *Merry is May-time, and merry our meeting.*
> *(271)*

The meter of this song is quite different from that of the "Tra-la-la-lally" song. Its lines are much longer and statelier, lacking the quick beat and rapid rhyme of the elves' first song. The theme of the first two verses, however, is quite similar to that of the elves' other songs. The first stanza sings of the night and its loveliness, using imagery that personifies Night as a lady in a tower, surrounded by a garden of silver lights. The instruction to "sing all ye joyful" seems to include more than the elven singers themselves: the "tree-top" and "heather" join the song as the wind breathes and rustles through them. The second stanza now adds motion to the scene. The first two lines encourage the light-footed dancing of the elves, while lines three and four bring the motion of the river and even the turning of the seasons into the dance. These first two stanzas show the animation that the elves perceive in the world around them. They do not merely sing about nature; they sing and dance with the natural world itself.

This is all very lovely and would doubtless make an excellent lullaby. In the last two stanzas, they make explicit the joke they are playing:

Sing we now softly, and dreams let us weave him!
Wind him in slumber, and then let us leave him!
The wanderer sleepeth. Now soft be his pillow!
Lullaby! Lullaby! Alder and Willow!

Sigh no more Pine, till the wind of the morn!
Fall Moon! Dark be the land!
Hush! Hush! Oak, Ash, and Thorn!
Hushed be all water, till dawn is at hand!
(271)

The third stanza, all about Bilbo's sleep and dreaming, is heavily ironic. The elves speak of singing softly when their song is so loud it has already woken Bilbo from a deep sleep, a fact that completely undermines their expressed intention to "wind him in slumber" and "leave him" there. I imagine their shouts of "Lullaby! Lullaby!" would be particularly raucous; Bilbo does say afterwards that they would "waken a drunken goblin" (271).

The fourth stanza pushes the joke even further, making as if to turn off all the noise and shut down all the lights in the countryside to ensure Bilbo's undisturbed sleep. The gentle breeze in the treetops and the flowering light of the moon that made up parts of the living and radiant Night, full of song, the elves now seek to chase away for Bilbo's benefit. Notice that even the rhythm of the lines is disrupted in that fourth stanza to reflect the breaking up of the melody and dance of the song's beginning. Bilbo is sleeping, so let all nature hold its breath and be dark and still until dawn!

The elves, of course, are teasing Bilbo outrageously. The primary purpose of their song is to make a joke at Bilbo's expense. They wake him up with verses about the loveliness of the night he is sleeping through and the fun of the dance he is missing out on. Then they draw attention to the fact that they have woken him up by pretending, loudly, to be putting him to sleep. They end with absurd shushing gestures to all the gentle, soothing night noises. The song is quite funny, and Bilbo takes it in the right spirit, laughing with them and teasing them back.

But why do the elves do this? I think that we can see how the song fits into the larger concerns of this last chapter, but I also think it is clear that its primary purpose is to illustrate the merriment of the elves. The elves are "Merry People," as Bilbo calls them (271). They are not distant and ethereal, all solemn faces and trailing robes. Tolkien's elves romp, play, and tease like good-natured children. And we must remember that these are not some lesser kind of elves who lack the dignity of the great elf-lords. All of the evidence we have in *The Hobbit* suggests that the elves of Rivendell are the High Elves with whom the Wood-elves were contrasted back in Chapter Eight. The elves singing "Tra-la-la-lally" are most likely some of the elves who returned to Middle-earth from Faerie in the West over the sea. The laughing singers under Bilbo's window may well include survivors of the fall of Gondolin itself. By including this paradoxical mixture of high and low in his depiction of elves, Tolkien seems to be trying to convey the sense that we are encountering something fundamentally outside human experience.

I cannot help but think, though, that there is some significance in the fact that the elves tease Bilbo for sleeping. There can be no real criticism intended by the elves, of course; if the poor hobbit is not to sleep in the middle of the night, when *is* he supposed to sleep? But the song nevertheless works to draw his attention to what he is missing. While he is wrapped in oblivion, the night, with its sights and sounds of beauty, goes on. Once his initial weariness is cured, Bilbo takes his hosts' lead and has "many a merry jest and dance, early and late, with the elves of the valley" (272). A life of rest and stillness, of song and contemplation, is not a life cut off from the world, but a life in tune with the world in a more active and profound sense.

Bilbo is heading home, retiring from his life as a burglar out in the Wild. I suggested earlier that on the way home, Rivendell seems to sit on the boundary of the Great and the Small. As Bilbo prepares to cross that boundary for good, he is taught new lessons about the value of small things and how to appreciate them.

Bilbo's Nature: Homecoming

As Bilbo sets out from Rivendell with Gandalf to return home at last, "wind and rain came up to meet them" (272). Bilbo makes an odd comment at this moment. He observes that "our back is to legends and we are coming home. I suppose this is the first taste of it." When he left Rivendell, Bilbo did indeed cross a boundary between the legendary and the mundane worlds, and given the insight that Bilbo has already shown on his return journey, it is not very surprising that he should be conscious of the significance of the moment. What *is* odd is that he seems to associate "coming home" with an unpleasant and uncomfortable experience. He has been longing for this moment for so long that it seems strange to hear him say that wind-driven rain in his face is the "first taste" of home! He seems to be suggesting the possibility that life in Bag-End might actually be dull and miserable, as "sad" and "dreary" as the elves said he looked when he came back to Rivendell (270).

Bilbo has been changed by his journey, and as he approaches his home, he seems increasingly uncertain about what his homecoming will bring. When he finally sees the Hill itself standing before him again, he stops suddenly and gives voice to his feelings in a poem. The song is not the first poem he has ever composed; that honor goes to his earlier efforts in the well-established literary genre of spider-aggravation verse, back in Chapter Eight. This song is also spontaneous, but it is rather more contemplative. The Hill has been Bilbo's goal for a long time, and it is perhaps not surprising that the new Bilbo, at the end of his adventures, would make a poem to commemorate his return at last.

The content of the poem might perhaps surprise us, though:

Roads go ever ever on,
 Over rock and under tree,
By caves where never sun has shone,
 By streams that never find the sea;
Over snow by winter sown,
 And through the merry flowers of June,
Over grass and over stone,
 And under mountains in the moon.
  (273)

Bilbo's song is not a song in praise of home, but a look back at his journey. The first stanza consists entirely of description. It mentions the places that roads go—not any particular road, just "roads." It emphasizes the surroundings, the variety of the settings that roads pass through. Roads go everywhere in the song, over grass and under mountain, through winter and summer. There is an elvish kind of appreciation of the natural world here, as if Bilbo were looking back over his journey as the singers in Rivendell might do, marveling only at the variety of the natural world.

Notice, however, that the stanza remains completely impersonal—Bilbo himself appears nowhere, nor do any of the events of his adventure. Several of the settings he describes sound familiar and are no doubt inspired by scenes he is recalling in this moment. The sunless caves and "streams that never find the sea" might make us think of goblin tunnels and a subterranean lake. We might remember Beorn's garden full of "merry flowers," and we might recall a hungry and fearful walk along the feet of the mountains in the moonlight, with the howling of wolves ringing through the night air. Bilbo is almost certainly reflecting on these things, but the first stanza is completely detached, recognizing that even the many and varied places that his journey has taken him are only a few of the places that roads go.

The second stanza moves a little closer to Bilbo's own experiences:

> *Roads go ever ever on*
> *Under cloud and under star,*
> *Yet feet that wandering have gone*
> *Turn at last to home afar.*
> *Eyes that fire and sword have seen*
> *And horror in the halls of stone*
> *Look at last on meadows green*
> *And trees and hills they long have known.*
> *(273)*

The second stanza begins by generalizing the path of the roads, noting that all roads go "under cloud and under star," but it then approaches the central event of the song: a homecoming. Notice that although the song is getting intensely personal, it remains distant; Bilbo never speaks of himself in the first person or mentions *his* homecoming. He does introduce a central figure, but that figure is disembodied. He talks about wandering feet returning home, and he talks about eyes that have seen battle and "horror in the halls of stone" and are now looking at last on familiar trees and meadows once again. It is as if Bilbo, in his song, is considering this phenomenon objectively, taking for the subject of his contemplation a wanderer returning to his quiet home from wild adventures.

There is a pressing but implicit question contained in that

second stanza. When such a wanderer returns from "fire and sword" to "meadows green," what happens? The last two lines are completely neutral, stating the fact that the eyes of the wanderer look on these quiet and familiar things, but saying nothing at all about what the wanderer feels, or what his experience is like. Bilbo knows that he has changed, and he knows that the home he has longed for again and again over the last year will never again look quite the same. Will he find that the taste of home is not sweet and restful after all, but sad and dreary? The song Bilbo sings at the sight of the Hill is not jubilant, but uncertain and even anxious. Bilbo's homecoming is not a simple fairy-tale ending, but a complex emotional experience.

Gandalf's response to Bilbo's song acknowledges Bilbo's doubts and worries. He recognizes that Bilbo has indeed changed, noting, "You are not the hobbit that you were" (274). The fact that Bilbo is expressing his thoughts through poetry is enough to prove that. Bilbo returns home with the memories of diverse settings like those in the first stanza and of divergent experiences like those described in the second stanza. His eyes have been opened, and he now sees even old things differently. He certainly is not the hobbit that he was.

Gandalf's reply to Bilbo, however, is gentle and reassuring. After responding with a tender and affectionate "My dear Bilbo!", Gandalf teases him gently with his comically exaggerated "Something is the matter with you!" (274). Bilbo's uncertainty is understandable, but Gandalf's jest suggests that he might be worrying needlessly. The Hill that Bilbo finds at the end of his quest will not be exactly the Hill he left at its beginning, but Gandalf doesn't seem to think he will find the change as unpleasant as he seems to fear.

As we consider Bilbo's uncertainty about what returning home will be like, we should also remember the strange dream that Bilbo had back at the end of Chapter Six, when he was sleeping in the eagles' eyrie. He "dreamed of his own house and wandered in his sleep into all his different rooms looking for something that he could not find nor remember what it looked like" (104). I said in Chapter Eighteen that at some point during his journey Bilbo stopped merely looking backwards and wishing he could return home and began striving toward his home as the endpoint of his journey—being resolved to go There before he went Back Again. This dream of dissatisfaction in Bag-End, of looking for something that was missing in his longed-for home, comes after his first turning point, the first time he has to set his own will to surviving and continuing his adventure. I wonder if perhaps the dream shows a glimpse of what might have been, a premonition of what would have happened if he had turned back, or even if he had never left. A fulfillment of his frequent wish to be suddenly transported back to his fireside and his whistling kettle might not, in fact, have led him to satisfaction. Once adventure had come in through his front door in Chapter One, Bilbo began to change. Escaping or denying that change, as was his wish for quite some time after the experience began, might well have ended up poisoning his peace of mind, even amidst the quiet comforts of Bag-End.

When Bilbo returns from his journey, however, he finds no such discomfort. To his delight, Bilbo finds that when wandering feet have returned at last to their home from afar, the eyes that have seen "fire and sword" are opened to the beloved scenes "they long have known" with a new wonder and a greater appreciation. Bilbo is "quite content; and the sound of the kettle on his hearth was ever after more musical than it

had been even in the quiet days before the Unexpected Party"
(275). Bilbo's experiences have not made his mundane home
seem dreary; they have infused it with wonder. His old clock
on the mantelpiece now has a magical sword hanging above
it. His front hallway now holds a marvelous coat of silver
mail. He still enjoys going on long walks, but now his walks
may take him to visit elves. You may still find him relaxing in
his garden and blowing smoke-rings, but he may also be composing a poem as he does so.

The Desolation of the Dragon: A Cautionary Tale

Not everything is perfect back in the land of Bilbo's home,
of course. Bilbo has "lost his reputation" among his neighbors, for one thing (275). The narrator playfully emphasizes
the shallowness of their perspective, noting, "It is true that
for ever after he remained an elf-friend, and had the honour
of dwarves, wizards, and all such folk as ever passed that way;
but he was no longer quite respectable." Since Bilbo's reputation was chiefly founded on his utter predictability, on the
narrowness of his mind and his experiences, such respect as
his neighbors gave him before was not really worth all that
much. Bilbo obviously takes the opinions of the rest of the
people in the wide world a little more seriously.

Bilbo's neighbors prove themselves to be not only small-
minded but venial. When Bilbo disrupts the auction at his
home with his unexpected return, we find that "not everybody
that said so was sorry" to find the presumption of his death
wrong (274). Their ill wishes to Bilbo are motivated by simple, if small-scale, greed. The "people who had got specially

good bargains at the Sale" resisted returning Bilbo's posses-
sions, not because they had any real doubts about his identity,
but out of sheer possessiveness. Bilbo's cousins, the Sackville-
Bagginses, he suspects, even sink as low as petty theft, stealing
Bilbo's silver spoons and remaining on unfriendly terms with
Bilbo ever after.

The actions of Bilbo's neighbors not only show that the
home Bilbo is returning to is no idyllic paradise, but they also
suggest that he was right to refuse most of the reward that
Dain offered to give him. Bilbo's lesson in caution about the
dragon-sickness is well learned. It may seem unlikely that "war
and murder" would have broken out among Bilbo's neighbors
if he had brought wagonloads of gold home with him, but
their own minor corruption suggests that it would have been
possible. The Sackville-Bagginses, in particular, might benefit
from hearing the cautionary tale of the Master of Lake-town.
The Master's end, fleeing into the Waste with bags of gold
and dying of starvation, "deserted by his companions," is the
perfect illustration of the results of dragon-sickness, if it is allowed to run its course (276). The Sackville-Bagginses, priori-
tizing their desire to possess Bag-End for themselves over their
family relationship with Bilbo, would have been in real danger of contagion. Bilbo has protected his neighbors and relatives from this danger by declining to bring home much treasure, and even more so by freely giving away much of what he
does bring home.

Luck: The Hand of Providence

The Desolation of the Dragon, we learn, has been thoroughly
healed. The land itself has been cleansed; we learn that "all the

valley had become tilled again and rich, and the desolation was now filled with birds and blossoms in spring and fruit and feasting in autumn" (276). Even more importantly, "there was friendship in those parts between elves and dwarves and men." The old songs have come true, and in the rebuilt Lake-town they are now making new songs celebrating the prosperity that they enjoy once more.

Bilbo expresses some surprise when he hears that "the old songs have turned out to be true, after a fashion!" (276). In Gandalf's reply, the wizard finally addresses openly a truth that has been increasingly clear as we have studied Bilbo's story. "You don't really suppose, do you," he asks, "that all your adventures and escapes were managed by mere luck, just for your sole benefit?" Gandalf confirms that what Bilbo and the narrator have been calling "luck" the whole time was more than simply chance. Bilbo's adventures have been "managed" by divine Providence for a purpose far greater than the enrichment of one small hobbit. As we have seen, Bilbo was one of the chief instruments of Providence in this story, but Bilbo's story has been thoroughly blended with the voices of many other instruments, contributing to a symphony whose score incorporates everything from the tea parties of hobbits to the motions of the moon and stars.

Bilbo's reaction is a perfect snapshot of Bilbo after his journey. He has learned wisdom and humility, and his cheerful "Thank goodness!" shows that he is quite satisfied to learn that he has not really been the protagonist of his story, after all (276). Bilbo is at peace, and our final image of him is a fitting one. Bilbo, laughing around his parlor table in Bag-End with Gandalf and Balin, hands the tobacco jar to his friend, as they all smoke their pipes together in contentment.

The Writing of *The Hobbit:* Bilbo's Memoirs

The last scene of the book begins with Bilbo writing his memoirs. His proposed title, *There and Back Again, a Hobbit's Holiday,* is both cavalier and self-deprecating, speaking of his great adventure as if it were only a little interlude in his life, a vacation he took one year to get away from home for a while. The title shows, with some comical exaggeration, how thoroughly Bilbo has integrated the experience of his journey into his life, in which the marvelous and the mundane are now "blended in measure."

Lighthearted as the title is, however, this glimpse of Bilbo's story written down as a real book reminds us of the stature that Bilbo's adventure has achieved. Ever since Chapter One, the odd little story of this clueless hobbit, his bumbling dwarf companions, and their ill-planned quest has come into contact with higher and greater legends. Bilbo's own tale might seem in the beginning like a farce, but even back on that first awkward Wednesday we are prompted to see Bilbo's journey as the unlikely final chapter of a saga that began with the fall of a kingdom and that has already encompassed goblin wars and passed beneath the shadow of the Necromancer's dark tower. By the end of the story, the increasing grandeur of its events and the solemnity of its tone have drawn us firmly into that world of legends. Like Bilbo, we have been swept into an adventure whose scope and significance we can only appreciate in retrospect.

The image of Bilbo writing his memoirs also has a powerful psychological effect on us as readers. In these last pages, we see that the book we have been holding for all these hours is derived from Bilbo's own diary; we are given a sense of continuity with Bilbo himself. In several of the early printed editions, Tolkien emphasized this connection on the dust-jacket of *The Hobbit*. He included a long string of dwarf-runes (which are really just Anglo-Saxon runes) which if transliterated read: "THE HOBBIT OR THERE AND BACK AGAIN BEING THE RECORD OF A YEARS JOURNEY MADE BY BILBO BAGGINS OF HOBBITON COMPILED FROM HIS MEMOIRS BY JRR TOLKIEN AND PUBLISHED BY GEORGE ALLEN AND UNWIN LTD." Tolkien puts himself forward merely as the compiler of Bilbo's memoirs, the transmitter rather than the creator of Bilbo's story.

Although it is only a fictional frame, the idea that the book we have been reading all along is actually Bilbo's own book provides a thrill, a sense that we are not only the audience but part of the story. We are given, though indirectly, a link to the world of marvels and legends that Bilbo discovers. The very book we are holding has been transformed into an artifact of adventure, almost like the map and key handed to Thorin at the beginning of the story. We too have found a secret door.

Acknowledgments

I am very grateful to all the people whose assistance made this book possible:

To my wife, Bridget, for her tireless efforts as an editor, proofreader, and inspiration.

To my son Nicholas, who was curious as to why I was writing a book about a book that had already been written.

To my son Matthias, who promptly gave me one of his own pieces of Christmas candy to reward me for finishing my book.

To my sister, Melissa, who has had to put up with me prattling on about Tolkien for longer than anyone else on earth.

To my brother Kristian, for his gentle but persistent requests for "updates" on my progress on the book.

To my brother Andy and my sister-in-law, Krystina, for their crazy photographic skills.

To Beth Lavin, for showing me the ropes.

To Joe Monti, my intrepid agent, who makes things happen.

To Ken Carpenter, for his patient guidance and excellent advice.

ACKNOWLEDGMENTS

To Alyssa House-Thomas, for much assistance in getting my facts straight.

To my Washington College students, for sharing my enthusiasm.

To the members of the Inklings book club, for years of good conversation and much encouragement.

To the staff of the Mythgard Institute, for their support and for all the help which they are still in the process of giving.

And especially to everyone who has listened to the Tolkien Professor podcast. Without you, this book would certainly never have happened.

Index of Names and Places